SHOTGUNS
AND
GUNSMITHS

SHOTGUNS
AND
GUNSMITHS
—The Vintage Years—

GEOFFREY BOOTHROYD

A & C Black · London

To Nancy, who read it and to Jean, who typed it, my thanks

First published in 1986 by
A & C Black (Publishers) Ltd
35 Bedford Row, London WC1R 4JH

Reprinted 1988

Boothroyd, Geoffrey
  Shotguns and Gunsmiths : the vintage years
    1. Shotguns—Great Britain—History—19th century
    2. Shotguns—Great Britain—History—20th century
  I. Title
  683.4'26'0941   TS536.8

  ISBN 0—7136—5552—6

ISBN 0 7136 5552 6

Printed and bound by Adlard and Son Limited, Letchworth, Hertfordshire

Contents

CONTENTS

About this book

The selection of articles from *The Shooting Times* for this, the second volume on the shotgun, has been even more difficult than for the first one. This is because the choice of material has been made from a large number of articles and a decision had to be made either to treat one aspect of the subject in detail or to include a smaller number of articles on a wide subject range.

I conducted a survey amongst readers as to what should be included and the consensus was that the material on gunmakers should be given prominence, and this has been done. Then a choice had to be made as to which makers should be included and which should be left out. This was not easy, and as far as possible the selection has been made on the basis of specific reader interest. I hope that the choice is one which meets with the approval of the majority.

The period covered is one of considerable interest: it extends from the fourth quarter of the nineteenth century to the present day. The subject matter is confined to shotguns and to shotguns of British manufacture. This, of course, excludes repeating and automatic shotguns. This is a period which saw the introduction of the "hammerless" shotgun. Hammer shotguns continued to be made, although in decreasing numbers, and were certainly widely used even after the hammerless shotgun gained popular acceptance. For this reason the hammer shotgun will still be encountered in the following pages.

The closing years of the nineteenth century also saw the introduction of smokeless powder as a propellant to replace black powder. The problems which this new family of propellants introduced were speedily overcome, and except for certain special applications the use of black powder became as rare as using a flintlock. Smokeless powder is not photogenic, and a study of the subject is largely a matter of chemistry, ballistics and commerce. If, in the future, a third volume is published, this could well include a history of the cartridge and explosives industry.

The early years of the twentieth century saw the reintroduction of the vertical arrangement of double barrels, and the British gunmaker made a significant technical contribution to what became more widely known as the "Over and Under". Production of the O/U gun in this country was never large and the guns made were, with few exceptions, complex and extremely expensive. They are of considerable interest, and for this reason mention is made of them later on in the book. Single-trigger mechanisms also found a degree of acceptance but since this is a very specialised subject I have not included any detailed discussion of these mechanical marvels.

The list of people who had a hand in gathering the information on which these articles have been based is almost endless. This is why I have restricted acknowledgements, in general, to the professional members of the gun trade. This is solely because there happen to be fewer of them, not because their contribution was more than that provided by the amateur or, to use a better word, the enthusiast.

Photographs, unless otherwise acknowledged, are entirely my own responsibility and have been taken under very varied conditions with a wide range of 35 mm and 2¼ in. cameras. For most of them Ilford film and paper have been used.

Once again it is a pleasure to thank *The Shooting Times* for publishing this material in the first place and agreeing to its republication in book form; and although they are not acknowledged individually I most warmly thank all those people, past and present, who have written to me and aroused my curiosity, extended my horizons and greatly increased my knowledge of that fascinating subject, the British shotgun.

Geoffrey Boothroyd
Glasgow, 1986

ACKNOWLEDGEMENTS

Birmingham Gun Barrel Proof House – Mr. Roger P. Lees
David McKay Brown, Gunmaker, Bothwell, Hamilton
Bailons Gunmakers Ltd. – Mr. L. Onions, Director
A. A. Brown & Sons, Alvechurch, Birmingham
Christie's, King Street, London – Mr. C. Brunker
Peter Dyson Ltd., Honley, Huddersfield
John Dickson & Son, Edinburgh – Mr. A. Sinclair
DEVA Altenbecken, G.F.R.
Eley Ltd., Witton, Birmingham
Gunnerman Books, Auburn Hgts., Mich., U.S.A. – Mr. L. Barnes
Gun Trade Association – Mr. N. S. Brown
John Harris, Gun Stocker, Birmingham
Matched Pairs Ltd., Durham
Alan Myers, Gunmaker, Garstang, Lancs.
D. A. Masters, Beare Green, Dorking, Surrey
Bill McGuire Inc., East Wenatchee, WA, U.S.A.
Mr. Harry Lawrence, O.B.E., James Purdey, London
John A. Richardson, Gunmaker, Liphook, Hants.
Sotheby & Co., New Bond St., London – Mr. Jim Booth
W. & C. Scott (Gunmakers) Ltd., Witton, Birmingham – Mr. P. G. Whatley

I

The Shotgun Action
Some mechanisms described

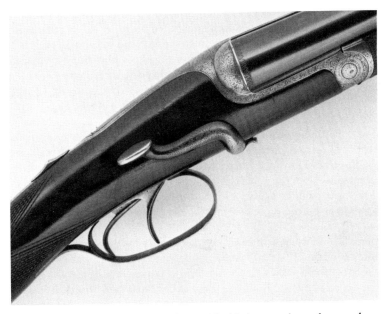

Dickson "Round Action" in 16 bore with side-lever and wood covered
action.

When guns were loaded at the muzzle most shotguns could easily be described under three simple headings: lock, stock and barrel. The lock was attached to the side of the stock, and in the days of the percussion shotgun the mechanism could either be in front of the axle upon which the hammer or cock was swung, in which case it was "bar-action", or behind the axle or tumbler, when the lock was known, appropriately enough, as a "back-action" lock.

These terms continued to be used into the breechloading era and on into the hammerless period since guns with sidelocks are, of course, still being made. You will encounter guns with bar-action sideplates and back-action lockwork and guns with internal lockwork fitted with sham or dummy sideplates.

If to the lockwork we then add the mechanism for holding the barrels of a breechloader in the closed or bolted position; the extractor and ejector work to remove the fired cartridge case, and safety bolting devices, the term "action" can then be used to describe a number of contrivances located in the metal "body" of the shotgun. From the fairly simple lockwork of a hammer sidelock we reach, by the turn of the century, a period where the mechanism for loading, firing and getting rid of the fired case had become quite complex and sophisticated.

The shotgun stock had not changed much from that used on guns made by the Mantons. It was still made of wood, mainly walnut, and in spite of modern synthetic finishes the "best" London gun is still finished in the traditional way. Instead of the stock being in one piece as it was on the muzzle-loader, it was now, with few exceptions, made in two pieces, the butt stock and the fore-end. The latter was removable and permitted the gun to be dismantled.

The barrel(s) of a shotgun form a study entirely on their own. During the period the material of construction changed from "Damascus" to steel, the latter being formed from steel bar by a fairly complex series of mechanical operations, which, in the early days, relied on the skill of the barrel borer. The skills and strength of the men who forged Damascus and twist barrels were largely replaced by machinery and the traditional "browning" process which had revealed the pattern of the Damascus and twist barrels was becoming very nearly a lost art with the introduction of various "blueing" processes for steel barrels.

Except in the odd isolated instance, British quality shotguns are still largely made by the techniques of the nineteenth century. Machine tools, jigs and fixtures are used to reduce the hard work involved in the removal of large lumps of metal. The tools are, in essentials, powered files and chisels. Both these hand tools are still used widely to shape and form metal so that each shotgun is a "one off", an individual artistic creation, a sculpture in wood and metal. The use of these traditional techniques is dictated by low production runs. Sophisticated tape-controlled or computer-controlled machines could be employed, as could the latest numerically controlled electric discharge machines for the manufacture of many components of a traditional shotgun.

Where the production is numbered in tens rather than in hundreds or thousands it is far too expensive to employ highly specialised machine tools. Even to hire such machines has been shown to be non-cost-effective, and only where the machines are on site and over seventy per cent utilised for other work can spare capacity be justified for traditional shotgun manufacture. Under these circumstances the high standard of accuracy which can be attained is a useful plus for some operations, but in general high technology is more expensive than the highly skilled gunmaker when the numbers involved are relatively small.

In this part of the book some of the mechanisms which were evolved are described. They are quite remarkable when it is appreciated that many of these systems were invented a century or more ago.

A device which would project a small quantity of lead shot under the personal direction of one man could no doubt be developed today. Such a "projector" would look very different from the side-by-side double game gun that has been used for sporting shooting for the last hundred years or more. It is not inconceivable that such a device would be far more effective than the traditional shotgun. One such device (I cannot call it a shotgun) has already appeared in America, the O/U Ljutic and no doubt others will appear in the years to come.

The use of shooting machines such as the Ljutic or repeating or automatic shotguns for clay shooting is all very well, but not for game shooting. Here the rules, both written and unwritten, preserve a sport which, although many would call it anachronistic, is still a rewarding, fulfilling and delightful activity. There are only four "sports" – huntin', shootin', fishin' and the pursuit of women. To use a repeating shotgun for game shooting (in the British sense) is as inappropriate as the use of a hand grenade for fishing. The British game gun evolved over a period of many years to meet the considerable demands which were made on it at the turn of the century. That it survives in its present form is largely because of the survival of a highly specialised type of shooting – once that is lost the game gun will be relegated to the Museum and gun collectors' cabinets, and in my opinion life will have become that much more tedious and commonplace.

PAULY BREECHLOADER

Most ammunition companies acquired collections of firearms, some almost by chance. Visitors to the 1984 Game Fair had the opportunity to see part of the Eley Collection on that company's stand, and with the kind co-operation of Eley I was able to see and photograph one of the most important pieces in the collection – the double-barrelled centre-fire, breechloading cartridge arm which bears on the sideplates "Brevetée à Paris" and "Invention Pauly". Before we look more closely at the gun itself it is worth asking: "Why is it important?" We also want to know something about the inventor, Pauly, because to the question: "Who invented the breechloading shotgun?" most people would answer "Lefaucheux".

Samuel Johannes Pauly was born in Switzerland in 1766. He was a Sergeant-Major in the Artillery and, in the early years of the nineteenth century, he became interested in balloons. His first balloon ascent probably took place in France in 1804. Pauly then moved to Paris and, in 1812, he was granted a patent or brevet for 10 years. The patent, which closely resembles the Pauly sporting guns and pistols, also describes the cartridges, as does the later British patent No. 4026 of 1816.

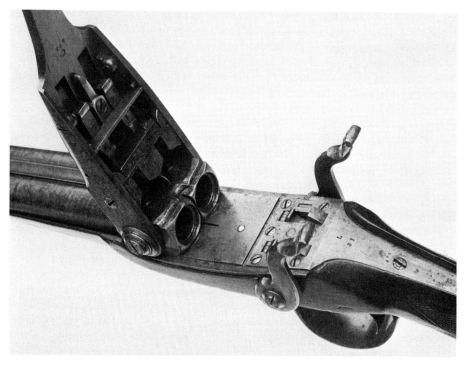

A Pauly breechloader with the hinged breech lifted to show the internal mechanism.

The gun in the Eley Collection is fairly plain except for the decoration of the stock, which is in the French manner. The barrels are conventional with a central rib and they have trunnions on which the hinged lifting breech is mounted. The mechanism of the gun is below the action plate, which is firmly attached to the stock. Underneath the plate are the locks and mainsprings; the locks are cocked by the external cocking levers. The strikers or firing pins are in the hinged breech, which is opened by a long lever extending to the comb of the stock. With the breech open, the cartridges can be inserted into the chambers; the breech is then closed and with the action cocked the gun is ready to fire. The gun is simple to operate and very well constructed. We can, of course, look at the Pauly sporting guns which have survived and wonder what the shooting men in France thought of them. We are, in this respect, quite fortunate, since a report on the gun was made by M. le Baron Delessert, apparently at the request of Pauly and a gunmaker called Prelat, whose place of business was No. 4 Rue des Trois Frères, Paris. In his report the Baron tells us that he fired 300 shots without either a hangfire or a misfire.

He paid special attention to the reliability of the system and, in a further series of trials carried out by the French "Society for the Encouragement of National Industry", the following points were stressed. (1) The same barrel cannot be loaded twice. This was a hazard with muzzle-loading guns and one attended by considerable danger.

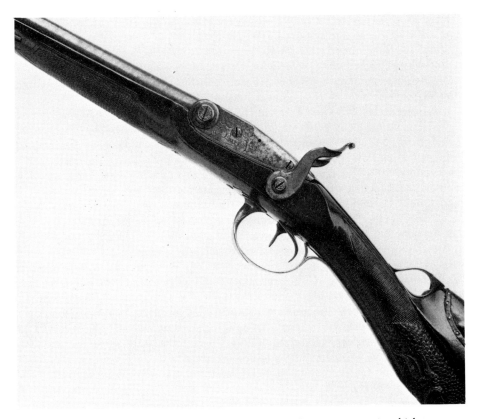

The smooth lines of the Pauly are evident, as is the neat manner in which the operating lever is blended into the comb of the stock.

(2) The gun is easy to unload if one wishes to change the load or to put away the gun. Unloading muzzle-loaders was neither easy nor always safe. The best way to empty a muzzle-loading shotgun was to fire it, often up the chimney! (3) The action of the gun is enclosed and is not affected by damp or rain. (4) Loading is quick and easy and can be done even when walking. With the Pauly it is possible to shoot as often as if one were using several muzzle-loading guns.

The Pauly cartridge was similar to the modern paper-case shotgun, with a metal head containing the percussion powder and a paper tube for the charge. How effective this cartridge was in use I cannot say. Trials under controlled conditions are one thing, protracted use in the field is another. One of the reasons for complaints against the earlier Forsyth gun was simply the fact that the users were unfamiliar with a new system, they had inadequate knowledge and didn't take sufficient care with cleaning and maintenance.

The Pauly shotgun was sold in a case with a very complete set of tools and accessories. The gun was capable of firing both shot and ball; a bullet-mould was provided, also cartridges and cleaning tools. Possibly one reason why the Pauly system did not progress further in France was because the inventor moved from Paris to London. By 1814 he had obtained a British patent for a system of compressed-air ignition and subsequently his interest reverted to "Aerial Conveyances". In this venture he had the help of a fellow Swiss, the noted London gunmaker Durs Egg. After a considerable sum of money had been spent the balloon venture came to naught and, after 1817, we hear no more of Samuel Johannes Pauly.

It does not seem likely that he returned to Paris, where the business had been carried on by Henri Roux. Roux made modifications to the Pauly design and he continued to manufacture guns on the modified system until the business was taken over by Eugène Pichereau. Pichereau again modified the gun by providing external hammers which fired a copper cap. This effectively converted the Pauly gun into what today we call a capping breechloader – a breechloader with external ignition. Pichereau was then succeeded by Casimir Lefaucheux, whose name was to become synonymous with the term "breechloader". Lefaucheux made guns with the hinged "lift-up" breech on the Pauly system, but with external ignition. He then abandoned the fixed barrel and lift-up breech for the hinged, drop-down barrel system which became so closely associated with his name. His French patent of 1834 shows a drop-down barrel gun, but again this has external ignition. Two years later he patented what was to evolve into the first widely-adopted breechloading system – the pinfire.

In spite of having been discarded by Lefaucheux, the Pauly system was not entirely forgotten. Another gun with a hinged lift-up breech was introduced by Robert in 1831. This had a "hammerless" action; the cocking levers of the Pauly were dispensed with and the locks were cocked by lifting up the breech with its long lever.

It is important to differentiate between the inventions which were applied to the mechanism of the gun and those inventions which altered or improved the cartridge. When it comes to cartridges another Frenchman (about whom we know regrettably little), Houllier, is of great importance since his pinfire cartridge, patented in 1846, was the first reliable *gas tight* cartridge and, as such, it made the breechloader a truly practical proposition.

Today we hear little of Pauly or, indeed, of Houllier. To Pauly must go much of the honour for an invention which foreshadowed later events and which was, perhaps, invented too early to be commercially successful. Serial numbers up to 475 have been recorded, but one has the feeling that the guns were regarded more as an interesting curiosity than anything else. A particularly fine example, serial number 178, is in the Royal Collection at Windsor Castle. This example was bought from Durs Egg for £65 and sent to Windsor Castle on 13 August 1835. The provenance of the gun in the Eley Collection is unknown and we must be thankful that it has survived. No doubt it will be displayed on the Eley stand at future Game Fairs to delight those who have an interest in the history and evolution of the sporting shotgun.

NEEDHAM'S NEEDLE-FIRE

Have you ever thought how very much simpler your shotgun would be if you did not have to extract the fired case? Even with simple single-barrel guns the mechanism

The Needham bolt action needle-fire double shotgun as made by John Rigby, showing the left-hand barrel and lock, with the lock "bolted" on "safe".

would be much easier to operate, and with double-barrel guns the lack of selective ejectors would greatly simplify manufacture, increase the speed of loading and reduce costs. When you consider a repeating or automatic shotgun the situation becomes even more advantageous.

As with many things connected with firearms, the problem was solved many years ago and shotguns were built which did not require you to remove the empty case either by hand or with the aid of an additional mechanism. The patent was taken out by Joseph Needham in 1852 and describes a breechloading gun and a suitable cartridge. Most of the Needham guns appear to have been made by John Rigby of Dublin, as was the Needham gun illustrated, as shown by the Rigby "trade mark" of the deeply etched Damascus barrels and the inscription "Rigby, Dublin" on the barrel and lock.

From the illustrations you can see that what we have is essentially a double-barrel gun with a bolt-action type of breech. The bolt, when opened, because of the quick-start thread, moves the bolt-head to the rear, allowing the bolt to be hinged outwards, thus permitting the cartridge to be introduced into the breech. In the illustration overleaf I have removed the bolt or breech-plug, and the lock-cylinder has been returned to show the external screw and the long firing pin or "needle". It had another feature in that it was one of the few British shotguns with fixed barrels, other than rifle conversions like the Martini.

The Needham/Rigby was the first "hammerless" gun to enjoy the acceptance amongst sportsmen and the distinction of being one of the very few guns using a special cartridge to receive acclaim. Success depended upon a number of factors. The first was the need to manufacture the gun to the highest standards and although the mechanism to modern eyes is by no means complex, to the gunmaker of the mid-nineteenth century it posed problems which required the skill of a gunmaker such as Rigby to overcome. The claims made by those who sold the Needham and those who

The Needham bolt system dismantled.

used it were that it could be more rapidly loaded than the muzzle loader and that it was safer both in loading and in use. Someone already familiar with the handling of powder, shot and wads could make the cartridges for himself, and unlike the pinfire, the cartridges were relatively cheap and did not have to be removed from the breech after the gun had been fired. With the needle gun, a metal plate and base remained behind after firing and were pushed ahead of the next cartridge when this was loaded. However, the Needham needle gun suffered, as did all needle guns, from corrosion of the needle due to the escape of gas and less than perfect obturation. It is a matter of some regret to me that I have never been in a position to dismantle a Needham cartridge although I did make some effort to manufacture them many years ago, but with little success. Certainly Eley Brothers made the Needham cartridges for rifles in 75-, 90- and 110-bore but I have no certain knowledge that Eley's ever made the shotgun cartridge as well. It is regrettable that cartridges for this gun do not appear to have survived, as they would be of considerable interest.

Both Needham and Rigby remained staunch advocates of the needle principle until the establishment of the centre-fire cartridge, much as did J. D. Dougal with his advocacy of the pinfire.

The Rigby-made Needham shotguns were of a very high quality and it is reasonable to speculate that at least some of the success of the gun was due to this. One other factor, already mentioned, was the fact that empty cases did not have to be removed from the gun, a point heavily stressed by a contemporary user of the Needham. The

Needham family continued to make guns and to make a contribution to the development of the shotgun for many years until the Birmingham end of the business was bought out by W. W. Greener.

THE BACON BREECHLOADER

Most of us have seen and many have used the single-barrel bolt-action shotgun. Such weapons have been made in calibres such as the simple bolt-action No. 3 garden gun firing the No. 3 or 9 mm rim-fire shot cartridge, the popular .410 as made by BSA and Webley & Scott and the extensive range made in America by Mossberg, Stevens, Higgins and Marlin in calibres ranging from .410 up to and including 12-bore.

Also available in the years between the wars were a range of bolt-action shotguns based on obsolete military actions, such as the Gras, Chassepot and early Mauser, which were again to be had in most calibres up to 12-bore and which were to be found in most parts of Europe. All of these shotguns, including the Manufrance "Buffalo", made in 12 mm and 14 mm calibres, have one thing in common: they are all single-barrel guns. The bolt system of breech closure has much to commend it. Ease of manufacture, adequate strength and, where necessary, economy, are all factors which can be placed on the credit side of the balance sheet. Successive shots can also be obtained by employing a simple magazine system. The disadvantage of the bolt system is its lack of symmetry. This presents certain problems, particularly in the design and use of double-barrelled shotguns. In spite of this, coupled with the fact that at least $2\frac{1}{2}$ inches are added to the length of the barrels, at least one such double-barrelled, central-fire, breechloading shotgun was made, and enjoyed a measure of success. This was a long time ago and the gun was the Bacon.

The inventor, Fracis Bacon, a retired officer in the Marine Artillery, introduced his gun in 1870, and several modified types were to appear in the years which followed, one of which is illustrated overleaf.

The arrangement of the two bolts is shown in the second illustration, the right-hand bolt being in the open position. The firing pin or striker is driven by a coil spring and is withdrawn or cocked when the bolt is opened. When the cartridge is inserted into the breech, the bolt is pushed forward and the head turned down by means of the bolt handle. The gun cannot be fired until the bolt is locked. An unusual feature of the gun is the method of removing the fired case. Unlike most bolt-actions, where the extracted and ejected case is expelled from above, in the Bacon the case is extracted and falls out of the gun through a ventral opening in the stock, as can be clearly seen in the illustrations.

The Bacon guns which I have had the opportunity of examining have been made to the highest traditions of British gunmaking; who made them, I don't know, but those seen carried Birmingham proof marks.

The introduction of the Bacon gun provoked a number of comments from sportsmen of the day, apprehension being expressed as to the likelihood of a premature discharge of the cartridge when the bolt was thrust forward. This was not as foolish a comment as perhaps it appears today, since a contemporary committee on

The later, more streamlined version of the Bacon breechloader
with rounded bolt heads.

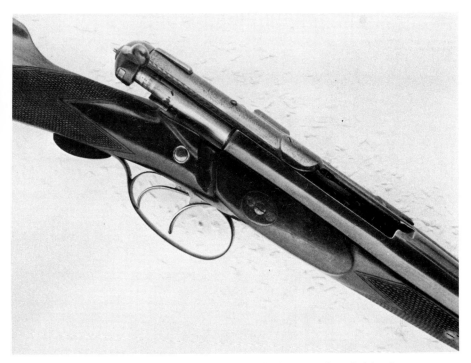

A disadvantage of the bolt system was the long travel needed for the
bolt; note the grip safety behind the trigger guard.

small arms had already come to the conclusion that the bolt-action system presented
certain hazards and that the impact of the bolt-head on the base of the cartridge was a
possible source of danger. The inventor, in defence of his system, stated that he had
fired 9,000 rounds from guns of his design without accident and pointed out that on the
occasions that bolt-action guns had exploded caps, the mark of the striker had been
evident and that the danger was entirely due to a protruding striker. Informed opinion
of the time agreed that the design of the gun was quite sound, and permitted economic
manufacture, and made the point that one barrel could be fired whilst the user was
reloading the other.

When the manufacture of the Bacon gun ceased is still unknown to me but certainly
I know of one that was in use until quite recently, a fact which I think amply
substantiates the inventor's confidence in the design.

THEOPHILUS MURCOTT'S GUN

Murcott, in whose name the patent for this gun was taken out in 1871, had his business
at 68 Haymarket, where he seems to have started his activities in or around 1861. His
previous history is at present a blank. His hammerless gun seems to have been put on

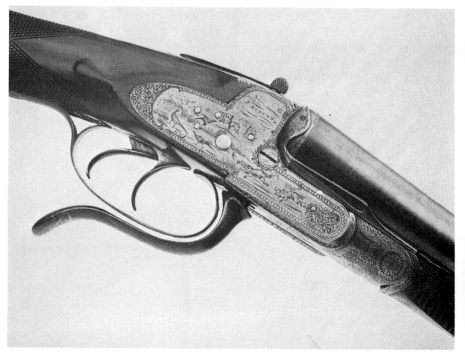

T. Murcott's hammerless breechloader of 1872.

the market early in 1872 and it is of particular interest since it was the first hammerless shotgun to achieve any degree of commercial success. It was not the first hammerless gun: George Daw, Green and, of course, Needham had all made guns which did not employ hammers, but Murcott's gun was the first adequately to demonstrate the practicality of the hammerless system and the fact that a gun built on these lines was acceptable to the general sporting public.

If one were to take off the odd-shaped lockplate one would find that the lever is extended upwards so that first of all it withdraws the retaining bolt which secures the barrels, while a further extension to the lever cocks the internal hammers or tumblers. Both locks are cocked by means of a projecting arm on the tumbler and the locks can be regarded as ordinary hammer locks with the hammers on the inside of the lockplate instead of on the outside.

Internal arrangements are conventional, and neither the owner nor a gunmaker would have any difficulty in understanding how the mechanism operates. It was probably this simplicity that gave the Murcott its appeal – nothing complicated and nothing revolutionary to go wrong. The only unusual feature, apart from the absence of external hammers, was the safety bolt, which can be seen behind the standing breech. This was pivoted at the rear and when the gun is held in the shooting position the safety lever is swung to the right to the "locked" or safe position. This safety bolt only bolts the triggers and does not prevent the release of the tumblers in a positive manner by interception. According to Theophilus Murcott his gun afforded a number of benefits to the user. These included a clear sight, rapidity of action, perfect security and simplicity of construction. The clear line of sight was achieved by the absence of external hammers. I suppose that some of the potential customers might object to this and state that they liked external hammers, since the ears provided a simple type of backsight. Against this, the absence of hammers helped in sighting for the second barrel. Rapidity of action was achieved by the fact that the underlever unlocks the barrels, cocks the internal "hammers" and, after reloading, locks the barrels again – quite simple and much quicker than having to cock external hammers.

From the security angle the gun was not quite so safe as it could have been, since the locking bolt did not lock the tumblers and a failure of the sear or a severe jar could cause the gun to fire with the safety lever applied and the triggers bolted. Quite a play was made by Murcott that the gun was safe because the word "Locked" appeared in gold letters and, of course, during the early history of the hammerless gun the need to know whether the gun was cocked produced quite a range of devices called cocking indicators.

The simplicity of construction was undeniable, and the Murcott deserved the success it enjoyed due to its mechanical simplicity, strength and reliability. It was also quite acceptable owing to the clean and graceful lines and absence of the odd projections that afflicted many of the early hammerless guns. That the design was "right" and the gun well made is difficult to deny since several are in satisfactory use today!

GEORGE GIBBS OF BRISTOL

Some years ago I used the illustration of the original Gibbs & Pitt lockwork from a partially complete gun. This was in a series on the development of the shotgun and this variant of the Gibbs design is illustrated in my earlier volume, *The Shotgun: History and Development*. The fact that this gun was incomplete allowed me to show the manner in which the lockwork was contained in the "case" which projects underneath the gun and in many ways is slightly reminiscent of the Gibbs-Farquharson rifle.

An illustration of a complete example of a Gibbs & Pitt was provided by Mr. Godbold. Mr. Godbold's gun is a very fine specimen and has that look about it which once you have seen you cannot possibly mistake. It is indefinable but quite positively identifiable – the look that a shotgun has when it has been made by a riflemaker! One other riflemaker produced shotguns which had this rugged handsomeness, Dan'l Fraser of Edinburgh. His shotguns always looked like double rifles to me.

But to get back to George Gibbs. The earliest example of which I have knowledge has a rotary underlever and external cocking levers. The levers serve as cocking indicators and can also be used to place the locks at half cock if required. As an alternative, the Gibbs & Pitt gun was offered with a snap-lever action and was in this respect similar to that illustrated above. Both types of action are as described in the Gibbs & Pitt patent of 1873. All of the surviving examples I have either seen or been advised of lack the external cocking levers and have, as an addition, a safety bolt. This

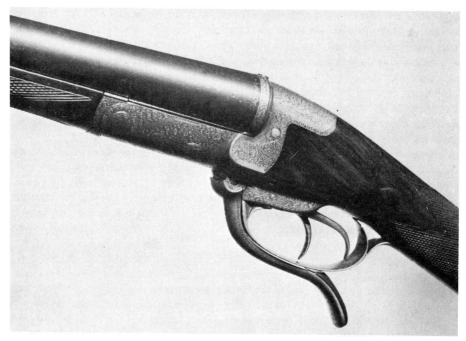

The Gibbs hammerless gun with the "push forward" underlever.

This Gibbs gun, with a rotary underlever, is a good example of the amazing variety found in British shotguns during the formative years.

is usually fitted on the right hand side of the gun and takes the form of a pivoting lever.

This type of lever continued to be used by Gibbs after the Gibbs & Pitt action was replaced by the type of action illustrated later in this book. With the lever in the vertical position the internal tumblers, or what Gibbs called "strikers", were bolted and prevented from touching the firing pins. When the gun was ready to fire, the safety bolt was rotated through 45 degrees to the rear.

Mr. Godbold tells me that his gun is in good condition but that "some clot had the barrels blued". I gather that this will shortly be rectified! It is very fortunate that this gun has survived in such good condition. This type of action, lever-cocking, was a sort of cul-de-sac of development and the lockwork, bearing as it does a marked resemblance to several of the lock systems employed for single-shot rifle actions of the period, was also to be short-lived.

The Gibbs & Pitt in its lever-cocking form with trigger-plate case-locks is a truly magnificent gun and exerts upon me the same odd fascination as that other anachronism, the armadillo.

MALEHAM'S HAMMERLESS GUN

For those of you who file the information away for the future, this offering should be filed under: shotgun, British, breechloading, hammerless, lever-cocking. There are readers who do this, as I know to my cost. So much so, that a few years ago I had to establish a special card index of my own so that I wouldn't be caught out.

The information here is based on a photograph supplied by a reader, Mr. Bulmer, who told me that the gun is original except for the grip safety, which he has made himself to replace the lever which was lost. From the illustrations we can see that we have a hammerless gun, bar-in-the-wood, with an extremely long top lever and a rather unusual appearance. The name on the lockplate reads "Maleham & Mirfin" and the extra long top lever tells us that the hammerless action is cocked by the lever and not by the fall of the barrels. This type of action was patented by C. H. Maleham and T. Mirfin in 1873 and, of course, it was not the first lever-cocking action, since three months earlier in the same year Gibbs & Pitt had brought out their better-known lever-cocking action. Because of the way shotguns were made in this country, we can encounter wide variations in the design in a short period. This is because much of the work was done by hand, and changes in the design or styling of the gun could be carried out without having to scrap half the machine shop and throw expensive machines, jigs, tools and fixtures on the scrap heap. "Old Joe", the action filer, was merely told to make the gun "this way, not that" and what was wanted was probably drawn in chalk on the workshop floor.

The original Maleham & Mirfin gun looked even odder than the illustration of the later version shown. If you take another look you will see that the other uncommon feature of the gun is the "ball fences".

To digress slightly, I have been asked by an American reader to write a short article on the names used for parts of guns, and since this hasn't been done yet, for those new

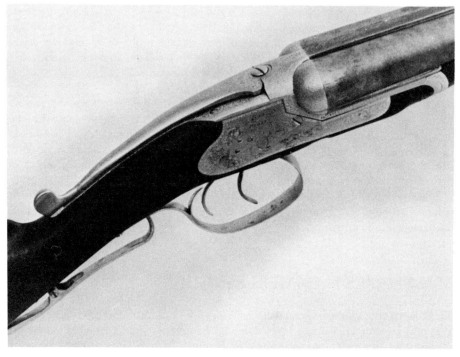

One of the very few actual examples of the Maleham hammerless gun.
The grip safety is a later replacement.

to the series the "fences" on a breech-loading gun are those parts of the standing breech which close the end of the barrels. They could, functionally, be square or rectangular blocks of metal and before the action filer gets at them this is what they look like after rough machining. However, to increase the aesthetic quality of the action body or receiver and to reduce weight – I nearly said "increase lightness" – several styles of "fence" appeared. The style on the Maleham is known as a "ball fence" simply because that is what the fences look like! They could be ball-headed, with a bead between the ball and the action body, and on the earlier version of the Maleham the fences were what is known as "percussion fences". They looked very similar to the styling to be found on muzzle-loading percussion guns. When centre-fire breechloaders appeared, the percussion nipple was replaced by the centre-fire nipple, striker and spring. The distinctly odd feature of the early Maleham was the inclusion of what looked exactly like a centre-fire nipple/striker assembly, and one looks for the hammers on the gun! There are, however, none. What appears to be the nipple and striker are "loaded" indicators. With a cartridge in the breech the indicator pin stands proud like a striker or firing pin. What the system does not indicate is whether the cartridge is live or has been fired. Loaded and "cocked" indicators were very popular in the early days of the hammerless breechloader until the common-sense attitude prevailed: treat all guns as loaded.

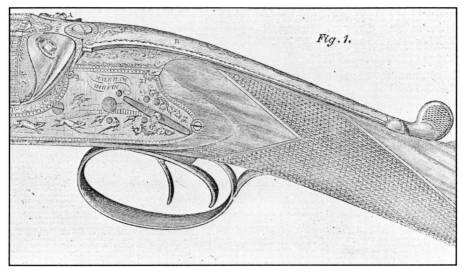

It is interesting to compare the illustration of the Maleham in a
contemporary magazine with the actual example. Note the long cocking
lever, and, in particular the "loaded" indicators which give the
impression of a hammer gun without the hammers.

How long it was before the original Maleham & Mirfin lost its "loaded" indicators
and acquired its modern ball fences I cannot say. The original patent was taken out in
1873 and "it was noticed" by the sporting press in 1874. We have no indication of when
the gun illustrated was made, but it has lost its "loaded" indicators, percussion fences
and styling and acquired a lever or grip safety. One feature which was also "noticed"
at the time was that the gun had a snap action. The lever was pushed across to the right
allowing the barrels to fall. The lever was then allowed to return to its original position
in line with the barrels. The cartridges were introduced and the barrels closed with a
"snap". The lever remained in line with the barrels "not diverging to one side as when
opening".

The gun does not seem to have been very popular, since within seven or eight years it
was no longer offered, and guns based on Scott patents were being advertised by the
firm of Chas. M. Haleham of Sheffield.

Although we know nothing of Mr. Mirfin, we know quite a lot about Maleham.
The firm was founded in 1830 by George Maleham. He was joined by his nephew,
Charles Henry Maleham, in about 1860; he continued until his retirement from the
business in 1910. Arthur Turner, who had served his time with Maleham, became
Manager and ran the business until his death in 1941.

The firm passed on from father to son, Charles Henry Turner also starting as an
apprentice in 1914 and taking control of the business in 1941. The firm became a
limited company in 1946 with C. H. Turner as Chairman, a position he held until his
death in 1966. The chairmanship passed to Miss Louisa Turner, Charles Henry's
sister, and then his daughter Judith Ann became a Director in 1966. John Clarke, who

had been Manager since 1966 married Judith Ann and he became Managing Director in 1975. There is, therefore, a family connection going back for over a hundred years and the history of the firm goes back even further.

It is to be regretted that no records exist of the firm's activities prior to December, 1940 when the original premises at No. 5 West Bar were totally destroyed during the blitz on Sheffield. Today the company are to be found at 33/35 West Bar, Sheffield and they celebrated their 150th anniversary in 1980.

ANSON AND DEELEY ACTION

It doesn't matter what language is used to describe the action of a shotgun, sooner or later you will find someone either making or selling shotguns, "System Anson & Deeley". W. Anson and J. Deeley, both of whom worked for the firm of Westley Richards in Birmingham, took out patents in 1875 for an action with internal hammers which were cocked by the fall of the barrels. How was this done? In the case of the sidelock it is possible to get at least some idea of how the mechanism works if the locks are removed. All the parts can be seen and with a little imagination it is not all that

Anson & Deeley's hammerless action in the full cocked position with the barrels open.

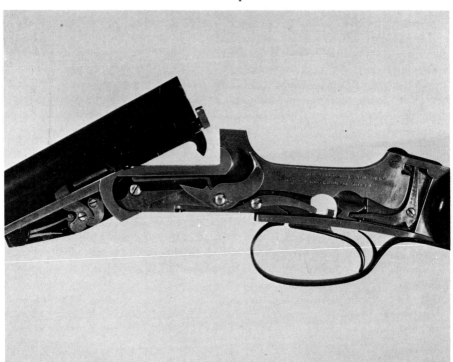

difficult to visualise what happens when the barrels drop down, the cocking lever is moved and the tumbler cocked. It's not quite so easy with the A & D action. First of all, with one very noticeable exception, the lockwork cannot be removed since it is fitted into slots cut into the action body. The exception is, of course, the Westley Richards Hand Detachable Lock, a beautiful piece of mechanism.

Before Westley Richards introduced their detachable locks it must have been considered a valid selling-point to illustrate how their A & D-actioned guns worked, and through the kind services of a reader I am able to illustrate this article with a special cut-away demonstration action. Unlike many of the demonstration models which were made from actual guns, the example shown was specially made and is marked "Westley Richards Patent Hammerless Gun Mechanism". If we disregard the extra bits and pieces in the fore-end and the parts of the ejector mechanism, the gun mechanism can be seen to comprise three main components.

The first of these is the cocking lever. This is pivoted concentric with the hinge pin, and one limb projects through the joint of the action body and enters a slot in the fore-end iron. When the barrels are depressed, the fore-end rotates about the joint and carries with it the front limb of the cocking lever and so causes the rear limb to rise. Since the extension to the tumbler projects over the rear limb, it is raised until the tumbler is held at full cock by the sear, the third of the components in the lock.

The first illustration shows the parts in the position they occupy with the barrel depressed ready for "loading". Also you can see how the safety system on this later version of the A & D action bolts the triggers. The second illustration shows the parts as they appear after the trigger has been pulled. The safety slide has been pushed

Note the position of the limbs of the action when the gun has been fired.

forward, unbolting the triggers and the combined tumbler and striker is in the "fired" position. Additions to this mechanism were few, simply the ejector system patented by Deeley in 1886 and the later intercepting safety. Single-trigger mechanisms were also fitted and a very great deal of work was done, notably by Greener, to improve the basic A & D system.

That the Anson and Deeley system was fundamentally sound is more than adequately demonstrated by the fact that it is still being built in Germany, Belgium, Spain and Italy and, indeed, elsewhere, unchanged in all essentials. Many famous firms built their reputations by building guns on the A & D system, a system which has reflected great credit on two Birmingham gunmakers, W. Anson and J. Deeley for nearly a century.

NEEDHAM'S EJECTOR GUN

Have you ever wondered, as you push over the top lever and open your ejector gun, who first thought of the device which ejects the fired cases so neatly over your shoulder? If you think about it, the selective ejector is quite a neat and rather elegant piece of mechanism. For example, it wouldn't do to have both cartridges flicked out of the gun when it was opened if, for example, neither had been fired. You would have to practise the neat trick of catching ejected cases in the air; this, it must be admitted, looks rather splendid in a gun shop but couldn't be recommended for normal sporting use. Nor indeed, could you have a system which ejected the fired case from the right barrel and also the unfired case from the left. Then, if you think about it a little more, if the mechanism can be made to leave unfired cartridges in the chamber, you may wish to withdraw them yourself. So, to save fingernails, it would help if they could be slightly withdrawn, to permit a reasonable grasp of the head to be obtained with

Needham's ejector gun has that curious unco-ordinated look so common amongst the early hammerless actions, at least those which did not stand the test of time.

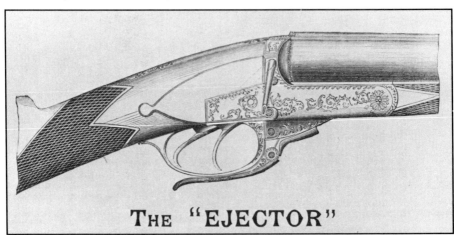

THE "EJECTOR"

perhaps cold fingers. All of these desirable features are available with an ejector gun and today are taken completely for granted.

When ejector guns first appeared the feature was not hailed with unmixed rapture. J. H. Walsh, the Victorian arbiter of shooting fads and fancies, did not see the justification for ejector guns since "If a loader is employed he has almost always plenty of time for extraction by the fingers" and "if there is no loader the gun becomes too hot to hold". Notwithstanding the condemnation implicit in Walsh's comments, the shooting man demanded ejector guns, and these were provided by the trade in plenty and in such a fashion as to arouse the admiration of even Walsh in "their great ingenuity".

The first ejector, the Needham, was not only the first but it also had all the desirable features outlined above. I have not been able to locate a Needham ejector gun so we will have to make do with an illustration of one taken from *The Sporting Mirror* of June 1882. As can be seen, the gun is a double-barrelled hammerless underlever cocking gun, but here the term "underlever" is used to describe a hinged lever, which should not be confused with the rotary underlever which is rather more common, even today. When this lever is pushed forward and down, the barrels are unlocked and they can be depressed. The opening of the barrels is used to cock the hammer or tumbler, to the front of which there is a long forward projection. In the lump of the barrel are two small levers, one for each extractor. When the hammers are cocked, the arms or projections of the hammers are clear of the extraction levers and consequently do not act upon them. If one or both barrels have been fired and the hammers are forward, the projections act upon the extractor and flip out the fired empty case.

The main objection to the Needham ejector system, the patents for which were taken out in 1874, concerns the appearance. The use of levers inside the lump resulted in a downward prolongation of the lump which produced a rather unsightly excrescence underneath the bar of the action. This is not particularly noticeable on Needham's gun, which employed an underlever, but guns on Needham's system were also made by other manufacturers under licence. The Lancaster ejector gun looked rather strange with the protruding lump, since Lancaster employed a top lever and consequently could not disguise the lump as did Needham.

Needham's ejector system was modified by W. W. Greener in 1881 and used with the Greener version of the Anson & Deeley action but, in spite of the system or a variant being employed by some of the most important gunmakers, it was eventually superseded by the type of ejector mechanism set independently in the fore-end. One type of ejector which does not depend on part of the mechanism being in the fore-end is that still employed by John Dickson in their "Round Action" gun, but this is the exception. Most modern ejectors are of the Deeley or Southgate type and, when you consider the job they have to do, they are still quite remarkable pieces of mechanism, even in this modern age of miracles.

AN UNUSUAL EJECTOR SYSTEM

After the complexity of the automatic or self-loading shotgun, the side-by-side double appears to be deceptively simple. This simplicity is the result of a considerable amount of work over a number of years by quite a lot of ingenious people. Not all the early attempts to provide the facilities required by the nineteenth-century sportsman displayed this desirable simplicity, desirable because usually the more complicated the mechanism the more likely it was to go wrong.

If you have a side-by-side double shotgun and if it has selective ejectors (the gun will only eject the fired empty case; the loaded cartridge is extracted, but not ejected) ask yourself how the gun tells itself what to do! If you own such a gun you may know the secret. If so, next time you are in the pub seeking a topic for discussion amongst shooting friends ask them – and see how many can describe the way in which a selective ejector system works.

The earliest of the selective ejector guns were made by Needham, Greener and Lancaster. One of the most successful designs was that of J. Deeley, which dates from 1886 and which is still used today. The other design is known as the "Southgate", and this dates from T. Southgate's patent of 1893. In the years before the First World War it was often a matter of pride with first-rate gunmakers to employ their own patent systems and this, of course, also extended to the new-fangled selective ejector. Many of the designs which appeared proved unsatisfactory, and the harsh lessons of history have shown up the weaknesses which appeared as the years went by. The problems of the gunmaker seeking fame and fortune from his own "patent" system, either because of pride or a reluctance to pay a royalty for the use of a proven and satisfactory system, were many. Not only had he to think of something new which would work, but he also had to avoid principles previously patented by his competitors.

One of the most fascinating designs which appeared was due to W. Anson. A reader kindly sent me an illustration of the system in a gun made by the well-known craftsman C. B. Vaughan and dates from the late 1880s. I cannot do better than quote the owner (who wishes to remain anonymous), and his explanation is that the method consists of "ejecting every time the gun is opened, but obstructing the path of the unfired cartridge".

To expand on this a little, the ejector is not divided as is usual. The ejector plate is spring-loaded and is normally retained by the hook, which can be seen below the plate. When the gun is nearly fully open, the extractor/ejector spring is compressed and the hook depressed so that the ejector is thrown forward. If neither cartridge has been fired, the two clips, which are hinged under the plate, will be in the closed or upper position and the tabs (the right-hand tab is broken off) will prevent the cartridges from being thrown out of the chamber. If either or both cartridges have been fired, the hammer corresponding to the fired cartridge pushes forward a short rod which protrudes through the face of the standing breech, and when the gun is opened the rod draws down the clip. When this is done and the gun opened there is no obstruction to the cartridge, which is ejected from the chamber. This was an interesting but unduly complicated method of operation which relied on several small and rather fragile parts. As we can now see, one of these parts has, in fact, broken, but when this happened I don't know. Even if it happened 30 years ago the system must have lasted for half a century, but I have the feeling that this method of selective ejection was perhaps not all that robust. However, it would be interesting to find out if any guns with Anson's system are still in use.

THE LANG HAMMERLESS SHOTGUN

With the invention of the Purdey double bolt in 1863, the sporting gun in the middle of the second half of the nineteenth century had evolved into a remarkably efficient and beautiful weapon with either a rotary underlever or a Purdey bolt with top lever and bar- or back-action locks.

At their best such guns were masterpieces of the art of gunmaking and here the word "art" is used advisedly. Fortunately many have survived and are still able to arouse our admiration, but the sportsmen of the time wanted something even better and the gunmakers strove to find answers to the problems, the most important of which was to simplify the loading operation. This could best be done by eliminating the need to cock the external hammers. The solution was, of course, not only to eliminate the need to cock the hammers but also to eliminate the hammers! If we except the Needham needle-fire gun, the first "hammerless" breechloader was the "Daw" of 1862. This was not as successful as the Daw hammer-gun which appeared at the same time and enjoyed but brief success.

Several other hammerless guns appeared before the Gibbs and Pitt; and then came the Murcott, which was the first of the lever-cocking hammerless guns to achieve success. The year 1876 saw the introduction of the Anson and Deeley, which was not only hammerless and cocked by the fall of the barrel but also abolished the traditional method of construction and brought a completely new system forward which was to last to the present day. Two years later Joseph Lang patented his barrel cocking action but, although guns were built on this principle, Lang had to abandon his design owing to the actions which were brought by Anson and Deeley against infringement of their patent. Lang, therefore, turned to underlever cocking to avoid the possibility of legal action.

Lang, however, does not appear to have had a suitable action on the "drawing board" and so he looked to an earlier patent obtained by E. Hughes in 1875, which he embodied in a modification of the design covered by patent in 1880. However, before this, in 1879, Lang had patented a variation of his barrel cocking action, and the design of this can be seen in the illustration overleaf: this shows the robust pivoted underlever and the hammers mounted on the trigger plate. At first one might be fooled into believing that this was a sidelock with underlever cocking, but an inspection of the illustration will show that this was not the case: this Lang is a trigger-plate action gun, and it is salutary to be reminded that in the same year MacNaughton of Edinburgh patented his trigger-plate action gun, many examples of which are still in use and very highly regarded.

The Lang, with its underlever cocking and dummy sideplates, represents an interesting example of underlever cocking. The system, as those who use it well know, has much to commend it, and one or two modern guns of foreign origin use this system, albeit slightly modified, and undoubtedly they have their staunch adherents.

The firm of Joseph Lang underwent several changes in style and direction before being bought out by Stephen Grant and Sons in 1925 and the name survived as Atkin, Grant and Lang Ltd. following the amalgamation with the firm Henry Atkin in 1960. A

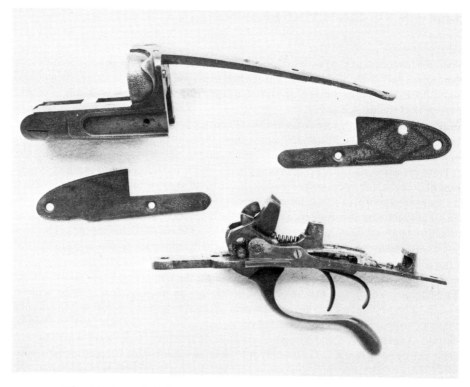

The sideplates of the Lang gun are dummies; the lockwork is mounted
on the trigger plate.

further amalgamation took place with the firm of Churchill in 1971 but the Churchill
Atkin Grant and Lang grouping finally ceased to trade in 1980.

It would be of interest to discover how many of the Lang lever-cocking guns have
survived and, knowing something of the astonishing longevity of best British guns,
how many are still in use.

THE LANG LEVER-COCKER

Previously I have described the Lang hammerless lever-cocking shotgun. At that time I
only had an illustration of the action body and lockwork, and it was used to show how
this interesting action functioned. As a result of this article I received a number of
letters on this type of shotgun and entered into a quite lengthy correspondence with
several readers. Mr. Kilfedder of Northern Ireland let me have photographs of a very
interesting Grant hammerless gun which I will be describing later.

I had been keen to see a complete Lang lever-cocking gun and, as with most things, if
you wait long enough someone will turn up with exactly what you want. This, of

course, is just what happened. My very good friend Allan Paton produced not one but three very interesting guns. All will be the subject of future articles, but among the collection was a complete lever-cocking Lang. I sometimes can't help thinking that we have not progressed as far as we might like to think. The Lang gun is an example of this. Admittedly it is a 16-bore and it is a non-ejector, but how well it handles! The lines of the gun are graceful and the operation is easy and convenient. I sometimes get the same feeling when I compare my pre-war Leica 35 mm cameras with the post-war up-to-date 35 mm reflex cameras. The Leica was a true miniature and you could pop it into your pocket; but carry my largest 35 mm reflex around your neck for an afternoon and you'll know all about it!

To be quite fair, I don't suppose the underlever is quite so convenient as a top-lever and certainly, since this lever has to cock the action, it is not as easy to open as is the top-lever which, apart from drawing back the bolts, has merely to move the safety. On the other hand, the barrels open and close very easily because all the work they have to do is to perform the primary extraction of the fired cartridges.

On the Lang the safety is mounted on the tang, but it swings across to the side instead of moving back and forth. Also this gun has two cocking indicators which are small, gold-plated pins which rise up when the action is cocked; this system has the advantage that you can both see and feel whether the locks are cocked. On the tang or

The Lang lever cocked with the sideplate removed.

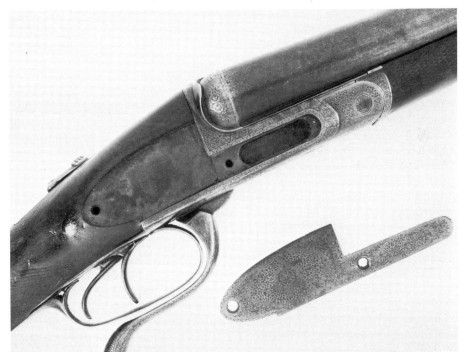

top strap, just in front of the safety lever, is to be found the words "Lang's Patent" and on each of the lockplates is the legend "Joseph Lang and Sons".

Those of you who remember the earlier articles on Lang will recall that the term "lockplate" is really a misnomer, since these plates do not carry the lockwork. They are complete dummy plates and whatever you may think of the use of dummy sideplates, they did tend to strengthen the gun at this point. Such additional strength was an advantage, since much of the stock was cut away to provide a space for the lockwork.

As far as the visual appeal of an action with or without dummy sideplates goes you will have the opportunity to judge for yourself, from the section which follows on the Grant hammerless gun, for this action does not have dummy sideplates. Unfortunately, we can't tell with absolute accuracy how the Lang handled originally, since at some time in the past it has been rebarrelled. Instead of the top rib bearing the name and address of Joseph Lang we have the name "Bambridge & Co., Eton" and the statement "New Barrels by". The gun was originally made by Lang in about 1881. I haven't been able to trace Bambridge & Co. so I can't tell when the barrels were fitted.

MR. GRANT'S HAMMERLESS GUN

A number of readers have written to me about Mr. Grant's gun (examples of which they have), and about comments on the gun in J. H. Walsh's book, *The Modern Sportsman's Gun & Rifle*, published in 1882. Walsh (who also wrote under the name "Stonehenge"), was at one time editor of *The Field*, and his writings represent what one might call eyewitness accounts of events which are of increasing interest to those studying the development of sporting firearms.

Walsh tells us, on page 217 of his book, that he had reported in the spring of 1872 on Mr. Grant's gun and that his report had given "considerable offence to some of Mr. Grant's customers"; despite this, Walsh tells us that "he saw no reason to alter his opinions". On the following page of the book there is a fine engraving which shows the mechanism of the Grant gun. The engraving reveals that this lock can be regarded as a trigger-plate lock with coil mainsprings.

Before we look more closely at Mr. Walsh's critical comments, let's have a look at the Grant gun. Grant was in partnership with Mrs. Boss after the death of her husband. He then started up in business at 67a St. James's Street in 1866–7. He became renowned for building the highest-quality guns of perfect symmetry and proportion; in the opinion of many his sidelever hammer breechloaders were perfection itself. In 1889 the firm became Stephen Grant and Sons and, in 1925, the first of many mergers took place. This first was between Grant and Joseph Lang Ltd. The story of the firm after that date has been dealt with in previous articles, so having sorted out the historical background let's go back to 1872 when, Mr. Walsh tells us, "he first noticed the Grant gun".

Locating the patent for any gun is a great help, but this is particularly the case when there is comment about it. No patent in the name of Stephen Grant can be located which resembles the gun illustrated by Walsh, and no mention is made in Greener of

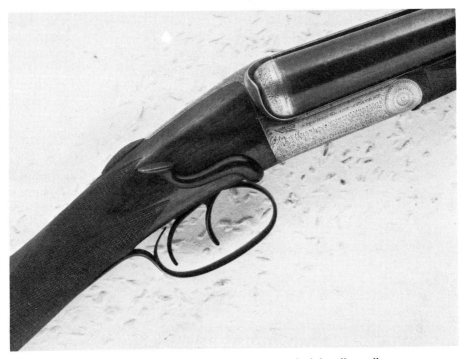

The Grant sidelever, nice lines and a gun which handles well.

the Grant hammerless gun, so we must turn to examples of the gun which have survived.

Most of those readers who expressed interest in the Grant gun live miles away from me. One lives in Australia! So, it was with very considerable delight that I welcomed Mr. Meachin, the owner of a Grant gun, to Boothroyd's Booth at the Strathallan Game Fair. Mr. Meachin, a gentleman of great perception, at once appreciated that I could not examine the internal workings of his Grant gun at the Fair, first because there simply wasn't time and, second, because it is damned difficult to find lost screws in long grass! With a generosity that I have now come to expect from my readers Mr. Meachin suggested that I have the gun on loan, to photograph it and examine its innards. I accepted this offer.

The gun is a 12-bore, $2\frac{1}{2}$ in. chamber, No. 2 of a pair (No. 5015). It is, of course, a non-ejector and bears the original London proof marks and later Birmingham nitro proof marks. The barrels bear the mark "HW"; they are Damascus and 30 inches long. The gun has a sidelever which, when depressed, cocks the internal locks, sets the safety and withdraws the barrel bolt, allowing the barrels to fall for loading. Depressing the lever is easy – the pressure required is not excessive and unlikely to be tiring even after a long day in the field. As one would expect, the gun is nicely balanced and I think I could shoot well with it.

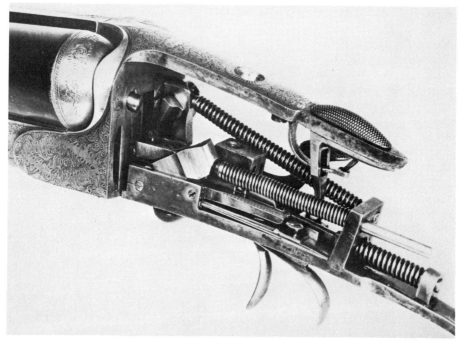

The "works" of the sidelever cocking Grant gun; note the treatment
of the bar of the action on this example.

With the stock removed we see that the lockwork is as shown in Walsh. The
sidelever draws back the bolt and then presses against the hammers, rotating them and
compressing the coil springs which surround long rods extending rearwards. The
trigger and sear mechanisms are present in conventional, though modified, form,
because of their situation on the trigger-plate, and the safety, which is set by the lever,
blocks the triggers only. This was Mr. Grant's first mistake, since Walsh objects to this
kind of safety – he requires (most definitely) that the safety be of the intercepting type
which guards against the accidental discharge of the gun should the sear become jarred
out of the bent.

Walsh also condemned the absence of any means of reducing the admission of gas to
the action through the striker holes. This problem was reduced in later years, not so
much from improvements in the mechanics of the gun, but because of improvements in
the construction of the cartridge case. Walsh also expresses dislike for coil springs and
has a strong preference for flat springs. Interest in coil springs as an alternative to the
more expensive flat spring no doubt arose with the use of coil springs for striker-fired
weapons (such as bolt-action rifles) and the introduction of the Martini-Henry which
was provisionally approved for service use in 1871.

Coil springs were used in the Adsett of 1879 and in the earlier Woodward of 1876 but
in spite of the ease with which coil springs could be made and in spite of their low cost,

shotgun actions continued to use flat springs, as they do to the present day.

One of the earliest of the hammerless actions was that offered by Theophilus Murcott of 68 Haymarket. Walsh tells us that Murcott "patented his plan" in 1871. This we know to be true since the patent number is easy to remember, 1003 and the actual date is 15 April. We must now ask ourselves why Walsh didn't tell us about the Grant patent. One reason could be that he didn't know about it (which is unlikely) or that the patent was taken out in the name of someone else. But why did Grant state, on the gun: "Stephen Grant's Patent"? The Murcott gun was well received by Walsh; it used flat springs and conventional locks and it was not until some time later that Walsh commented on the lack of an intercepting safety. Fewer Murcott guns seem to have survived than Grant guns and I have had no reader comment from Murcott owners extolling the merits of their gun, whereas a number have commented favourably on the Grant.

Was the patent taken out by someone else? A search around the 1872 date (when first mentioned by Walsh) provides no clues, and the only patent which remotely resembles the Grant is one taken out by H. F. Philips in 1879. The number of the Grant gun places it after 1880, so one wonders if the date given by Walsh is wrong. A search of *The Field* for 1872 would answer this question.

There are a number of other avenues that still remain to be explored since, at present, we have more questions than answers. If anyone has a Grant hammerless gun, sidelever cocking, similar to that illustrated, I would be interested to have details, serial number and so on. Meanwhile I will go on with the search.

Just in case I had overlooked something, and to make certain that I hadn't done something silly, I had a chat with David Baker, who is working on Volume 2 of *The British Shotgun*. This deals with hammerless actions and, since David must have worked his way through the patent jungle, I value his opinion. His comment was that the Phillips patent was the nearest he could find and that, to the best of his knowledge, no patent for this action had been published in the name of Stephen Grant. So the mystery remains.

A search of *The Field* was carried out, and there is no mention of the Grant action during 1872 but early in 1882 we find the comments on the Grant and the illustrations which were reproduced in Walsh's book. From this we can safely say that the date 1872 is in error and it should be 1882.

Mr. Meachin still uses his Grant and likes the action very much and he tells me that he shoots well with his vintage Grant which by now has passed the century!

AN UNUSUAL WILLIAM POWELL GUN

My good friend Colin Haygarth, knowing my recent interest in William Powell guns, very kindly arranged to send me an unusual Powell double 12-bore. As you can see from the illustration, the gun is an early hammerless model with underlever cocking. One point which becomes apparent when one looks at it is the absence of a safety device. This is odd, since each of the "back-action" sidelocks refers to "William A. Adams Safety Locks, July 1884". Is one to presume that the locks are so safe that they

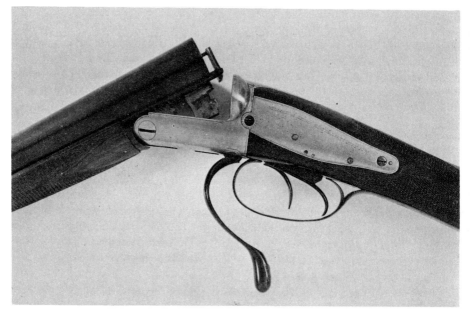

Hammerless underlever gun by William Powell of Birmingham.

do not require any additional safety device? A further search for clues brought to light the statement, on the breech flats, that this was "T. W. Patent No. 651". Last of all there was the maker's name on the barrel, "William A. Powell & Son, 13 Carrs Lane, Birmingham". The gun is, of course, a non-ejector. A careful examination of the outside of the locks indicated that they were not normal back-action sidelocks as might be imagined by the external shape, but were striker-fired locks – and for this reason this type of lock has no tumbler. Instead there is a cylindrical striker which, when released by the sear, is impelled forward by a coil spring.

In the unlikely event of your having a gun of this type do not be deceived by the statement, "Safety Locks": the locks are anything but safe when removed from the gun. If you press the sear (as would happen if the trigger were pressed) the striker is released. If held at an angle of five degrees above the horizontal and some three feet above the ground the striker will be propelled about ten feet and the coil spring about two feet. As you can imagine, this could be dangerous – if not lethal – for someone who might be in the way! The only possible excuse for referring to these locks as "safety locks" is the addition of a front intercepting sear which, of course, does not prevent the release of the striker if the rear sear is operated: it will only act if the rear sear is jarred out of the bent.

The locks and action of this gun are built under T.W.'s patent. T.W. was the noted Birmingham gunmaker, T. Woodward, a man with many patents to his name, but his lock lacks the additional interception sear, so we can assume that this was due to the foresight of Mr. William A. Adams, although I have not been able to trace any record of this modification.

This gun is of considerable interest and it teaches us several lessons. First of all it is extremely light, simple and well balanced. It illustrates the fact that often, with increasing complexity, come penalties which can partially or completely cancel out the advantages which complications are sometimes claimed to provide. Most shooting men who have handled these early hammerless breech-loaders have commented upon their lightness. The situation is rather similar to the 35 mm camera. The Leica, when originally introduced, was light and could be carried in the pocket. With the passing of the years one arrived at the Zeiss Contarex which was heavier than a 2¼ in. reflex and considerably more complicated.

The other lesson that this gun can teach us is one of caution. If, like me, you are cursed with an insatiable curiosity, do be careful when you open an unfamiliar gun. At best you may not be able to put it back together again, you may lose some parts or you can hurt yourself if you do not take care.

Oh! I almost forgot: how is the gun cocked? Well, the other end of the underlever projects inside the stock and when it is pushed forward the top end moves to the rear and in so doing engages two projections on the strikers. The strikers are pushed rearwards until fully cocked. The mechanism is simple and easy to operate. This is just one of several unusual guns which have been made over the years by Powell of Birmingham.

The locks of the Woodward "Acme" gun (see page 42).

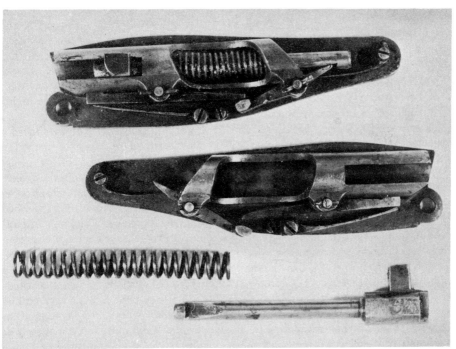

THE WOODWARD ACME GUN

Readers will have seen the outside of these locks. They are attached to the gun illustrated in the preceding section. Although I mentioned the unusual locks (which when removed from the gun and "fired" can project the strikers for ten feet) I didn't show an illustration of what the inside of the lock looked like. Several readers have expressed an interest in strikers, coil springs and locks, so here is what these locks look like inside.

The right-hand lock (at the top of the picture on the previous page) is assembled. The sear, which engages with the bent in the striker, can be seen, and also the secondary sear, which engages with a notch in the front of the striker. Each sear is provided with its own spring. Each lock has, therefore, two single leaf springs and one long coil spring. Leaving out the springs and "pins" there are two "limbs" and the striker to each lock. You can see what the striker looks like in the lower illustration, which shows the left-hand lock dismantled. You can also see how long the coil spring is, when released. The projection on the striker (this, incidentally, was the term employed by Woodward when he described the lock) is provided so that the arm of the underlever acts against it when the lever is pushed forward to open the gun. Since the projections are inwards and facing one another you can understand how the centrally disposed lever can cock both locks.

"COMMUNITY" GUN

The Woodward action was sold in London by J. Beattie & Co. of 104 Queen Victoria Street, London E.C. as the "Acme" hammerless gun. In 1882 the Acme sold for £20 in the "Best Quality" and for £14 in "Second Quality". For those who did not want to spend any money on ornamentation the Acme was offered as the "Community" gun. This gun was suggested as being suitable for exportation since, if any part broke, a replacement "could be made by an unskilled person on the spot". For this quality the price fell to £12 10s. and even lower with a non-automatic bolt – £10 10s.

The Acme differed in one important respect from the Woodward pattern gun illustrated in the previous article. The Acme was provided with a safety bolt. The virtue of this was marginal, since it bolted the triggers only and if the sear were released by a jar the safety would not prevent the gun discharging if loaded. William A. Adams' modification to the original Woodward lock would prevent an accidental discharge of this type, since the secondary sear would prevent the striker from being released. The Beattie gun had one feature absent on the Woodward/Powell namely, cocking indicators. These were very fashionable, in the early days of hammerless guns since, without external hammers, it was not possible to tell whether the locks were cocked merely by looking at the gun. At least one "improved" Woodward Acme gun has survived. I cannot help wondering if one of J. Beattie's Acme guns has managed to escape destruction?

THE SIDELOCK

Have you ever wondered how a sidelock double shotgun works? Let's take just one aspect: how are the locks cocked? If you have a sidelock and have taken off the locks to clean them you will have noticed that the mainspring either lies in front of the "hammer", in which case you have a "bar-action" lock or it lies behind the "hammer", in which case you have a "back-action" lock.

Today, because the hammer is inside the lock, it is called a tumbler. The tumbler has

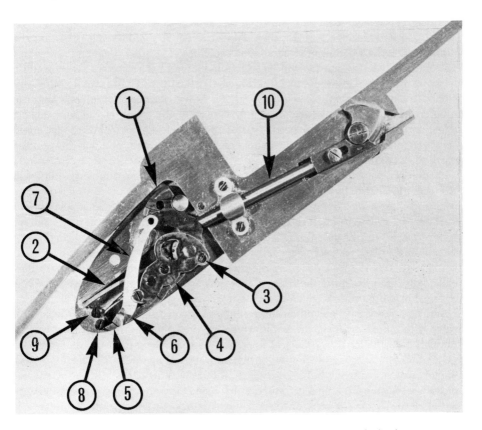

This gunmaker's test piece illustrates how the mechanism of a back-action sidelock operates when the barrels are depressed to cock the mechanism. (1) The tumbler is under the influence of the mainspring (2), the tumbler being mounted and supported by the bridle (3). The tumbler is held back when cocked by the sear (4), the tail of which (5) is pushed upwards by the trigger bar (not shown). At the same time the tail of the safety sear (6) would also be raised moving the top of the sear (7) clear of the tumbler. Both sears have their own springs (8 & 9) and the tumbler is cocked by the cocking rod (10) in the bar of the action.

to turn, so it is mounted on an axle, the bearings of which are at either side of the tumbler, and one in the lockplate itself (quite often the end which lies flush with the outer surface of the plate has a gold-filled slot which allows you to see whether or not the lock is cocked). The other end of the axle has its own "outrigger" bearing which is called the bridle. The tumbler can therefore pivot easily on its axle between the two plates, the larger being the lockplate and the smaller the bridle. Before the tumbler can do any useful work it has to be provided with a spring, which, when compressed, stores energy which can be released when required, the energy being imparted to the striker by the tumbler to fire the cartridge. The mainspring, which does all this work, is mounted, as we have seen, either in front or behind the tumbler.

In the lock which we will use for demonstration, the mainspring is behind the tumbler and it is, by definition, a back-action sidelock. The main advantage which this type of sidelock has is that the bar of the action does not have to be cut away to house the mainsprings and it is theoretically stronger. The mainspring has two limbs, one of which is fixed to the lockplate, while the other is either attached to or bears against the tumbler. The lock under consideration does not employ a link swivel between the spring and tumbler; instead it bears against the tumbler direct. A little roller could have been introduced here, but the maker considered the benefit of doing this was not worth the extra expense involved.

In addition, we require some sort of prop or catch to hold the tumbler at full cock. This is accomplished by cutting a notch or "bent" in the tumbler into which the nose of a centrally pivoted lever can be inserted and so prop the tumbler in the cocked position. This lever is called the "sear" (from the Latin *sera*, a bar), and in Shakespeare's time it was called a "sere" and it may also be spelt "sceare". So that the nose of the sear will properly engage the bent, it is provided with its own little spring, the sear spring, and when you press the trigger of your gun, this is one of the springs which you compress, since the trigger blade acts against the tail of the sear, which is extended at right angles to the lockplate for this reason.

At this point we have met all the main components on our sidelock: the sideplate on which is mounted the lock, the bridle which provides the additional bearing for the tumbler, the tumbler itself, the sear and the sear spring and mainspring. On good-quality locks there is one other component, the intercepting safety. The normal safety on most sidelocks merely bolts the triggers; it does nothing to prevent the accidental release of the tumbler. This can happen owing to dirt interfering with the proper seating of the sear in the bent, or to mechanical damage or failure. A lock with any of these defects can be released by an accidental jar and, if the gun is loaded, the user will be fortunate to get off with just a fright. To avoid this, the lock is provided with an intercepting safety which is disengaged if the trigger is pulled but which will prevent the tumbler from rotating fully if the sear is jarred out of engagement.

We can, of course, examine the lock when it is removed from the gun but we can't see how it is cocked, since it must be fitted to the gun for this to take place. What we need is an inside picture of what happens. In the lockwork illustrated this has been provided. The lock is, in fact, part of the training programme for gunmakers, and it is mounted on a section of metal representing the action body of a gun complete with fore-end.

On this type of mechanism, instead of using a cocking lever, a cocking bar or rod is employed and we can see how, when the gun is opened, the rod is pushed to the rear against the breast of the hammer. As the rod moves to the rear, the hammer or tumbler is rotated until the sear engages the bent and the lock is cocked. Of course, on a complete gun the rod would not be mounted by means of the bracket which can be seen but would, instead, operate through a hole drilled in the action body.

No really startling developments have occurred in the design of gun locks for many years and today's locks are the result of years of slow and painstaking improvements. The fact that most people who use guns have little idea of how they work is testimony to the skill of the lockmaker and to the care with which locks are made. The mechanism of the best guns will last for years and years without giving any trouble. But abuse and neglect, rust and oxidised oil can cause trouble, so if you are in any doubt have a competent gunmaker check the locks on your gun just to be on the safe side.

SIDELOCKS AND BOX-LOCKS

One of the first books on guns which I bought was *Shotguns, their History and Development*. The author was H. B. C. Pollard and the date of publication 1923. This book is quite fascinating, since it reflects the attitude of a period not so long ago measured in years but separated from us today in so many ways that it could have been written on another planet!

However, I intend to use this book to illustrate something else. In the chapter which deals with the selection of a gun it is interesting to see the illustrations which are used. The first is of a Boss double trigger 12-bore sidelock. The second illustration is of a Churchill "best" quality 12-bore sidelock, the third Holland's sidelock 12-bore with detachable locks and the fourth a Purdey sidelock 12-bore.

Pollard says "The 'best' gun is usually made with sidelocks instead of the box action of the Anson and Deeley type. These locks make the arm more expensive and in no way add to its efficiency, but they make it rather more delicate in balance, graceful in appearance, slenderer and more tapered at the action than can be achieved with the Anson and Deeley type."

Greener, writing 13 years before, a staunch advocate of the Anson and Deeley type of lock, stated that the A & D lock gave quicker ignition and almost the sole advantage of sidelocks was that they could be easily removed. Even this advantage was not allowed, because Greener stated that ease of removal was "not a matter of importance since a well-made box-lock will work well for years without any attention".

In 1906 Henry Sharp had pointed out that by using the Westley Richards box-lock, ease of dismantling could be offered with their hand-detachable lock. Sharp condemned the sidelock on the grounds of over-complication, and in his book *Modern Sporting Gunnery* all the illustrations of "best" guns are of Anson and Deeley type actions.

Coming closer to our own times, Gerald Burrard, writing in 1931, comes out in favour of the sidelock because on his system of assessment the sidelock is the better "in five out of six points", some of the aspects being considered including safety, efficiency, strength, trigger pull, ease in cocking and quickness. Burrard, like Pollard before him, mentions the question of beauty. He goes on to say that this aspect should not be thought unimportant, and that the lines of the box-lock cannot compare with those of a really well-designed bar-action sidelock.

In considering the appearance of the sidelock we must bear in mind that there are three basic types; first, the bar-action with the mainspring in front of the tumbler and lying along the bar of the action; second, the back-action, in which the mainspring is behind the tumbler. In back-action sidelocks we have two types, the first looking exactly like a normal bar-action lock except that the pins are in a different place on the lockplates. The earlier type of back-action sidelock cannot be mistaken, since the lockplates are of a completely different shape. The third type of "sidelock" is that in which a box-lock action has had dummy sideplates fitted in imitation of a sidelock. Although there have been occasions when someone has purchased a box-lock with these sideplates and thought he had a true sidelock, no reputable firm would practise such deception. Such dummy actions can be detected by the fact that the triggers are much further forward than would be the case with a sidelock and the sideplates lack the necessary pins.

Let's come up to date and see what is said in 1970 about the merits of sidelocks. We can take the opinion of Gough Thomas in his book *Shotguns and Cartridges*. Times have changed since Burrard wrote his comments but "G.T." agrees in the main, "a more elegant weapon than the box-lock, usually better balanced and with superior trigger pulls. Everlasting in the best grades if well treated". One could, of course, write just as convincingly about box-locks but, like it or not, the sidelock has that certain indefinable something about it. The appraisal of the relative merits of sidelock and box-lock can provoke heated arguments, but Gough Thomas, I think, is as impartial a judge as any; he puts the benefits of both systems forward and leaves you to decide.

THE TARGET GUN

This article could equally well have borne the title "The Ward gun", or "The Rylands gun".

The story starts several years ago with two of my pet obsessions: "The use of coil springs in shotgun actions" and "What went wrong with the British gun trade?" In pursuit of both these interests, I encountered the "Target Shotgun". This followed an article I wrote on trade marks, which brought to light the use of a "Target" or "Bull's Eye" by the Birmingham firm, Ward & Sons. Founded in 1859, Ward were one of the last of the Birmingham makers to manufacture flintlock "Trade Guns" and the "Long Dane" guns from their Central Gun Works at 24–7 Bath Street. They continued to make breech- and muzzle-loading guns, rifles, revolvers, African guns and firearms of every description until just after the First World War. By the mid-1920s they made both bar- and back-action hammer-guns, and also ball-and-shot guns, and imported a range of very low-priced Belgian guns. In addition, they offered three grades of the "Target Hammerless Gun". The prices were £11, £12 and £13.

Sold by Armstrong of Newcastle, this gun bears the correct patent dates
of 1917 and 1918, and the Ward "Target" trademark. Note the single pin
in the action body.

The gun illustrated is the mid-range No. 2 Model. If you look carefully you can see
two of the features which make this gun unusual: the first is the shape of the fences,
almost conical, and the second, the single screw at the rear, lower part of the action
body.

I eventually got my hands on one of these guns and was able to dismantle it. Some
time later I obtained the patents which covered an unusual and interesting action. The
action employed coil springs instead of flat springs and could be regarded as a later
development of the famous A & D action. The development simplified the manufacturing processes, rather than improving the action. The patents, which covered a
period from 1904 until 1918, were in the name of Charles Rylands. Those concerned
with shotguns covered two distinct types of action, one with the coil spring in front of
the hammers and one with the coil springs behind the hammers.

I have yet to encounter a Rylands patent gun of this first type, i.e. one with what one
might call bar-coil springs, but the second type of action covered by the patents of 1917
and 1918 appears to have been sold by Ward & Sons and it bears the "Target" trade
mark on the flats of the action.

In work of this nature, things go well for a period and then tend to lie fallow for a while unless much energy and expense is devoted to stoking the fires of hot enquiry. I had tended to let the fires die down somewhat and it wasn't until the 1983 Game Fair that I realised that I had seen a number of guns with the curious conical fences I had come to call "Ward fences" for want of a better term. John Bond brought the first one along, nicely engraved, Greener-type cross-bolt, but with no name or trade mark anywhere. The "Target" guns all seem to have a top-lever wedge-fast bolt, not the Greener cross-bolt, so, in spite of the shape of the fences, I thought that perhaps this was not a Ward gun. Also, this was an A & D-type action, judging from the location of the pins through the action body. Then along came another gun with Ward-type fences. This was brought by Mr. Goodman, again with nice engraving but no names, patent dates or any identification. And, once again, an A & D-type action.

Then I struck gold: Dr. Scratcherd produced a gun with the true Ward-type fences and signed on the rib "Armstrong, Newcastle-on-Tyne". No doubt about it, this was a Ward Target Gun and with the kind permission of the owner the barrels and fore-end were removed. There was the "Target" trade-mark and the Rylands patent dates of 1917 and 1918.

Ward Target Guns have a curved back to the action, whereas the Armstrong Target Gun has a straight back. In spite of this I am confident that the gun was made by Ward and it has the Rylands action with the coil springs behind the hammers. There is no Greener cross-bolt and just one pin in the bar of the action.

There are other small differences between the Target Guns illustrated in the Ward catalogue of 1928 and the Armstrong gun. These tend to make me think that perhaps the firm of Armstrong placed a special order with Ward for Target Guns to their own pattern. I have not been able to trace anything about Mr. Charles Rylands other than the fact that he may have worked for Chas. Osborne early in his career. At the turn of the century he described himself as a "Gun Maker" and he lived at Bittall Road, Barnt Green, Worcestershire, between Birmingham and Bromsgrove. From a study of the series of patents which were taken out in the name of Charles Rylands it becomes

The Ward "Target" gun as advertised in the 1920s. The fences are a distinctive feature.

TARGET HAMMERLESS GUN.

obvious that here was a man trying to adapt a shotgun long made by traditional methods to manufacture by machinery. Manufacture of the Target shotgun appears to have ceased during the depressed years of the 1930s and was never restarted. That the gun had merit can be gauged by the fact that a number have survived, quite a surprising number in view of the likely total production. It is to be greatly regretted that the enterprise was not more successful. If it had been, we might still have machine-made guns from Birmingham.

The other lesson to be learned is that because of the way in which the vast majority of our shotguns have been made, the variation possible is immense. So, when you see "just another box-lock" take a closer look at it; there are still lots of things which remain to be discovered, lots of things which have been forgotten and lots of questions needing answers. Who, for example, was Charles Rylands?

THE SIMPLEX DETACHABLE GUN

As the years have gone by my files on British shotguns have grown and are now replete with useful information. This has been culled from contemporary writings, from gun catalogues, and from the examples themselves, the guns which have survived legislation, lack of attention and just plain wear and tear. In this task I again acknowledge the enormous help given by the readers of *The Shooting Times*.

By now I have a reasonable chance of providing at least some information on the gun or guns about which enquiries are made. Sometimes I feel rather sad that I cannot say more about a gun which is obviously a cherished possession, but gunmakers, with a few notable exceptions, were not given to the use of the pen: the file was their chosen tool! One special section – the "mystery file" – has now been devoted to those weapons about which I know nothing.

The story of the "Simplex" gun started with a letter from Mr. G. A. Liggett, who told me that according to his information the gun was one of only three made. He dates it to the turn of the century and told me that 28 in. steel barrels were fitted. The name "Simplex Demountable" can be seen on the bottom tang behind the trigger guard, and according to Mr. Liggett the name "Hill and Smith, Price Street, Birmingham" is also to be found on the gun. Hill and Smith were certainly in business at No. 13 Court, Price Street, Birmingham in 1900. Patents were taken out by Hill and Smith, very possibly the same two people, in 1894 and 1895 but neither covered detachable lockwork of the type illustrated.

During the first decade of the twentieth century Hill & Smith continued their development work and in 1906 they patented an ejection mechanism. In 1908 we find the patent for a gun "carrying the whole of the lock mechanism upon a detachable trigger-plate". The lever which releases the lock is mounted on the bottom strap behind the trigger guard, and swings out to the side to unfasten the trigger-plate.

The best known detachable locks are those of Holland & Holland with the special pin mechanism and equally well known are the modified A & D locks and the hand-detachable lock fitted to Westley Richards guns and rifles. The system employed by the Simplex differs from both the H & H sidelock and the WR lock since, apart from other considerations with the Simplex, even the trigger mechanism is detached! This must have been quite a handsome weapon in its pristine state. I have to confess to a liking for "bar-in-the-wood" actions and the Simplex is a good example of this style of stocking. Nothing, to my mind, beats the old "Edinburgh" action of MacNaughton and, of course, this was also a trigger-plate action gun. If there were only three Simplex guns made it is rather too much to hope that the other two have survived.

A number of questions remain unanswered. Who were Hill & Smith? Are all three Simplex guns the same, or are there variants, with improvements made, one after the other? Indeed, one has to ask if three Simplex guns were made? Lastly, did any other maker produce a similar type of gun to the Simplex as made by Hill & Smith? We have the answer to the last question since a similar gun by Thomas Bland of London has been notified to me but so far no illustrations. One cannot help wondering if Hill & Smith ever published a catalogue and, if so, did one survive?

SHAM SIDELOCKS

The argument as to which is best, the sidelock or the box-lock, has been with us ever since the development of these two types of action became static and easily externally recognisable. The specific points which the expert will happily debate until closing time fall under six main headings: ease of cocking, quickness, efficiency, safety, strength and, lastly, appearance.

There were, of course, some noted champions of the box-lock action, and the feelings of W. W. Greener show through quite clearly when one reads the statement made in his catalogue of the 1920s regarding the Greener sidelock: "This type of gun – so beloved of the London Gunmaker – is preferred by some sportsmen as an English Game Gun and although guns made with sidelock mechanism are rather slower in firing and more complicated, the shape affords admirable opportunity for decorative effect."

Leaving aside technical considerations there is little doubt that most people prefer the look of a sidelock to a box-lock. We are, of course, talking about the bar-action sidelock since, for some years now, the back-action sidelock, although still made, is externally indistinguishable unless one looks closely for the screws in the sideplate. The fact that the lockplate outline for the back-action lock is rarely any different from the bar-action, lends weight to the statement that popular opinion prefers the smooth sweeping outline of the "standard" English sidelock of traditional pattern, whether the sideplate conceals bar- or back-action lockwork.

Because of this general preference for the outline of the sidelock, a number of box-lock guns have been built which were fitted with dummy sideplates. In external appearance they were very similar to the true sidelock and one occasionally finds mention of this type of gun in old catalogues. The usual description was "Fine quality, fitted with imitation sidelock action." How many of this type of gun have survived I cannot say, but there are most certainly quite a number owned by people who think they have a genuine sidelock gun, as I know from personal experience. This, of course, poses a slight problem, since one cannot gratuitously denigrate someone else's gun and

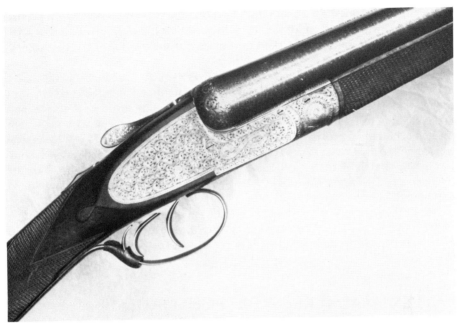

The Dickson "Round Action" with dummy sideplates.

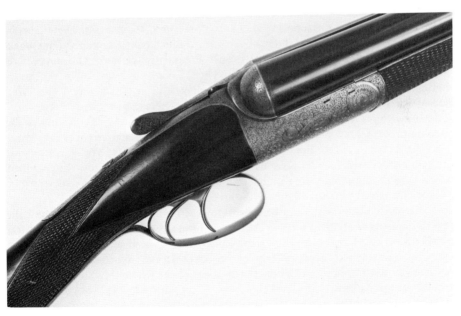

The true "Round Action".

I normally would not draw attention to the fact that a prized sidelock, a gun greatly liked by the owner, was not all that he perhaps thought it was. In addition to box-locks, a number of continental actions were fitted with dummy sideplates, particularly over-and-under shotguns.

One type of shotgun that, in my own personal opinion, is even better-looking than a sidelock is the "trigger-plate action" gun. This type of action is fairly common in Europe and is seen to the best advantage in those guns made by Dickson and MacNaughton of Edinburgh. The MacNaughton "Edinburgh" gun with the wood-covered action is particularly pleasing, as is the Dickson Round Action. Why anyone would want to use this action as a basis for an imitation sidelock I cannot understand. Nevertheless, a short time ago I had the opportunity of examining what I at first thought was a Dickson sidelock. Closer scrutiny revealed that this was a Round Action with imitation sideplates.

One of the photographs shows a standard Round Action made in 1910; the other shows a "sidelock". There is only one screw to be seen in the rear of the lockplate – the screw which holds the dummy sideplate in position. If you own a sidelock gun, have a closer look at it. Is it all it appears to be?

STYLES HAMMERLESS BREECHLOADER

One of the more fascinating aspects of the development of the modern hammerless breechloader is the actual pattern of development itself, the appearance of a sound but revolutionary idea, followed by the translation of this idea into wood and metal. Few such ideas have been an instant success from the beginning, possibly because of the innate conservatism of the shooting man but, more often, because of the problems of manufacture. In retrospect most of us have said, at one time or another, "That was a good idea, I wonder why it didn't catch on?" Frequently the good idea appears, is poorly translated into practice and fails. Then, taken up again, with the faults eliminated, it becomes a success. Equally, we have the case of a sound idea, well carried out and very successful. The success encourages imitators and "improvers" and here we have the reverse situation: the failure not of the original idea but of the later "improvements". In no other field of endeavour can this pattern of development be so clearly seen as in the firearms of the late nineteenth century. The appearance of the hammerless breechloader gives us the opportunity of studying how the problems which were encountered were recognised and then overcome.

As we have seen, the early hammerless breechloaders relied on the use of a lever to cock the mechanism; this could be a push-forward type of underlever, as with the Murcott and many others, a turning underlever, as used by Alex Henry or the top lever employed by MacNaughton. All of these ideas can be classed as "improvements". A new and fundamental idea was that of Anson & Deeley. Not only was the lock mechanism new but here was a completely new system where the fall of the barrels cocked the mechanism.

That lever cocking did have its disadvantages can be seen by the length of some of the levers which were to appear. The levers were made longer and longer to reduce the effort needed both to open the gun and to cock the mechanism. Some went so far as to have two levers, one for each task! Anson & Deeley used a very much longer lever, already to hand, the barrels themselves, and barrel cocking became THE system. I think that the A & D system was one of those which was an unqualified success from the beginning. Many, many "improvers" followed in their footsteps and both the inventors improved on their own idea, but the original concept was right from the start.

Once barrel cocking had been adopted, the ingenuity of the gunmaker and inventor was directed towards the best possible way of putting the idea into practice. There is no doubt that they had quite a problem, since the original idea was so good. The A & D system used a lever pivoted in the same axis as the hinge bolt. One end, projecting through the knuckle, engaged a slot in the fore-end; the other end acted upon the tumbler or internal hammer. As an alternative to a cocking lever, the famous Birmingham gunmaker Scott employed a cocking rod, and Greener went to a considerable amount of trouble to devise alternative arrangements to the original Anson & Deeley. All types of system that man could devise appeared; some enjoyed brief fame before hard use highlighted a defect, others were enjoyed by a knowledgeable few willing to accept minor idiosyncrasies because of real or imagined benefits, or purely for the cachet of owning the unusual.

Many systems are to be found by browsing through the patent files. One wonders if some of them were ever translated into metal and if anyone actually bought and used a gun based on some of the ideas described and illustrated. One such system was patented by T. Keight in 1884. It was an automatic cocking system for drop-down guns where the cocking pieces, one for each tumbler, are attached to the fore-end iron. As the barrels fall, the cocking pieces are drawn forward. The ends are provided with a hook which engages with a notch in the hammer or tumbler so that the hammers are raised to full cock. The only disadvantage to the system appears to be the slight additional problem of taking the gun apart because of having to withdraw the cocking pieces. Unless the gun was dismantled the owner wouldn't know he owned anything unusual. The only Keight-action guns I have encountered have been made by J. G. Styles & Co. of London and Birmingham; if there are any others I should be pleased to know of them.

OPENING MECHANISMS

One of the most satisfactory and widely adopted methods of securing the barrels of a "drop-down" gun to the action has been the "Purdey bolt". Dating from 1863, the patent described a "sliding plate" operated by a pivoted underlever. The early Purdey actions used this system, with the underlever being pushed forward by the thumb, and the trigger guard having a large irregular hole at the front to permit the thumb to be passed through the hole and so push forward the short lever. Such a system is easy to operate as I can testify from experience, and the barrels are easily closed since this is, of course, a snap action.

Some years ago when writing about the development of the shotgun I mentioned

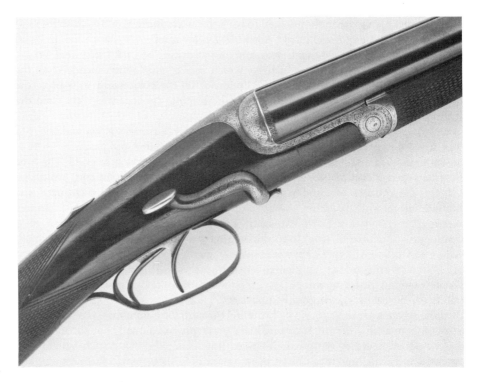

Dickson "Round Action" in 16 bore with side-lever and
wood-covered action.

that one simple line of development was that which ensured that the hands remained in
contact with the gun! Speed and simplicity of use were the two main objectives of the
British gunmaker and the less the hands have to move during the sequence of
operations required to fire a shotgun the quicker the whole operation can be carried
out.

Levers around, in front of, inside or part of the trigger guard dominated the thinking
of the gunmakers until Powell of Birmingham introduced his "lift up" lever, although
not in combination with the Purdey plate or bolt. This was created by Scott who, in
1865, patented what we today call the Scott spindle. This combination of the Purdey
bolt with the Scott spindle and top-lever has most successfully withstood the test of
time.

Levers in front of the guard and around it and now top-levers, both lifting, as in the
Powell, and pushing over to one side (moving laterally): where else could one fit the
lever? Purdey produced one system where the action was opened by pushing down a
stud or large button on the top strap, just about where the modern "safety" is. This did
not appear to have a great deal of success, but one alternative which was popular over
the years was the "sidelever". I have some doubts as to whether a patent was ever
taken out following a definite invention. Certainly various actions had appeared by the

mid-1870s which offered, almost as an alternative, operation by a sidelever. Possibly one of the earliest was that employed by Hollis. A year later in 1876 the Scotts mention an action employing a sidelever, and throughout the nineteenth century a devoted band of sportsmen remained closely attached to this form of lever. Capable of being fitted for either left- or right-hand operation, it was particularly attractive when used with hammer-guns and was also used with the later barrel-cocking hammerless actions. Not successful when employed with lever-cocking hammerless actions, since the leverage was apt to be too small for effective cocking of two mainsprings, it looks best of all when fitted to trigger-plate guns such as the Dickson.

Few Dickson Round Actions with sidelevers were made, compared with the more popular top-lever actions but the photograph shows very adequately how attractive the side-lever action can be, especially when we also have the Dickson in perhaps its most classic form, "bar-in-the-wood".

COMB-LEVER OPENING

Once people stopped loading their shotguns from the front end, a means of introducing the cartridge from the breech end had to be sought. Ease of opening and, of even greater importance, strength and surety of closure were desirable attributes which the gunmakers of the nineteenth century pursued with keen assiduity.

The defects of the Lefaucheux, the first practical breechloader, were early recognised by gunmakers in Britain and efforts were made to overcome them. Important inventions concerned with breech closure were the Purdey bolt, the Westley Richards top lever, and a combination of Purdey bolt with top extension and top-lever operation giving the "treble grip". In 1873 W. W. Greener brought out his widely publicised "treble wedge-fast" breech mechanism which employed the double-grip snap action and a round cross-bolt through the barrel extension. Also widely employed was the rotary underlever, but this had a basic disadvantage as it was not a snap action.

The Purdey bolt had the undoubted merit of convenience. One opened the gun by pressing the top lever to the right, which allowed the barrels to fall open. Closing was even simpler: the curved lump pressed back the bolt until the "bites" were reached, when the bolt sprung home automatically. The vertical-spindle top lever was convenient and it had the additional merit that it could be seen to be closed. In spite of this, other lever systems were devised and many gained acceptance amongst sportsmen. Perhaps the most popular was the sidelever, usually on the right of the action but sometimes fitted on the left.

The earliest of the lever systems was the simple "push-forward" lever in front of the trigger guard, and the early Purdey used this type of lever. Snap action underlevers of all types have one disadvantage, not always apparent until you use one: the right hand cannot work them without losing grip of the stock.

The more you think about it, the top lever, even the vertical lifting lever as used by Powell, has a great many advantages. The leverage is more than adequate and set on top of the gun it will not catch in the clothing.

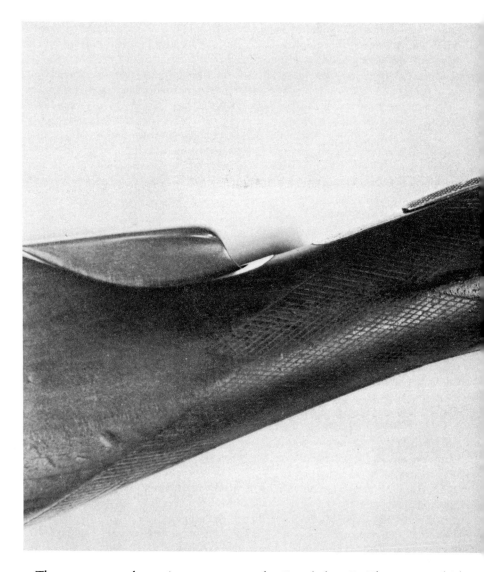

The most unusual opening system was the "comb lever". The patent which protected this idea was granted in 1885 to Jones & Taylor. I have hoped that one day I would see and handle this type of lever, but this hasn't happened yet, though through the good services of a reader, Mr. A. W. Collinson, I have seen the next best thing, five really superb prints of a double 12-bore hammerless gun with the Jones & Taylor comb-lever opening action.

You can see from the illustration that the lever is just in front of the comb of the stock. When this is depressed by the ball of the hand the bell-crank lever inside the stock draws back the locking bolt by means of a connecting rod. At the same time as

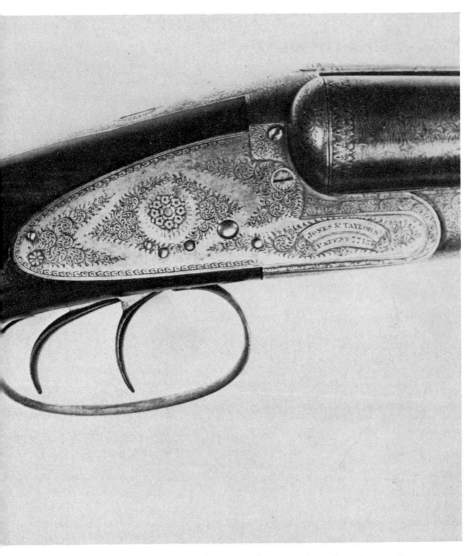

Jones & Taylor's patent comb lever cocking gun. Signed on the top rib,
"Robert Jones, Monarch Gun Works, Manchester Street, Liverpool".

the bolt is withdrawn, the safety bolt is also moved to block the triggers. The barrels,
which are Damascus, carry Birmingham proof marks and, in addition to the double-
bite Purdey bolt, a "doll's head" top extension is also fitted. The top rib bears the
legend "Robert Jones, Monarch Gun Works, Manchester St., Liverpool, No. 58". I
know little about Robert Jones. He was in business in 1848 at 9 Waterloo Road, and by
1900 the firm seems to have gone out of business.

Double 12 bore, by the London Armoury Company, showing the cocking indicators.

COCKING INDICATORS

If you pick up a German gun catalogue it is likely that in the section devoted to A & D-actioned guns you will encounter the phrase "mit seitliche signal stifte". Translated, this means "with lateral signal pegs" or "with side cocking indicators". These are the little pegs which pop out when the lock is cocked so that this fact can be verified both by sight and touch. There are many other cocking indicators where the indication is visual only. If you have a good-quality sidelock you will find that one of the little "axles" which pass through the lockplates has a gold strip across it. This is the cocking indicator, and from its position you can tell whether or not the lock is at full cock.

Long ago such things were not needed. Guns had large external hammers and both you and whoever happened to be near you could see whether or not the locks on your gun were cocked. Even when the hammers vanished inside the lockplate one or two gunmakers still produced guns with "dummy" hammers on the outside of the lockplate so that you could tell at a glance if the internal hammers were cocked. Two things were important in those early days of the hammerless gun: were the locks cocked and were the chambers loaded? With the pinfire gun you could see if the chambers contained a cartridge, since you could see the pins. If the hammers were down on the top of the barrels then the cartridges were fired (or were dud). With rebounding locks this was not possible, as such locks were used to fire central-fire cartridges which lacked external pins.

The earlier locks did have a half-cock "safety" position, but rebounding locks could be let down on live cartridges or on empty chambers and the external appearance of the gun remained the same. Many people turned up with bright ideas to show whether or not the chambers contained cartridges. Few shotguns today have these indicators but more than a few quite modern automatic pistols have them. Cocking indicators lasted quite a bit longer on shotguns than did "loaded" indicators – up to the present day in fact – although few guns now have them and the range of devices employed is also smaller. I thought that I had seen all of them and, in fact, written about most of them – vertical pegs, Scott "windows", MacNaughton indicators and so on – but just when I thought that there were no more to be discovered, along came a new, but at the same time familiar, device.

It is this constant factor of "something new" that prevents me from becoming big-headed or self-important about guns. The moment I am about to make a pompous, dogmatic statement I think back to the last time I did so and was found out! I was about to say that I know all about cocking indicators, when a gun was put into my hands with the statement, "I've kept this on one side for you to see; quite a plain gun but I think you might find it of interest." I was about to make some non-committal remark when I noticed the lockplates and what was on them! A new type of cocking indicator; one I hadn't seen before. You can quite clearly see the form it takes from the illustration. There in the middle of the plate is a large indicator. Where had I seen one like it before? Why, on the side of the old Martini-Henry rifle. Patents for the Martini had been taken out in Britain in 1868, 1870 and 1871. The cocking indicator first appears in the 1870 patent, the rifle itself being officially adopted by the British authorities in 1871 and named the Martini-Henry.

I have been unable to discover whether or not the type of cocking indicator which you see on the shotgun illustrated (the gun is by the London Armoury Co., incidentally) was ever patented for *shotgun* use, but certainly this type of indicator is clearly described in the 1870 patent of Von Martini.

So, if nothing else, here is yet another cocking indicator. It has had a long and interesting life and, if we are to judge by some German makers and, for that matter, some of the makers of best sidelocks, the people who make the guns still think it worthwhile to fit them. Do the people who use guns find them of value in the field?

2

The Gunmakers

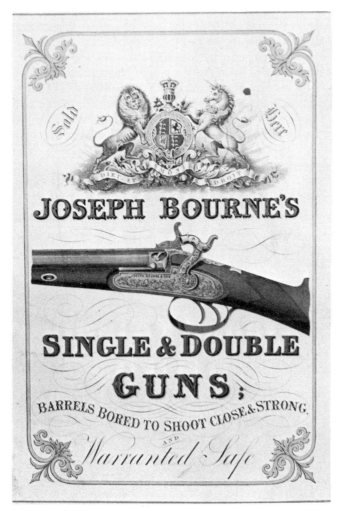

One of the earliest of the Bourne advertisements to have survived. This card would have been displayed in a country gunmaker's to advise the potential purchaser that guns by Bourne were stocked and available.

This section of the book is the longest; it could have been considerably longer, and the problem of choosing what to use and what to discard has been considerable. Some of the names have already appeared in my earlier volume and also in the first part of this one – the latter indicating that the firm or individual made some significant contribution to the art of gunmaking.

The term "gunmaker" is largely a courtesy title, for the majority of those who described themselves as "gunmakers" were, in fact, "gun-vendors". Some gunmakers made important contributions to the development of the British shotgun: Anson & Deeley, Beesley, Greener, Westley Richards come to mind, and there were many others whose names are now lost to us. Other gunmakers made their contribution not by some technical advancement or significant patent but an insistence on work of the highest possible quality. They established standards by which others were judged, and through their workshops passed many men whose training and ability allowed them to establish businesses of their own. Others, again, had made guns, possibly in the far less complex days of the muzzle-loader. Away from the main centres of gun manufacture, as guns became more complicated, these firms had guns made for them by the London or Birmingham trade, guns which had their name and address on the rib and lockplate and which often were made to a special house style, to distinguish them from the "run of the mill" guns made for the gun trade.

An important element in the structure of the industry was the man who is best described as an entrepreneur. He did not make guns or even parts of guns himself. He organised the manufacture of sporting guns by a group of independent craftsmen. It is

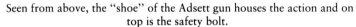

Seen from above, the "shoe" of the Adsett gun houses the action and on top is the safety bolt.

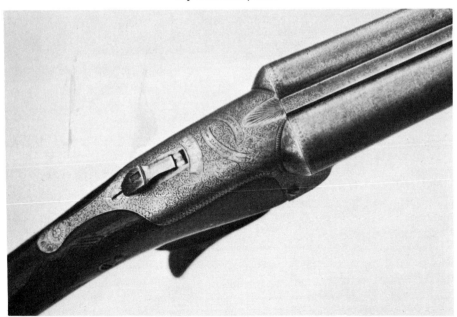

possible for one man to make an entire gun by himself; it has been done. It is more efficient and more economical, however, for the job to be split up into the separate crafts: barrel-boring, action-filing, stocking and finishing. At one time nearly fifty separate categories of gunworkers could be encountered in what had become a highly specialised industry, largely, but not entirely centred on Birmingham. Many were family businesses and many of the highly skilled craftsmen were unknown outside the confines of the gun quarter. This reliance on hand work gave the gun trade considerable flexibility. The entrepreneur merely increased the number of outworkers who did work for him when orders were many, and reduced the numbers when orders were few. No one was "laid off " and no machines were idle, but there was less work to go round and belts were tightened.

Even today the gun trade is remarkably diverse in the way it is organised. Regrettably, we no longer have large factories making sporting guns, and production on the scale of Italy, Spain or Japan is unknown here. There are, nevertheless, a surprising number of people building guns in Britain today, and in the pages which follow you will meet some of them. Guns made in this country have remarkably long lives if taken care of; many are still in active use though over a century has passed since they first left the workshop. With the possible exception of mechanical clocks I can think of no other reasonably complex mechanical artifact that can still be used in the same manner and for the same purpose as that for which it was originally intended. If we add to this the fact that a Purdey sidelock made in 1882 could be taken to a shoot in this country today and no one would notice that it was unusual in styling, performance or handling, the remarkable character of the British sporting shotgun becomes a little more evident.

So in addition to the gunmakers of the present you will meet the gunmakers of the past. Their names no longer glitter in gold characters above the gunshop windows but they appear on the lockplates and barrels of guns held in high regard by their modern owners. Their interest in the guns they own and use and in the men who built them contributed in no small measure to what follows.

JAMES ADSETT, CANTERBURY

The introduction of hammerless, self-cocking actions in the fourth quarter of the nineteenth century stimulated a flurry of inventive activity which makes this period of the history of shotguns one of the most fascinating. The previous 25 years, from the middle of the century, had seen the dominant position of the muzzle-loader challenged and usurped, and then, the public having become used to loading the gun from the breech instead of the muzzle, the type of cartridge was changed from pin-fire to central-fire.

To many, the underlever hammer breechloader was the acme of perfection and, indeed, many preferred to use a hammer-gun even when the hammerless action had become generally accepted.

Without doubt the significant development of the hammerless action was that due to W. Anson and J. Deeley in 1875. This design represented a totally new approach to the problem and its elegant simplicity has ensured that this type of action has remained in world-wide use unchanged in its basic elements from the day of its inception over a century ago.

However, although the excellence of the A & D action is acknowledged today this was not self-evident in 1875, and no doubt many were distrustful of the quantum leap the design represented and preferred the more gradual development based on tried and true designs. Such a design was the Murcott of 1871, which employed conventional bar-action sidelocks with provision for self-cocking. This was achieved by an extension of the bolt which locked the barrels bearing on a stud on the tumbler carrying the striker. When the underlever was pushed forward, the barrels were unlocked and the strikers cocked. Similar to the Gibbs & Pitt of 1873 was the Scott of 1874 in which the locks were placed above the trigger plate. None of the mutant sidelock designs were particularly attractive, mainly because of the need to have an unsightly protuberance under the action, but by 1876 Scott had developed a pleasing sidelock design which was to become widely copied and used by other makers.

The search for a satisfactory self-cocking hammerless gun was not confined to the gunmakers of Birmingham and London. Interesting designs which could have developed further were placed on the market by a number of provincial makers, and one of the most intriguing was that introduced by James Adsett of Canterbury some time after 1877. James was in business at 4 Upper Bridge Street in 1869. This is the address given on the gun illustrated on page 62, with the additional information that the gun is Patent No. 3. We also find a James Adsett listed in Guildford from 1839 until 1866 and a Thomas Adsett in Faversham, Kent in 1869. A Thomas Adsett survived in Guildford until 1900, and possibly longer, but at present the relationship of the various gunmakers bearing the name Adsett remains unknown.

If we move to the gun bearing the name James Adsett our first problem is to decide what to call it! It is not a sidelock, it is not a trigger-plate action and it is not a box-lock. Perhaps the best thing to do is to commemorate the inventor and call it the Adsett action.

As can be seen from the illustration, the backward extension from the top of the standing breech is very substantial and it is from what I would call the "top plate" and what Adsett calls "the breech shoe" that the mechanism is suspended. This is, if you think about it, a reasonable and logical development. Other designs were based on the lockwork being mounted on the trigger-plate, which at the height of its development gave rise to actions like the MacNaughton and the Dickson; others have the lockwork on sideplates and, as a "sidelock", this design is still with us. Others had the lockwork in the bar of the action and, although known as "box-locks" today, a better description is "A & D" after the names of the inventors.

The Adsett is a hammerless, self-cocking design which employs the push-forward underlever to cock the combined tumbler and striker, and there is a safety or locking bolt which is pushed forward to prevent the gun from being fired. Both James and Thomas Adsett were responsible for a further development of the shotgun action, for, in 1879, they patented an action which employed coil springs in a manner similar to the better known "Acme" action of Woodward, which has already been described in this series. After this the inventive genius of the Adsetts seems to have been exhausted and the literature is silent on their further activities.

That I now know that at least one Adsett action has survived is due to Mr. John Ashcroft, who very kindly supplied me with details of his gun and, even better, sent me the negatives from which the illustrations used were taken. Regular readers of my articles will know what comes next! Are there any other similar Adsett actions in existence? The design may not have been stable so variants may have been made and may have survived. Are there any of the later Adsett actions with coil mainsprings still in existence and lastly, does anyone have any information on the firm of Adsett?

NICHOLAS ANDREWS & SON

Some time ago I had a letter from a reader, Mr. H. C. Evans, asking for information about a 10-bore percussion muzzle-loader with the name "N. Andrews & Son" on the lockplate and "Gateshead" on the barrel. A search through my records, recently augmented by yet another reader, John B. Friedman, with names culled from American catalogues, showed no N. Andrews. Not only was Mr. N. Andrews absent but so was the name of Gateshead.

This happens quite frequently and serves to emphasise the quite large gap there is in our knowledge of gunmakers in the U.K. in spite of the painstaking work which has been carried out on this subject over the years. So often I am asked to comment on a gun when I have no description and no name. The next step in the process is to try and find someone with the records of the locus. The best plan is to try the local library. Some libraries have a special local study group and have made an effort to collect all the information on the locality in a manner which allows it to be used for research.

This was apparently the case in Gateshead since, when Mr. Evans wrote to the library he received a letter which provided the following information. The Andrews family had a tallow chandlers' business in the 1780s which continued to function until 1834, when Nicholas Andrews retired. We learn from the directories that Nicholas Andrews is described as a "gentleman" in the 1838–1850 directories. Then we have more good fortune: the 1851 census tells us that Nicholas Andrews was 51 in that year and his son 28.

In 1850 Nicholas Andrews & Son took over the established business of J. Marshall, ironmongers, and in 1852 they opened up a nail business, but the firm went bankrupt in 1856. We have no information as to why, after three-quarters of a century in business, the firm should fail. The founder, Nicholas Andrews the elder, retired early and over-expansion may have been a contributing factor. The year 1856 saw the end of the Crimean War and the outbreak of war between Britain and Persia. Neither of these events is likely to have influenced the fate of Nicholas Andrews & Son, and we are left in the dark as to what happened to the firm and to the family in the years to come. However, all is not lost for, from Gateshead, I received a copy of the advertisement in the 1851 directory, and this is reproduced here.

Underneath the advertisement for the Roker Baths Hotel at Monkwearmouth we find the advertisement for Nicholas Andrews & Son which tells us that they are in business at 16 Bottle Bank and at their Nail Manufactory at Sunderland Road End, Gateshead-on-Tyne. We have confirmation that they are wholesale ironmongers, offer

EDWARD BROWN,
ROKER BATHS HOTEL,
MONKWEARMOUTH.

This Hotel is a short distance from the Sunderland terminus of the York, Newcastle, and Berwick Railway, and there are cabs and conveyances meeting every train. The accommodation and charges are as under:—

Including Chambermaid, Waiter, Boots, and attendance of every description,

Board,	£1 8s. per week
Ditto, in a private room,	1 18 " "
Bed-room,	from 8s. to 1 12 " "
Double-bedded rooms,	from 13s. to 0 16 " "
Private sitting ditto,	from 12s. to 0 15 " "

USE OF DRAWING ROOM SIX-PENCE PER DAY EXTRA.

Persons not having apartments, nor taking their meals regularly:—
Breakfast, 2s.; Dinner, 2s. 6d.; Tea, 1s. 6d.
Bed and Breakfast, £1 1s. per week.

CHARGES FOR BATHING;

Vapour Bath,.......... 2s. 6d. | Warm Bath, ... 1s. | Shower Bath,.......... 6d.

BATHING MACHINES AND ATTENDANCE REGULARLY ON THE BEACH.

NICHOLAS ANDREWS AND SON,
16, Bottle Bank, and at their Nail Manufactory,
SUNDERLAND ROAD END, GATESHEAD-ON-TYNE,
WHOLESALE IRONMONGERS,
CUT AND WROUGHT NAIL MANUFACTURERS,
STOVE AND KITCHEN RANGE MAKERS,
DEALERS IN
Guns, and every description of Gun Furniture.
JOINERS' TOOLS, WARRANTED OF THE BEST SHEFFIELD MANUFACTURE.
BRUSHES, MOPS, ETC., ETC.

N.B.—The Public are respectfully invited to inspect their WHOLESALE PATTERN SHOW ROOMS, which contain the LARGEST ASSORTMENT of KITCHEN RANGES, REGISTERED and SHAM STOVES, at the most Reasonable Prices.

Country Orders punctually attended to.
PRINTED LISTS SENT TO ANY PART.
GENERAL SMITH-WORK DONE CAREFULLY TO ORDER.

The 1851 Directory advertisement for N. Andrews & Son.

stove and kitchen furniture, joiner tools, brushes, mops, etc., and make cut and wrought nails. We also find that they are dealers in guns and every description of gun furniture. The advertisement is of interest since it was published in 1851 but, according to the records, the firm did not take over the ironmongery and nail business of Marshall until 1852. From this we must assume that they were already in the ironmonger business before acquiring the business of Marshall.

I was also interested in "registered and sham stoves". A "registered" stove I understand to be one in which the air flow can be regulated by a sliding plate but I am at a loss to understand a "sham" stove. This incidentally illustrates one of the major hazards of research, getting side-tracked down fascinating byways and losing sight of the original goal, or at least mislaying things for a while: very interesting but very time-consuming!

Since I haven't seen the gun myself I have to assume certain things about it, the most important being that Andrews did not "make" the gun but probably bought it in from the trade in Birmingham. So from a very unpromising start we have quite a lot of useful information, and the gun now has "connections" which make it all the more interesting.

BAILONS OF BATH STREET

Bath Street first appears on the street maps of Birmingham in the late eighteenth century. Whittall Street and Weaman Street, which ran from Steelhouse Lane to Bath Street, were already the haunt of gunsmiths, barrelmakers, dealers and factors, but it is not known with any certainty when the gun trade moved into Bath Street; very probably it was during the expansionist period of the nineteenth century.

During the past century not only did the gunmakers and outworkers practise their craft in the area around St. Mary's Church but many also lived there and the self-contained community with church, cathedral, school, hall and recreation ground, not forgetting the public house, grew up, a community with its own standards, background and traditions. Some of the establishments grew to an impressive size: Greener's, for example, occupied the whole end of the block bounded by St. Mary's Row, Loveday Street and Bath Street. Changes took place, changes dictated by the fluctuations in trade and the development of the area, notably the building of the General Hospital in Steelhouse Lane.

Throughout the twentieth century the overall picture has been one of continued contraction, old-established businesses such as Webley & Scott moving out of the area and others closing their doors. It is for this reason that the establishment of a new business in the traditional gunmaking quarter is an event of some importance, and its continued prosperity of concern not only to those who earn their living in the gun trade but to those who employ the services provided.

Although the firm of Greener dates back to 1829, the impressive factory, with over 40,000 square feet devoted to gunmaking, was not built until 1896 and it was from the St. Mary's Row factory that guns and rifles went in a steady flow to all parts of the

All that was left of Bath Street, Birmingham, in 1970 – the former factory
of Joseph Bourne is at the right end.

world. Not only did the factory make firearms, it also trained people in the art and craft of gunmaking. Greener's is, alas, no more. Where the factory stood the St. Chad's ring road sweeps across, leaving on one side St. Mary's Church and on the other a defiant Gunmakers Arms, the last outpost of Bath Street, mute memorials to a past which is fast vanishing.

As we look down from the new road on to all that is left of Bath Street, the eye is drawn to a neatly painted factory frontage proudly bearing the name "Bailons Gunmakers Ltd". You can search the old records for the name of Bailons without success, for no gunmaker with this name has ever appeared in the long history of the gun trade. Nevertheless, this is a firm with long traditions in the trade and a firm whose very existence today bears testimony to the resilience of the Birmingham gun trade and to a reluctance to leave an area where guns and gunmaking have been carried out for generations. The co-directors of Bailons Ltd., Mr. Bailey and Mr. Onions, have spent most of their working life in the gun trade. Mr. Bailey started with W. W. Greener as an accountant, becoming, in turn, sales manager, production manager and eventually commercial director. As a balance to this commercial expertise, vital for survival in this day and age, Mr. Onions brings to the enterprise a thorough and unusually broad grasp of the practical side of gunmaking, a "know-how" gained as a result of three decades with Greener, from the workbench, through the machine shops until he became manager of the gun-work department. Mr. Onions bears a name which can be traced back through the history of the gun trade and he is a nephew of Mr. Albert Onions – of whom, more later. Both men could have joined Webley & Scott when this firm bought the Greener assets; instead they chose to set up, on their own account, across the road from Greener's back door.

With them came many of the former employees of Greener's, men who brought a vast fund of essential and specialised knowledge, including that doyen of the gun trade, Mr. Albert Onions. Uncle or "Nunky" Onions is now over 70 and he is one of that select group who are held in equally high regard by both the old and the young members of the trade. Not only is Mr. Onions a stocker of high repute, he also is regarded with affection and respect by the many men he has trained in his craft over the years.

Commercial "know-how", technical expertise and craft technique are all essential but, in addition, specialised tools are required, and Bailons are fortunate in having these as well. In the ground-floor machine shop there are barrel-boring and deep-drilling machines and here we find Mr. Billiards, an expert in the art of spill-boring and a man well versed in the many and complicated machine operations required before a pair of tubes becomes a pair of gun barrels. The machine shop has facilities for chambering, for machine barrels for refits and for sleeving.

On the second floor we find Mr. Gordon Salisbury, stocker, and here also is yet another remarkable man, now over 70, Mr. E. Southwick. Mr. Southwick is an action man, a man whom I could have watched and listened to for hours as he described the intricacies of gun locks and mechanisms.

You may think that too much time has been spent and too much emphasis placed on the past. However, it must be remembered that a very large number of guns from the past are still in use, and those whose job it is to repair and adjust them have to be familiar with a quite astonishing range of mechanisms. The men who invented and made them are long since dead and there are no instruction books to consult when a problem arises. In the event of breakages and honest wear and tear, there is no recourse to factory-made spares, so the necessary springs and components have to be hand-made. Guns which have given good service for half a century or more deserve good treatment, and deserve the same skilled attention, the same integrity of craftsmanship as that employed in their original creation: men such as Mr. Southwick can provide such attention.

To those who use quality guns of yesteryear there is always the problem of deciding whether or not an old gun, often inherited, is worth repair and restoration. An assessment can be made on the basis of hard financial fact; what will it cost to repair and how much would I have to spend to buy a new gun? Any firm of repute will provide an estimate of the cost of repair and will also indicate whether or not a gun is worth repairing. The difficulty lies in assessing the intangibles, the affection you may have for an old friend, and what one might refer to as rapport. In other words, the fact that you shoot well with a particular gun. These considerations are based on emotion, difficult to assess but to many equally difficult to ignore.

Today, if something breaks down, the immediate reaction is to throw it away and replace it. Our society is geared to the philosophy of planned obsolescence. Many of us cannot entirely share this attitude, for things, be they guns, pipes, shooting coats, comfortable old armchairs or treasured moth-bitten pullovers, acquire a character of their own and consequently exert a compelling though perhaps irrational influence on our emotions. People who have this feeling for things, and I am not ashamed to admit that I am one of them, have cause to be thankful that firms like Bailons exist. Sentimentality has little place in modern business and it is fortunate that this company, which has survived the initial difficulties following formation, has in Mr. Bailey and Mr. Onions a complementary and balanced approach to management which augers well for the future. Emphasis is on the repair and restoration of firearms; whether or not the same skills and business acument will be devoted to the manufacture of new guns is a question for the future.

Perhaps one day we may see a gun bearing the name "Bailons" on the top rib; maybe we never shall. It is enough for me that Mr. Bailey and Mr. Onions have created an enterprise which can cater for people like me, people who take pleasure in using the worthwhile creations of past gunmakers. Gun-lovers are fortunate that Birmingham still has several firms of this type in business, and it augers well that Bailons have joined this select company of craftsmen.

JOHN BLANCH & SON

The influence of the brothers Manton runs through nineteenth-century British gunmaking like a golden thread. I suppose it would be possible to discover how many gunmaking firms were founded by apprentices who learned their craft at the benches of John or Joseph Manton. Like Joseph Manton, John Blanch received his training at John Manton's before setting up on his own in or around 1809 in Fish Street Hill.

Unusual engraving on one of a pair of Blanch guns. (Photograph courtesy of Christie's Ltd.)

Blanch is better known from the Gracechurch Street address where the gun illustrated was made around 1910.

This is one of a pair of 12-bore sidelock ejectors which has a most unusual style of engraving. As can be seen from the bunches of grapes on the lockplates and fences the engraving is based on highly stylised fruiting vines. This style of engraving is quite different from that which is seen on ninety-nine per cent of British-engraved quality shotguns and it would be of considerable interest to learn something more about who did the work and whether or not it was done to special order.

I have recently illustrated a gun by Alexander Henry of Edinburgh which was engraved in a manner not normally seen on British-made guns. From past experience I know that some makers offered a type of engraving which was quite special to that firm and that firm alone. One example of that was the "Celtic" engraving which could be had on guns made by Martin of Glasgow. These guns were offered in 1939 at £150 a pair and were best-quality sidelock ejectors. I hope some day to get an illustration of this very unusual style of engraving, since to the best of my knowledge no other maker offered a gun engraved with this particular intricate pattern of strap and knotwork.

There is some evidence that Blanch may have made a speciality of the unusual with regard to the decoration of guns built just prior to the First World War. You will see that there is nothing altered in the style of the gun – only in the engraving. Other makers have attempted to change the shape or form of the gun but usually, unless there happened to be a basic mechanical reason for such changes, they have not been popular and after a brief period of sheer curiosity value such ideas have been discarded. I suppose that fundamentally we want our guns to look like guns – like the guns we have come to know. This is not strange, since a very great deal of effort went into the development of the British style of double sidelock and this style was copied throughout the world.

This also applies to the type of engraving which became known as English engraving and was generally based on scroll work. This could be fine scroll or open scroll. Some makers might incorporate flowers with the scroll work, while others would use the term "bouquet". The use of the term "scroll" might be qualified by the use of "London scroll" and this generally meant an extremely fine scroll pattern, often of such quality that the true skill and craftsmanship of the engraver could only be appreciated with the aid of a magnifying glass!

The appreciation of fine engraving takes some time and effort to cultivate. A well-executed border of good quality is far better than having the whole of the action covered in poorly done "scribble". Good quality English-style engraving never goes out of fashion and is never boring – one can look at it time and time again and still obtain pleasure from the contemplation of the skill of the engraver, whether the work was done last year or a century ago.

C. G. BONEHILL, BELMONT WORKS

Some years ago, when I was attempting to obtain details of Birmingham gunmakers, I started my task of compiling a list of names and addresses. Amongst these names was C. G. Bonehill, Belmont Row, Birmingham. Belmont Row, although not too far from the Birmingham Proof House, is not in the gunmaking quarter and I was not able to follow up my enquiry with a personal visit. However, from friends in the trade, I was told that Bonehill's had been a first-class factory and that Christopher Bonehill was a pioneer of the interchangeable system.

Mr. Bonehill and his factory were then put into the rather cobwebby recesses of my mind and the data obtained was filed. Then, early in 1973, through the good services of Colin Haygarth, I was shown a Bonehill gun. This was a 12-bore with 28 in. barrels which had been re-stocked. The address was given as the Belmont Firearms and Gun Barrel Works, Belmont Row and it was also marked "Interchangeable". This is the gun shown in the illustration. You can see that it is a nice A & D-action gun with a top cross-bolt and Scott top-lever work. Also note the sunk side panels, for although the gun has been re-stocked the style of the original has been carefully followed.

All was quiet again until I received a letter from Mr. W. J. Willis. Mr. Willis very kindly sent me a trade label for E. M. Reilly and Company which had been taken from an old gun case. His letter told me that he had a catalogue of guns made by C. G.

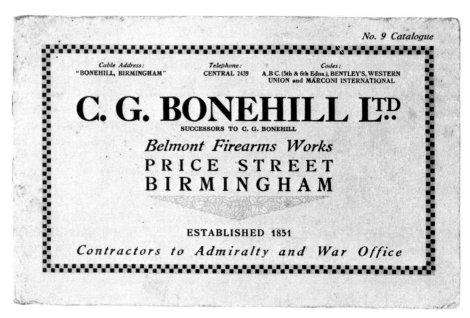

Front page from the C. G. Bonehill Catalogue No. 9.

Bonehill and that he had known the last of the Bonehill family. His offer to lend me the catalogue was accepted with alacrity: catalogues are of vital importance to any study of nineteenth-century sporting guns, and too few of them have survived. It is believed that this catalogue dates from about 1904 and in the 212 pages much of what the sportsman was buying at the turn of the century is listed. The catalogue tells us that the firm was founded in 1851 and that by 1870 it was able to undertake the supply of military rifles for the French government. In order to take advantage of the number of orders which the firm was receiving, Bonehill took over the factory of the National Arms and Ammunition Company in Belmont Row. The factory was re-equipped with new and up-to-date machinery and the techniques which had been employed in the manufacture of military rifles was adapted to the manufacture of sporting guns, with particular emphasis on the American market.

Unfortunately, the catalogue does not refer to the "Interchangeable" gun, and it is likely that this was an earlier production. It is of interest to record that Bonehill was responsible for the Britannia Air Rifle. This was one of the earliest British-made air rifles and certainly one of the most powerful since it could literally blow a .177 pellet to pieces. Bonehill also made "Britannia" air rifle pellets, and these were highly regarded by the Midlands air gunners – in those days air rifle shooting was a very popular sport in the Birmingham district.

But back to shotguns. Bonehill made the "Belmont" range of A & D-actioned shotguns and a very pleasant range of sidelock guns, all of which could be had with removable sidelocks and optional single triggers, the latter for £10 extra. Top-lever hammer guns were also offered and the hammerless range was available as a pigeon or trap gun chambered for $2\frac{3}{4}$ or 3 in. cartridges.

The range included ball and shotguns having rifled choked muzzles, and combination rifle and shotguns were made. These were to be had with the right barrel chambered for 12-bore shot and the left rifled and chambered for the .577/.450 Martini or the No. 2 Musket cartridge. Double Express rifles in all calibres from .600 Nitro Express down to the .303 were made and also – and this was probably the logical outcome of Bonehill's experiments with interchangeable manufacture – his range of "Standard" guns, which repeated the range already described, but at less cost. All these guns employed A & D actions and were finished in five grades from quite plain to full engraving; pigeon guns had side clips. Extra fine work could be had, including inlaying with gold "suitable for the most exacting requirements of Oriental taste". A stag's head, with horns, cost 14 shillings per head.

Single-barrel guns were also sold, in addition to single- and double-barrel muzzle-loading shotguns for the "Central and South American Markets". The catalogue also illustrates a wide range of rifles from the Martini to the Mannlicher. It is a splendid catalogue, and Mr. Bonehill must have been very proud of his firm and of its products. Belmont Firearms and Gun Barrel Works was still standing a few years ago; I wonder if it has escaped the developer and the ring road?

CHARLES BOSWELL'S HAMMER-GUN

In the past I have written about the men who made guns, men who designed them, used or repaired them. For a change I would like to write about a gun, just an ordinary gun. Perhaps I had better qualify that last remark: an ordinary gun *for the period when it was made*. I can't say very much about the maker, Charles Boswell. When this gun was built he was in business at 126 The Strand, London WC. This dates the gun, for the business appears to have been established at this address in 1884, so my Boswell can't be older than that.

How long Boswell stayed in the Strand I can only guess – probably until just after the First World War – for I know he had moved to 7 South Molton Street by the late 1920s. When the firm went out of business does not appear in my records; I do have a note that it was founded in 1869, but where Charles Boswell learned his trade is not mentioned.

Each time I do a little research into a maker I go through my old gun catalogues to see if, by some miracle, they have multiplied and something new has been added since I last looked through them. I did look again this time but no catalogue for Boswell could be found so we are left with the gun itself. As you can see from the photograph it is a rather nicely made hammer-gun with bar sidelocks and a rotary underlever. The quality is, I think, self-evident. Just have a look at the shape of the hammers. Have a close look at the fences. This is the part of the gun around the strikers. The changes that have taken place in this area of guns from the days of the flintlock are truly quite remarkable; changes there have been, many of them, but you can trace the evolution of the fence for nearly two centuries. On this gun the fences are particularly fine. Viewed from any angle the shape of the metalwork delights the eye, and if one is in a reflective

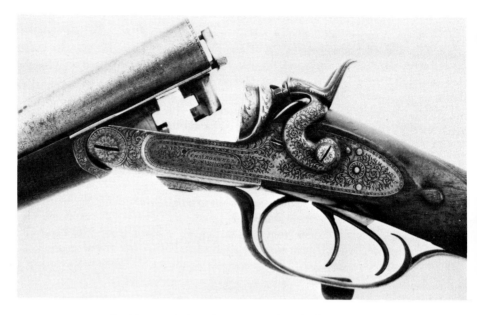

A 16 bore underlever hammer gun by Charles Boswell.

mood a short time spent in quiet contemplation of the skill and craftsmanship – nay, better still, artistry – of the man who formed the fences is time well spent.

The locks, as one might expect on a gun of this age, are rebounding, and based on Stanton's patent of 1867. The inside of the lock bears the name Grainer and this could be the maker, Stanton's name being found inside the lock as well, since he, of course, was the patentee. The locks inside are quite delightful, retaining their colour hardening. This has all gone from the outside of the lockplate but the pleasant scroll engraving makes up for the loss of colour.

This gun is a 16-bore. It is therefore quite light, and for this reason very pleasant to shoot. The barrels are Damascus, and so one has to be careful what sort of cartridges are placed in the breech; but it is a gun which has given me much pleasure and doubtless also the previous owner or owners would say the same if they were alive. This gun must be representative of many similar high-quality "London" guns which are still in use. Many will have passed modern nitro-proof tests and in spite of hammers and underlevers will give their owners a great deal of pleasure and satisfaction.

CHARLES BOSWELL

It is now some six years since I last wrote about Charles Boswell and from the number of guns by this maker which are still in use and the interest displayed in the firm which made and sold the guns I feel that a reappraisal will not be out of place.

The original article in 1975 generated much correspondence and a lot of interesting information but little in the way of hard fact. One reader wrote to me saying that his grandfather was a gunmaker and that many years ago he had built an addition to the gun shop to brew beer for the workmen. The beer proved to be so successful that he closed down the gunshop and made a small fortune from the brewery!

In response to my request for information I received a letter from Mr. Singleton in May 1975 which told me that Charles Boswell had started in business in 1869 in Upper Fore St., Edmonton. By 1884 he moved to 126 Strand. This is the address found on most of the Boswell guns including the hammer-gun illustrated. This is the only Boswell hammer-gun photograph I have and can be compared with the hammerless gun also illustrated. The latter was photographed at the 1977 Game Fair and then belonged to Mr. Harnett. The number of this gun is 15376 and one is advised that the charge is 38 grains of Smokeless Diamond and 1¼ oz. of shot. An alternative powder was suggested – 48 grains of Amberite. The trade label is of the same period and tells us that Charles Boswell is a "practical gunmaker" and advises that the firm, or guns made by the firm, won 40 cups open to all England.

An earlier label which cannot be reproduced is taken from a gun case from the Edmonton period and this tells us more about the firm than the smart later leather label does. We gather from the Edmonton label that the cups mentioned above must

Boswell, Anson & Deeley double gun with sunk side panels, No. 15376.
Note the treatment of the fences and the side clips.

Leather trade label from Boswell's Strand period.

have all been won *before* 1884, since this is the number of cups mentioned on the earlier label. We also learn that Boswell will convert muzzle-loaders to breechloaders and that Mr. Boswell is happy to take "old guns in exchange". Double breechloading guns were from £7 to £40 each and breechloading revolvers could be had from 12/– each (just over 50p). How I would like to have a time machine and be able to visit this shop in Edmonton!

In 1914 the business was taken over by the son of the founder, Osborne George Boswell and in 1922 the firm moved to South Molton St., W1 where they remained for but a short time, moving in 1932 to 15 Mill Street, Conduit St., W1, where in 1941 the business was destroyed by enemy action. O. G. Boswell died in the same year and this appears to be the full story of the firm. I gather that a grandson still survives, but whether there is any further information available time will tell. Certainly Charles Boswell made high-quality guns of character and distinction and I would like to know a little more about the founder and see a catalogue of their guns if possible.

BOSWELL REVIEW

Many letters have passed through the slot in my front door, a lot of mail has been sent to far distant places, hundreds of miles have rolled beneath my car and a lot of film has passed through my camera – all, I might add, to do with Charles Boswell and the guns made by this important firm. It all started with an article in the 24 April 1975 issue of *The Shooting Times* when I described a 16-bore Boswell underlever hammer-gun I had owned and enjoyed for many years. This produced one or two letters and then things took off, with the receipt of a photocopy of a Charles Boswell catalogue from Roy S. Smith of Ontario, Canada.

Advertisements taken from *The Shooting Times* of 1884, a gun-case label and a fine Boswell A & D action gun with sunk side panels illustrated the next article on the firm, which was published on 10 December 1981.

I then started "trawling" in earnest, flinging the net over the side and using my "letters" column to keep things going. As a result of this I was able to meet Professor Charles Boswell. I had some facts to go on: the first gunmaking Charles Boswell had served his time with Mr. Gooch of Hertford, Charles Boswell being a native of that county and born in 1850. From Professor Boswell I had the opportunity to photograph the indentures of Charles and start the ball rolling to get some information about Gooch. In this latter endeavour I had stalwart assistance from Mr. Howard Day, who went to enormous trouble on my behalf. From Mr. Day's work we find that there are two firms by the name Gooch, one in St. Albans and one in Hertford. From the data collected it became apparent that the "Mr. Gooch" who was to train Charles Boswell for some seven years was Thomas Gooch who is first listed in 1834. We can almost see young Charles starting work but can only wonder what life was like for him in Mr. Gooch's gunshop in Hertford. We then learn that he worked for the Royal Small Arms Factory at Enfield where he stayed for two years. By this time he was married, and he took the very bold step of setting up on his own without connections or capital. His premises were in Edmonton and his main work must have been repairs. We can assume that there must have been some worrying times before the business became established.

In addition to being a gunmaker, Charles Boswell was also an expert shot in the sport of live pigeon shooting. A connection was speedily built up, based on his prowess as a shot and skill as a gunmaker, and in 1884 he moved to more prestigious premises at 126 The Strand. Boswell guns went out to Australia, where they speedily gained an enviable reputation and, with Harry Ackland of Woollahra as representative, the business "down under" expanded. In the late 1880s Mr. Sayer, founder and secretary of the Melbourne Gun Club, was active in promoting Boswell guns. In South Africa a similar story is told. Overheads were kept down by the founder of the firm working on the bench himself, and quality was maintained by careful supervision of all aspects of gunmaking.

The firm survived the First World War but it was bombed out in 1940 and the direct family involvement ceased in March of 1941. The firm continued under various managements until the 1960s with an address in Connaught Street. My request for photographs and details of Boswell guns brought a splendid response. Regrettably some of the photographs cannot be used for publication and one or two determined people are doing a short course in firearms photography to raise their standards. From Robert Braden of Houston I have a fine series of photographs of his top-lever Boswell gun which show how the styling of the fences and percussioning has developed from the earlier underlever Boswell in my own collection.

The 1982 Game Fair brought more contributions. A splendid single-barrel Boswell, No. 17625, was brought by Stuart Hirst and the photographs of this sidelock top-lever gun are used to show you the quality of Boswell's work and to delight the eye. I can't tell you much about this gun since it is not shown in the only catalogue I have, but it does show how a skilled gunmaker treats the styling of a single, top-lever, sidelock hammerless gun.

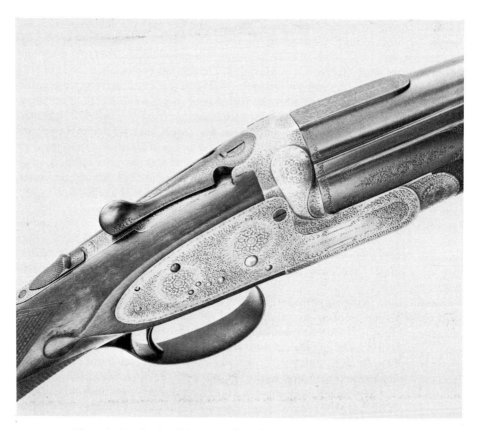

The right-hand side of the Boswell single barrel hammerless shotgun.

The three pieces on Charles Boswell show how, with the help of readers, a fuller picture of the life and work of a gunmaker can be built up. It is this interchange of information, extremely difficult to obtain by any other means, which has contributed in a very significant way to the total quantity of data now available on many gunmakers, most of whom were far less well known and who would have been undocumented otherwise. You will see "follow-up" pieces throughout this part of the book; they have been left in their original form to illustrate the importance of "reader participation".

JOSEPH BOURNE & SON

The history of the Birmingham gun trade has long fascinated me. Many of the Birmingham photographs I took in the recent past are now part of history, because the people and places they record have vanished. Whole areas of the old Gun Quarter have gone, streets have disappeared and buildings have been demolished to make way for new buildings and a road system that defies the laws of physics! Two streets, the names of which are synonymous with the gun trade, are Bath Street and Loveday Street. About one-third of the original Bath Street remains and most of Loveday Street.

James Bourne & Son, a firm typical of the gun trade, was once to be found at the corner of Bath Street and Loveday Street. The name of Bourne was connected with the very earliest gunmaking activities in Birmingham. A William Bourne appears on a Government contract dated 1693 for the supply of "musquettes" at the rate of 200 a month. The beginnings of the firm are not so well documented, however. They say they were founded in 1840, though the city directories do not list the firm until 1849, when they were to be found at 5 Whittall Street. There appears to have been some connection with Thomas Redfern, a firm also to be found at 5 Whittall Street, but the nature of this connection is now difficult to discover. In 1867 the style of the firm changed to "& Son" and by 1885 they had moved to 9 St. Mary's Row, still in the warren of streets and workshops between Steelhouse Lane and the Canal and with "St.

Joseph Bourne's premises in 1912. The building still exists (1980) in Birmingham.

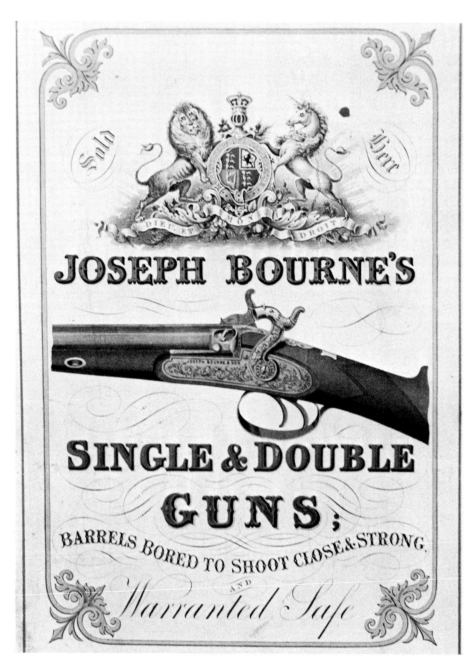

One of the earliest of the Bourne advertisements to have survived. This
card would have been displayed in a country gunmaker's to advise the
potential purchaser that guns by Bourne were stocked and available.

Mary's Chappell" giving its name to the area.

Here was a small, highly concentrated self-contained area, with chapel and school and almost the entire range of trades needed for gunmaking. In 1903 the firm of James Bott & Son, Tiger Works, Gun Makers to His Late Majesty the King of Portugal, was acquired, and the directories for 1900 show this firm to be at 100 and 101 Bath Street. The 1910 directories show Bourne established at the same address.

In 1907 Joseph Bourne acquired gunmakers Walter Edwards and then, in 1908, they made a further acquisition – the large and important business of Robert Hughes & Sons. This firm first appears in 1855 and in 1868 they adopted the name "Universal Fire Arms Works". A trade label of this period shows a very wide selection of revolvers and pistols and they advise that they "manufacture every description of breech and muzzle loading military and sporting rifle". Hughes sold a wide range of smooth-bore sporting guns converted from Enfield muzzle-loading military rifles and they also offered a range of muzzle-loading double percussion shotguns for the export markets.

By 1912 Joseph Bourne occupied premises at 100 and 101 Bath Street and they also extended down Loveday Street to numbers 89, 90 and 91 and 92. An illustration of the works at this period shows a handsome, three-storey building, the front of which gives us a clue about what we can expect in the twentieth century. In addition to guns, Bourne are by now obviously interested in bicycles.

As well as selling and manufacturing arms, Bourne also had extensive facilities for repairs. Their main business was, however, with the export market and with South Africa in particular. An early advertisement, possibly for display in a retailer's showroom, illustrates a double percussion shotgun and the potential customer is assured that Bourne guns "are Warranted Safe". A great comfort, no doubt! By 1912 the firm offered a double back-action, top-lever hammer gun with 30 in. barrels for £3 15s. 0d. The gun had rebounding locks and was nitro-proofed.

Oddly enough, the same gun, with the Jones underlever, known as the "Old Model", cost more, at £4. Top of the market in hammer guns were the top-lever bar-action treble-grip models, the most expensive of which was £30. As a concession to foreign buyers, sizes were given in centimetres as well as inches – and this was 1912! Hammerless guns on offer were the A & D-action 1912 Model Ejector at £16 and a sidelock with Greener-type cross-bolt at £15. Top of the range was an A & D single-trigger gun at £75. Also on offer was a range of pigeon guns, chambered for either the 2¾ in. or 3 in. cartridge, and a fine selection of double and single-barrel duck and wildfowl guns in 10-, 8- and 4-bores. To provide some indication of comparative prices, Bourne sold the five-shot Browning Automatic Shotgun for £13 10s. Converted Mauser and Chassepot rifles bored for 12-bore were £1, and neat conversions of the military Martini-Henry in .577/.450 could be had for about £4. A range of Lee Metford, Lee Enfield and Mauser and Mannlicher rifles was on offer from about £10 to £15, and good-quality double rifles in all bores up to .600 cost between £20 and £40.

Both automatic and revolving pistols from the famous makers such as FN, Colt, Smith & Wesson are illustrated along with "The Bulldog" revolver at a mere 50p! Air guns, walking-stick guns and air canes share the end of the catalogue with low-priced Continental shotguns, "a selection of which are kept, without guarantee, for the convenience of customers". Joseph Bourne also sold bicycles and motor cycles. I have not been able to discover if they actually manufactured them, but the motor cycle was a belt-drive side-valve sold under the name "Elmdon".

So far as the guns and rifles made by Bourne are concerned, it is likely that there are more guns by this maker in South Africa than in this country. Undisturbed by the developers and planners the premises at the corner of Bath Street and Loveday Street are still there, although now the factory houses a shopfitting centre. Last listed as gun and rifle makers in the late 1950s Joseph Bourne continued in business until quite recently, and the building at 101 Bath Street serves as a reminder of the diversity and far-flung interests of the Birmingham gun trade of the nineteenth century.

THE BSA SHOTGUN

As the cost of hand-finishing (I don't like the term "hand-crafted") continues its seemingly never-ending upward spiral, more and more people wishing to use a double shotgun turn to what used to be called "the machine-made gun". I am often asked "Why did the British gun trade never produce such a gun?" The answer to this question is long, complicated and involved but if I am restricted to three words my answer would be "But it did!" The name of the gun was BSA.

Little has been written about the BSA double shotgun. Hugh Pollard in his book *Shotguns*, published in 1923, merely stated that "a plain BSA hammerless shotgun – an admirable weapon – can be bought for as low as £11 11s. 0d". The advertisement at the beginning of that book tells us a little more. From it we learn that BSA had, over the past 60 years, developed the manufacture of rifles and guns on repetitive machinery to a remarkable degree of accuracy. We are assured that the parts gauge to within one thousandth of an inch and that the materials used are specially selected by skilled metallurgists. We are further told that the net result is great strength, perfect balance and "feel" and, because of the use of machines instead of expensive hand labour, phenomenally low prices.

The question one must inevitably ask is "What went wrong?" The price was, in 1923, just over £11.50 for a non-ejector and just over £14.50 for the ejector. A "Special" ejector gun was £25 and, until recently, I had never seen the BSA Special. I have still not actually handled one, but Mr. Ogden of Cheshire has a BSA gun of this quality, and he very kindly sent me the photograph reproduced here. On the top rib is the statement "Made by BSA Guns Ltd. England" and as you can see there is a rather nice fence, quite unusual in fact, and some scroll engraving and game. The top rib also bears the well-known "Piled Arms" trade mark of the Company.

By 1934 the prices had altered only slightly. The standard gun was then £13 13s. 0d. and the Special Model or "Ejector Model de Luxe" as it was now called, had been reduced in price and was £19 19s. 0d. This compares, incidentally, with the Webley & Scott No. 300 non-ejector at £21.

For a contemporary opinion of the BSA we can turn to Burrard, who said that "BSA have abandoned the top extension [did they ever use it?] but their guns are certainly strong. They are up to full weight and I am sure that the metal used in the action bodies is of better quality than many cheap guns ..." This, of course, is where the BSA

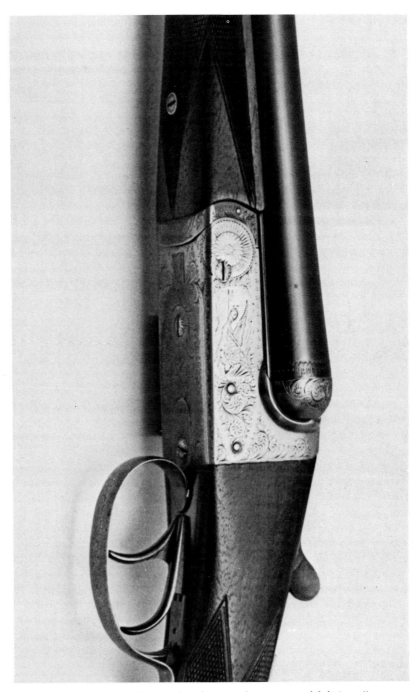

The British "machine-made" shotgun, the BSA "Model de Luxe".

metallurgists come in. BSA also used "chopper lump" barrels, as was the practice on "best" guns. However, BSA went a little further, and instead of brazing the barrels together employed a dovetail secured by two pins through the lumps. Burrard agreed that this method was strong and effective if made by machine, but he criticised the added width required for the dovetail, which resulted in what he called a "clumsy gun".

BSA made three different types of side-by-side 12-bore, the Standard, the Standard with ejector and the Special or Model de Luxe, again with ejector. All were for the $2\frac{1}{2}$ in. cartridge and they also offered their 12-bore wildfowling gun for $2\frac{3}{4}$ in. or 3 in. 12-bore cartridges.

Just to give some indication of comparative values, the F. N. Browning five-shot automatic in standard finish was selling for £9 in 1934 and the Browning over-and-under in standard finish was £25.

The BSA is a gun that has been grossly neglected by authors in the past and its merits largely overlooked. When it was first made is unknown to me, as indeed is the date when manufacture ceased. I would say its production ceased around 1939, although the Parker-Hale catalogue for 1941 still carried details of the BSA and the illustration of the Ejector Model de Luxe is almost identical with the gun illustrated here.

THE BSA SHOTGUN STORY

Publication of my article on the BSA shotgun in the issue of 19 April 1979 brought a splendid response. First to arrive was a photocopy of the 1932 BSA catalogue. This came from my old friend Colin Haygarth in Dunnett, Caithness. Then, from Dunedin, New Zealand, Alan & Anne Jerrard sent me photocopies of a Tolley, Birmingham catalogue showing the BSA, and, of great interest, a page from the catalogue issued in 1929 by Hammond & Turner Ltd., of Christchurch, New Zealand, giving details of the BSA.

An original catalogue was sent to me by Mr. Garrett of Cheshire and the illustration here is taken from this. Mr. Garrett told me that he had used the BSA Ejector Model de Luxe, which he had bought in Oswestry in 1930, for some 17 years. It had been bought in part-exchange and the price was £19 19s. od. in 1930, so that the catalogue is very probably later than this, since Colin Haygarth's 1932 catalogue shows the price to be the same, 19 gns. It is interesting to see what the price for the same gun was in 1929 in New Zealand. We learn from Hammond & Turner's catalogue that the Ejector Model de Luxe was £27, compared with the standard ejector model at £22 17s. 6d. This catalogue also shows us what the British gun trade had to compete with: for on the same page F.N. of Liège, Belgium, a firm very similar to BSA in origin and size, were offering an A & D ejector gun, with side clips and a Greener-type cross-bolt for £12, about half the price of the British-made BSA. One wonders what the reaction of the customers in Christchurch, New Zealand was when confronted by this choice between the British "machine-made gun" and the Belgian F.N.

Mention of the Greener cross-bolt on the F.N. highlights the fact that the BSA had no top "bite", such as the Greener cross-bolt, and that the BSA literature makes quite a point of this. The lack of any top bolt and the dependence on the Purdey under-bolt into the two "bites" in the lumps was stressed quite considerably by BSA, indicating that the people buying guns in this price range expected their guns to have some form of top-rib extension bolting. BSA went to some lengths to indicate that even "best" guns costing over £100 lacked any top bolt and did their best to brainwash the potential purchaser that he was not buying an inferior gun because it lacked the "third" bite.

Equally, BSA extolled at some length the virtues of their method of putting together the barrels and the high quality of the barrel steel they used. The barrels were forged out of Jessop's "fluid-pressed" steel and the lumps were integral with the barrel. The barrels were then dovetailed together, which certainly provided a strong and secure connection, but perhaps meant that the width across the breech was wider than that obtained with normal brazing practice. Throughout the catalogue emphasis is placed on the close metallurgical control exercised on manufacture and the high quality of the materials employed in the barrel, action, body and lockwork. Equal emphasis was also placed on the quality of the patterns obtained by the boring of the barrels.

A page from a pre-Second World War BSA catalogue.

That BSA had the "know-how" to make shotguns by machinery with the minimum of hand finishing is not in doubt; they had had great experience in the manufacture of the British service rifle and also in the manufacture of machine guns, but rather the question is whether or not the British shooting man was ready for the machine-made gun? What went wrong?

The range of shotguns offered to the public was based on one design, the BSA adaption of the classic A & D action, and a well-made shotgun manufactured by machinery from high-quality material is always better than a "hand-made" gun of poor quality made from inferior material. There is no inherent benefit from "hand-made" *per se*, it very much depends on the hands and how much their owner is paid! The use of a standard action resulted in lower costs and minimum tooling. As you can see, the action body was lightly engraved and standard chequering employed for the grip and fore-end. Only one calibre, 12-bore, was available, with either $2\frac{1}{2}$ or $2\frac{3}{4}$ in. chambers and 25, 28 or 30 in. barrels could be had, depending on the model.

Five different models were available, the Non-Ejector at £15, the Ejector at £18 10s. od., the Ejector Model de Luxe at £22, the Special Game Model at £25 and the Wildfowling Model, which was £16 10s. od. without ejectors and £20 with them. This model was chambered for the 3 in. cartridge. Extras which could be had were stocks to special dimensions at £2 5s. od. extra and a vulcanite butt-plate for 3/6d. extra. BSA also offered gun cases, cleaning rods and a well-known assortment of cleaning aids the names of which may well evoke memories among the older readers – "Cunirid", "Kleenwell" and "Safetipaste".

I have not used a BSA shotgun, but comments from readers who have either owned or used one over the years have all been quite complimentary. How many remain in use today is difficult to say. How many were exported is not known, although that New Zealand catalogue leads us to believe that efforts were made in the years between the Wars to export. When production started and who was involved in the design are not known but, knowing my readers, I expect that these facts will come to light.

BURNAND OF NEWCASTLE

My articles on William Pape of Newcastle aroused a remarkable degree of interest and, if nothing else, this interest again highlights the immense contribution made to British gunmaking by the provincial maker. True, many sought the greater rewards which came to some by moving to London but others stayed in their home towns and established firms which endured and prospered for many decades. Amongst the people who wrote to me about their Pape guns was Mr. E. J. Jackson of Ellesmere Port, Cheshire.

From Mr. Jackson I received a splendid photograph of his Pape hammer-gun and for good measure two other prints of a hammer-gun by Burnand of Newcastle. As can be seen from the illustration, this is a splendid example of an underlever hammer-gun with bar-action lockwork. Mechanically there is little that can be said about the Burnand gun; the locks are by Joseph Brazier, Ashes, and since Brazier's name again appears on the flats of the action it is not unlikely that this was a "Black Country" gun made by Brazier for the trade but made to special order.

As far as I can discover, the firm of Burnand was established in Newcastle about

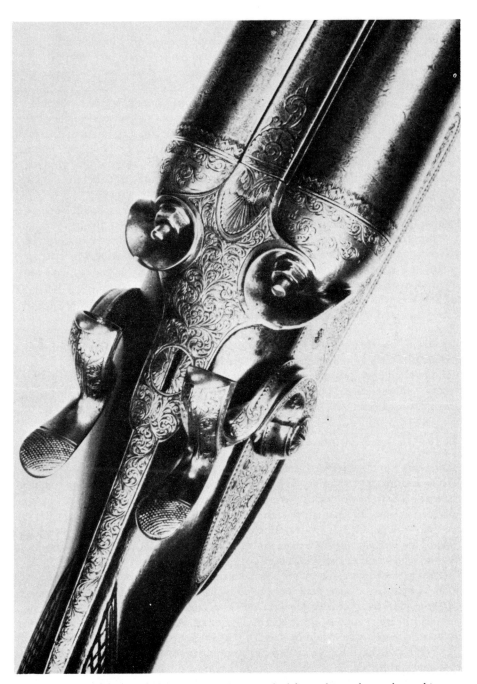

The Burnand hammer gun photographed from above; the workmanship
of the fences is worthy of particular notice.

1800 and probably by the time this gun was made, which could have been in the 1860s, the firm might have been in the hands of the second generation. Muzzle-loading guns were certainly made by the firm in the early days and one of its claims to fame is that W. Greener served his apprenticeship with Burnand.

Certainly, if you look at the side of this gun you cannot avoid being struck by the true sense of proportion, the balance and harmony, and it is quite possible to appreciate the feelings of a man who has used a gun of this type and quality being asked his opinion of the new hammerless guns. The shooting man of the mid-nineteenth century, fully accustomed to the elegance of his muzzle-loader and hammer breechloader, might well have regarded the early clumsy attempts to produce a hammerless gun with justifiable disdain, for it did take some time before the same degree of elegance was achieved with the hammerless ejector gun.

Without doubt the true beauty of this gun is brought out by Eric Booth's excellent photograph of its standing breech. This photograph repays some study. It is very well lit to bring out the engraving and form of the metalwork and you should look closely at the fences and the work around the strikers. This is not just gunmaking, this is artistry. I know few guns where the treatment in this area is quite so successful. This same attention to form is to be seen in the shape and design of the hammers. I am tempted to call this style the "Newcastle" style, since guns by Pape and Greener also have this same shape and style. I was able to see and handle the Burnand gun and I wasn't disappointed. In a way the Burnand was a very lucky gun for me because through it I was able to meet the owner, E. J. Jackson and the photographer, Eric Booth, and a number of keen shooting men from the Cheshire area.

Burnand and his guns continue to intrigue me. I have the feeling that there were at least three Burnands and I would be interested to hear from anyone with a gun bearing this maker's name.

THE COSTERS: A FAMILY OF GUNSMITHS

More years ago than I care to remember I was attempting to rebuild a rather battered Winchester Model 1873 rifle. Several of the parts were missing and I particularly required a small piece of metal to secure the fore-end. An approach was made to a local engineering firm and when my request was made known I was told that "they had just the man to help me". I was introduced to John Coster, who told me that he had worked in the gun trade for a time and with his help the part I wanted was produced and the renovation of the Winchester went on apace.

Of far greater importance to me was an introduction to George Coster, the father of John. George Coster was then retired and living with a married daughter, Peggy, in Glasgow. I spent several very enjoyable hours with George Coster who, although retired, still built guns in the kitchen. The table would be cleared of all signs of domesticity and a vice would be fixed to the table; then large old-fashioned tobacco tins were produced, full of small lock parts, tools, screws and the various impedimenta of the gunsmith's art. George was first and foremost a gunstocker and it was a delight to watch the old but firm hands guide the tools over a piece of walnut and to see the shape of a gunstock gradually emerge, until a thing of beauty had been produced.

Guns were re-stocked in the small kitchen and guns were built there too. The action, barrels and furniture were purchased through the trade and the whole put together with care and painstaking precision.

Engraving was done by Harry Morris in Birmingham. These two men had served together during the First World War, and later I was fortunate in being able to meet Henry Morris and spend some time with him in his workshop off St. Mary's Row in the heart of the old gunmaking quarter in Birmingham. The two old friends had, oddly enough, both been armourers, a most enlightened selection of trades, for the army does not always fit the round peg into the round hole. Henry Morris told me a little story about his friend, which serves to illustrate his all-round ability.

They were both aboard a troopship in the Middle East when, owing to some accident, a pair of sporting guns belonging to one of the officers was lost overboard. The guns, after some difficulty, were recovered from the sea bed, but the stocks were found to be badly damaged. George was asked to re-stock them and this he did, first of all making his own tools and then making and fitting stocks to both of the guns.

I was greatly interested in George Coster's history and shortly before his death I was able to gather enough information to thoroughly whet my appetite, but insufficient to satisfy it.

George Coster had worked for Alexander Martin in Glasgow from about 1930 until his retirement. George exhibited many of the weaknesses of the old gunmakers, one of which was a profound reluctance to divulge any of the secrets of his craft. A friend of mine who served his time at the bench in the workshop at Martins told me that if he was in doubt as to the method of tackling a problem he would walk round the bench to the side where George was working to seek advice. George himself would be working away and at my friend's approach he would take up a piece of cloth from the bench and drape it over his work so that the curious eyes of the apprentice would not light upon mysteries that were beyond him. For my part, three months of patient and courteous enquiry had to pass (and the best part of a bottle of whisky) before I was told the secret formula for browning gun barrels. The formula included "a piece of chalk the size of a nut" and in ignorance as to whether this was a monkey nut or a coconut I had to spend some time in research and experimentation before I was able to get the famous secret formula to work.

Prior to working for Alexander Martin, George Coster had been in business on his own account and a search of the records showed that the firm of George Coster and Son had started up in West Nile Street, Glasgow in 1920, going out of business in 1930. The title (George Ernest Julius) puzzled me, until I found that the firm was that of George Coster and his father and that the father had worked for Henry in Edinburgh and that he had served his time in Germany.

On this intriguing note I was forced to leave matters alone. A number of interesting questions continued to puzzle me. I had often wondered how the late nineteenth-century Edinburgh gunmakers had evolved the trigger-plate action made famous by MacNaughton and John Dickson. The similarity between these actions and the German Blitz actions, ideally suited to the building of combination shot and rifle guns, the Drillings and Vierlings, had given rise to conjectures, the foundations of which were, to say the least, shaky.

It was perhaps coincidental that an immigrant German gunmaker had arrived in Edinburgh and that shortly afterwards a series of patents had been taken out by both MacNaughton and Dickson for actions very similar to the German Blitz. A search through the patent literature showed that one Julius Coster had obtained patent protection for improvements in the extracting mechanism of the Martini-Henry rifle. In the patent dated 8 April 1885, No. 4335, Julius Coster explains how an extra lever inserted into the Martini action would overcome the inherent weakness in the extraction system of the Martini-Henry rifle. By this modification the extractor was operated by the finger lever instead of relying on the hinged breech block falling on the arm of the extractor, as is the case with the original Martini. Whether or not Coster's improvement worked I have yet to find out, but it is significant that this weakness in the Martini action was appreciated by BSA when they produced the Martini-International target rifle and provided "power ejection" to boost the system.

In Julius Coster's remaining patents we find more clues in building up the pattern of this man's working life. Though he was previously described as a gunmaker, we find in patent No. 5862 of March 1897 that he now describes himself as Works Manager to Alexander Henry Ltd., of 18 Frederick Street, Edinburgh. This description is in the Provisional Specification which, when completed in December of 1897, has the following alteration: Julius Coster, late of Henry Ltd., Edinburgh, now Works Manager to Charles Ingram, Renfield Street, Glasgow. So, between March and December, Julius Coster had left the famous Alexander Henry to work for Charles Ingram in Glasgow, a firm famous for its Match Target Rifles. The second patent refers to expanding bullets, the interesting feature of which is that the slits in the bullets are at the base rather than at the nose, as was accepted practice. Coster's third patent was taken out in June 1897 and again refers to extraction systems, this time for vertical falling-block actions like the Henry.

The last brick in the somewhat shaky edifice I was building came from that monumental work by Johan F. Støckel, *Haandskydevaabens Bedømmelse*. In this work on gunmakers and gunmaker's marks we find listed one J. C. Coster, Niedermeiser, about 1830–70. The question remained: had the Julius Coster, gunmaker, works manager to both Alexander Henry and Charles Ingram any connection with the J. C. Coster, Buchsenmacher of Niedermeiser, a small town some 25 kilometres from Kassel in West Germany? If so, when had Julius Coster left Niedermeiser and why? What were the circumstances that had made the move from Germany to Scotland seem attractive, and had Julius come directly to Scotland or had he worked elsewhere in the interim?

By this time I had become very interested in the history of this man, but lack of further information and also lack of time had resulted in the whole matter being shelved. From time to time I would again look through my notes, study the maps of late nineteenth-century Europe and read the history of these turbulent times; the fascination remained, but the problem seemed insoluble.

Then, one evening, a knock at my front door interrupted the evening's work. The visitor introduced himself: Hugh Gray, grandson of Julius Coster. Mr. Gray, a technician with a large Glasgow hospital, had decided to investigate the history of his family, and since guns and gunsmiths loomed large in the family chronicles he

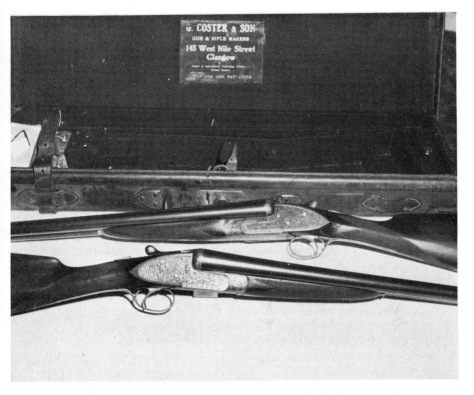

A pair of single trigger sidelocks by Coster, cased with the West Nile
Street label.

requested my assistance. Together we assembled the jig-saw, some of the pieces being
provided by Mr. Gray, some by myself. At last I had the answers to some of the
questions which had puzzled me for so long.

The first document I was shown, a copy of the baptismal record of George Ernst
Julius Koster, gave the father's name as Johann Christoph Koster, Buchsenmacher,
Niedermeiser. Here at last was the link between Julius Coster, gunmaker of Edinburgh
and J. C. Coster, gunmaker of Neidermeiser. From the record we learned that Julius
had been born on 4 July 1850 and we must assume that he worked with his father
before leaving Neidermeiser in 1869 at the age of 19. As to why he left his father's
business we can only surmise – perhaps a family squabble, or business difficulties, for
according to Stockel, J. C. Coster was not in business after 1870. On the other hand it
may have been because of the general political disturbance in Europe, due to the rising
ambitions of Prussia, for in 1870 the Franco-Prussian War broke out and Julius may
well have come to the conclusion that an ambitious gunmaker would find a better life
in the security of Britain.

Anyway, whatever the reasons, Julius came to Britain, perhaps first of all to
London, but in 1870–1 he was in Edinburgh working for Alexander Henry. Henry was

a man of some importance in the gunmaking world for, although his rifle had not been adopted, at least his patent rifling system had, and in 1869 the Martini-Henry rifle, a combination of Frederich von Martini's action and Henry's barrel, was the official British service rifle. Henry was perhaps one of the top six British rifle makers in the closing years of the century and as such his firm was an attractive one for a young gunsmith to work for. Coster rose to become foreman of Henry's workshops or, as he describes himself, "works manager", but in 1886 he left and went into partnership with Hunter. The firm Coster and Hunter opened premises in Frederick Street. The partnership was dissolved in 1890 and Julius carried on by himself until 1896. He then moved to smaller premises in Rose Street, finally leaving Edinburgh altogether late in 1898. The information conflicts somewhat with the facts as recorded in the patent specification and we can only assume that Julius had a separate business whilst at the same time working for Henry.

Whilst in Edinburgh, Julius had married Margaret Plenderleith, and when he moved to Glasgow his family went with him: George, his son and a daughter, Agnes. George was also employed by Ingram, no doubt learning his trade under his father's critical eye. After 22 years with Ingram the urge to start up again on his own resulted in the establishment of the firm of George Coster & Son at 145 West Nile Street, Glasgow.

In 1927 George Ernest Julius Coster died. The tradition of gunmaking continued. His son George carried on the business until 1930; he then joined Alexander Martin, staying with that firm until retirement. George had three sons, George, Ernest and John and also a daughter, Peggy, with whom he lived until his death. The son, George, also worked for Martin, being manager of the Aberdeen shop until his death in 1965. The story is not finished, for Julius' daughter Agnes had married John Gray, there being four sons. Hugh provided the data on which the latter part of this story is built and Douglas Gray carries on the tradition, being the gunmaker employed by the old-established firm of Arthur Allen at West Nile Street, Glasgow.

This is the end of the story. Whether guns may once again be made bearing the name Coster (or perhaps Gray) I cannot tell, but it would be a pity if this were not to be the case. The history of the Coster family of gunmakers may be even longer, for in the Stockholm Museum are a pair of flintlock holster pistols with carved ivory stocks signed "Jacob Coster a Maestrich", which can be dated between 1670 to 1680. Yet another Coster, Cornelis, worked in Utrecht about 1650. Having gone so far in the story you will appreciate that I now want to know if the Dutch Costers of Utrecht and Maastricht have any connection with Johann Christoph of Niedermeister and if they, or perhaps their sons, left the Lowlands during the eighteenth century to move across the border into Germany. If so, Douglas Gray, working away at his bench in West Nile Street, Glasgow, has a remarkable heritage of gunmaking to preserve.

DICKSON'S ANNIVERSARY

The first John Dickson was born in 1794. We know nothing of his early life except that he served his time with J. Wallace, whose shop was at No. 187 in the old historic High Street of Edinburgh. There is some evidence that Dickson entered into partnership with Wallace in about 1830 but certainly John Dickson was in business in his own right in 1840.

Edinburgh in the mid-nineteenth century was an important centre of gunmaking, and competition must have been keen. Little is known of these early years and, in fact, the records of guns made starts with No. 1590 in 1854. The firm was then trading under the style of John Dickson and Son, and John Dickson the Second was already in the business, having served the customary seven years apprenticeship.

The first double breechloader was sold in 1858 and although this gun, No. 1928, has not been traced we have a good idea of what it must have looked like. From the records we know that it was a 14-bore and that it was intended to fire $1\frac{1}{4}$ oz. of shot in front of $2\frac{3}{4}$ drams of powder. It would, of course, be a pinfire and very likely was supplied in a two-tiered case with the bottom compartment arranged to hold 100 pinfire cartridges. The gun itself was a double and we again assume that back-action locks were fitted and that the lever would lie forward under the bar of the action. Cleaning rods, brushes, oil bottle and a full set of pinfire reloading tools would also be contained in the case.

A very high proportion, if not all the work associated with gunmaking would have been done in Edinburgh at this time. Not all would have been done in Dickson's shop but certainly Edinburgh supported enough outworkers to the gun trade for all branches of work to be carried out. The shop was now well established in Princes Street, a thoroughfare whose fame was to exceed that of the old High Street, and it was from this shop that a never-ending stream of shotguns and rifles was to pour during the golden years of gunmaking prior to the First World War.

In 1859 Dickson's made their first pinfire breechloader with the lever curved round the trigger guard. This was certainly keeping up with the London fashions but, at the same time, of course, muzzle-loading guns and rifles were still being made and in 1865 a pair were built for the Duke of Roxburgh which were bought in a pawnshop 32 years later for 50s! The letter is still extant requesting information on these guns by the purchaser who also enquires as to whether or not they were built as breechloaders, for they were bought as breechloaders in 1897.

The year 1865 saw the production of breechloading guns with snap actions. The first of these was made under Brazier's 1864 patent and shortly afterwards Dickson's built another double gun with the Westley Richards doll's head snap action.

Old John must still have been shopping around – or perhaps it was his son – for in the following year they built another snap-action gun, this time on Horsley's patent and then later in the year the first double-barrel breechloader was made "of our own pattern". Unless gun No. 2683 comes to light we shall not know what their "own pattern" was, but it is likely that it would be a back-action pinfire with a double-bite rotary bolt. All was not settled, because towards the end of 1866 a 12-bore double was made with a "sliding action", and this would no doubt be a Bastin Lepage built to the order of a customer. Times were changing yet again, pinfire giving away to central-fire and in 1867 several Lancaster pattern guns were produced for central-fire cartridges, being followed two years later by guns with steel barrels and snap levers over the guard. Whether or not these were of the Purdey type is not known, but certainly Purdey actions of the 1863 pattern were made with back-action locks, and the same

John Dickson, born 1794, died 1886.

year saw the first of the top-lever snap actions manufactured.

The spirit of enquiry was still very much alive, for in 1871 yet another type of action was built, the Jones, which had been patented in 1870 and which was one of the earliest actions to have bolts at the top of the breech as well as on the lump.

To continue in business one needs customers to buy the guns and Dickson's had one of the most unusual customers a gunmaker ever had in Charles Gordon. He made his first purchase in 1875 and his last in 1906 and between these two dates Dickson's made over *three hundred* guns for their eccentric but valuable customer.

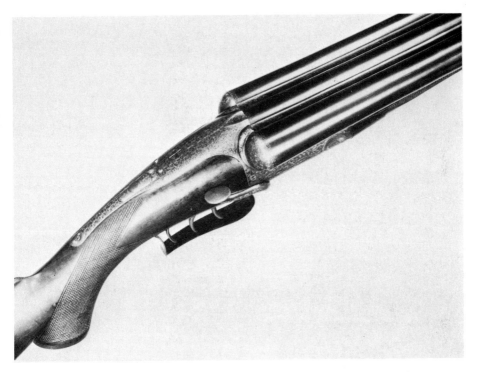

Dickson built several three-barrel shotguns; this example has the barrels, side-by-side-by-side, three triggers and sidelever opening.

Dickson's themselves could also be accused of eccentricity, for in 1882 they brought out their three-barrelled gun and two years previously the foundations for their famous "Round Action" gun had been well and truly laid, to be further improved in 1887. With the exception of MacNaughton's, yet another Edinburgh maker and a firm now incorporated with Dickson's, no other firm ever made a gun like the Round Action and well over half a century later this unique shotgun is still being made.

Even more unusual was the Round Action over-and-under which opens to the side.

With the exception of the Britt, which shares the side-opening feature, but not the lockwork, no other O/U shotgun remotely resembles the Dickson. Beauty, as Dr. Johnson remarked, is of itself very estimable, and should be considered as such and the Dickson Round Action is a really beautiful gun. It is also possessed of other qualities, one of which is longevity. The Round Action which advertises present production and which you will find on the cover of the current Dickson catalogue is the author's and this was built over half a century ago. How many manufactured articles of today can be advertised by an illustration of one made 60 years ago? Very few, I would think.

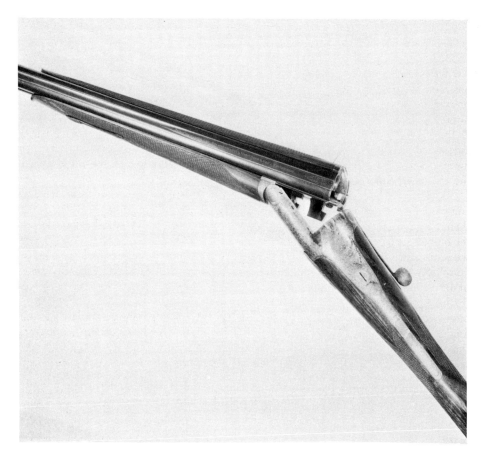

What at first sight appears to be a top lever triggerless shotgun is a top view of the side-opening Dickson Over and Under shotgun.

The last of the Dickson family left the firm in 1923 and shortly afterwards the premises were moved to Hanover Street, and then to the present premises in Frederick Street. Although this Edinburgh firm has a long and fascinating history, the people who work for Dickson's and those who guide its policy have their sights on the future and the shop in Frederick Street is modern and up-to-date. Possibly the only old-fashioned thing about Dickson's is their standard of service to sportsmen, a standard in keeping with their position as gunmakers in the capital of Scotland.

DISCOVERING THE FACTS

My readers' letters contain questions which fall into many categories. Mainly they are concerned with the background and history of particular guns, sometimes a favourite gun, more often than not, a newly acquired one. Within this category the questions generally asked are "Where was it made?" (if the address is not shown on the top rib) and "When was it made?" Then comes "What did it cost when new?" and, of course, "What is its value now?" Then I might be asked "Was X a famous maker?" If the gun has some unusual feature or marking then the owner naturally wants to know whether or not the feature was patented and, if the gun bears a patent number, what the number referred to.

The source of information which is likely to answer these questions is not one gigantic book on shotguns, a sort of helpful "enquire within". It is not one source but many: books, magazines, newspapers, trade journals, catalogues, printed literature, the guns themselves, gun cases, cartridges, letter-headings and bill heads.

Not only is there an absence of one source book or books – we do not even have one complete list of gunmakers' names and addresses! Even if such a list were available then it is absolutely certain that someone would have a gun with intriguing marks on the barrel, most probably placed there by the barrel-maker – if so, who was he? When we come down to the specialised craftsmen who contributed towards the making of a gun then we do have problems. By far the vast majority did not sign their work. Some of the barrel-makers placed their initials on the barrels. Some of the lockmakers signed the locks on the inside, and on the few guns which have silver furniture, these items might be hall-marked and signed by the maker. On Continental guns the engraver might place his name or initials on one part of his work, but this was the exception, in the case of British engraving, until quite recently. A very knowledgeable person might be able to identify the work of a particular craftsman but highly specialised knowledge is required.

The answer to "where and when made" depends very much upon the availability of some type of written record. Rarely does a gun have the date of manufacture marked on it. But military rifles did, more often than not. If you know how to read the markings, the model type and date of adoption as well as the year of manufacture could well be found on military weapons. In the case of sporting firearms one is left with the odd one which might have a presentation inscription or perhaps a note in the gun case – one is left to assume that the gun belongs in the case!

Serial numbers tell us the date of manufacture, provided that the maker's records are still extant and available. If no records exist then the serial number might help if another serial has been dated by means other than the maker's records.

The question, "Where made?" is often answered by the address on the top rib. Care

Early William Evans advertisement.

is taken today to replace the top rib if the gun is sleeved. If the gun is re-barrelled the convention is to place the name of the firm who re-barrelled the gun on the top rib and, of course, this is quite correct since much of the work in making a gun is in the making of the barrels and upon the barrels depends much of the performance of the gun. It is where the top rib is marked with only the maker's name or, perhaps, a general location such as London or Birmingham that more research is needed. One source is the advertisements in books of magazines. Let us take the advertisement placed in the book *Shot Guns* by Pollard, published in 1923. This was for guns and rifles by William Evans and it showed that Evans was "Gunmaker to H.R.H. Duke of Connaught". The correct address is given in full, together with some idea of the range and type of weapon that Evans offered. Second-hand guns and rifles were also available and the firm offered tuition at their private shooting ground.

Unfortunately, much information was missed out, including the date when the firm was founded and some idea of the skill and experience of the founder or the proprietors at that time. This could have taken the form of "Founded 1883" or more commonly "Established 1883". As to background, the advertisement might have stated "William Evans, from Purdey". I have this information from other sources. It is in trying to find out more about William Evans himself that a blank is drawn. The literature available to me for 1883 gives no mention of William Evans but it does tell me that in this year J. Purdey & Sons moved from 287 & 289 Oxford Street to South Audley Street and one wonders if it was this move that prompted William Evans to set up on his own. Royal patronage certainly must have helped to get Williams "established". Arthur, Duke of Connaught was Victoria's third son, born in 1850 and he held the title until 1942 when he was succeeded by the second Duke, who died in 1943. The appointment was to the first Duke and little can be learned from this other than William Evans was a maker of "best" London guns.

So, here we have a well-known, renowned but perhaps not quite "famous" gunmaker who has been in business for very nearly a century, yet we really know very little about the firm. Is it too late to collect together what facts are still available? Certainly, it's well worth a try, for each day that passes increases the possibility that some vital fact will be lost for ever. Let's try to tap one source of information I haven't mentioned yet: my readers.

J. D. DOUGAL: VICTORIAN GUNMAKER

J. D. Dougal was one of those men whose lives continue to arouse interest in the minds of those who are familiar with the development of the British breechloader. It is, I suppose, a slight blow to the pride of the British shooting man to have to accept that the early work on breechloaders came to us from France and it is to the gunmakers of the country which lies across La Manche that we owe one of the major steps in gunmaking – putting the charge of shot and powder in the rear end of the barrel instead of stuffing it down the muzzle.

The early breechloaders fired cartridges which Dougal insisted be called *douille*, which is the French word for "socket". It was Dougal's contention that since the device which contained the powder, propellant and means of ignition was in fact a temporary breeching at the moment of discharge, to call this a cartridge was a misnomer.

The cartridge was already well known as being a container to hold powder and ball for muzzle-loading rifles, while Eley's wire cartridge for holding shot was equally well known to the muzzle-loading sportsman. None of these devices contained the means of ignition as well as powder and projectile, and none formed part of the gun at the time of discharge.

Dougal was equally adamant that the word "socket" should not be used since in his opinion the word had an already widely established general use. In his book *The Art of Shooting*, Dougal painstakingly referred to what we would now call a pinfire cartridge as a *douille* and even instructed his readers that their order for pinfire cartridges should read "Please send me 1,000 *douilles*." He also suggested that the sportsman should give the word the English pronunciation, and it has intrigued me ever since I read Dougal's book as to whether any English sportsman ever used the word *douilles*. Certainly the literature is silent on the subject, except for Dougal himself.

Dougal came from Glasgow and later established himself in London, also becoming a director of a smokeless powder company. To the Englishman Dougal's middle name, Dalziel, is apt to cause as much of a problem as his *douilles* when it comes to pronunciation. The Scot would call him "Dee-ell", the whole of the middle of his name being unpronounced. Dougal was a keen advocate of the breechloading system and he mentioned that when in Liège in 1861 he saw upwards of 40 different breechloaders "in one room". He went on to say that all had a radical defect – want of locking power.

This defect was overcome in Dougal's own design, the rightly famous "Lockfast", in which the hinged barrel of the French Lefaucheux was combined with a rearward movement of the barrels by the use of an eccentric hinge pin.

Guns and rifles on the Lockfast principle were probably made for at least a period of 20 to 25 years, and during this time a variety of designs appeared. The earliest has a sidelever which lifts upwards and this is, of course, a pinfire. The locking system also changed and the majority of the Dougal Lockfast guns have levers which are pushed downwards.

Under licence from Dougal other firms made and altered guns to the Lockfast principle and, although there is evidence to suggest that he increased his manufacturing capacity to cope with the demand for his guns, one cannot help wondering how many were made, or in part made, by his friends in Liège. One of the more interesting aspects of the Dougal is that they were made throughout the period of transition from pinfire to central-fire. They were also so well made that they could well stand conversion. This is one of the interesting facets of the Dougal. There are a number which were undoubtedly made as central-fire guns from forgings and machinings intended for pinfire guns. There are also a number which were very definitely converted from pinfire to central-fire. On some the amount of work carried out would seem quite ridiculous by present-day standards but it has to be remembered that material costs were high in the late 1860s when labour costs were low.

By any standards the Dougal Lockfast was, and is, an extremely handsome gun. If one were asked which quality is represented, the best single word to use would be Victorian, for the Lockfast has the uncompromising solidity of a Great Western steam locomotive. The Dougal was one of that class of action known as the "Slide and Drop" in which over 15 patents can be traced easily, but the Dougal was probably the longest-lasting (though not the earliest) and, in my opinion, at least one of the best-looking.

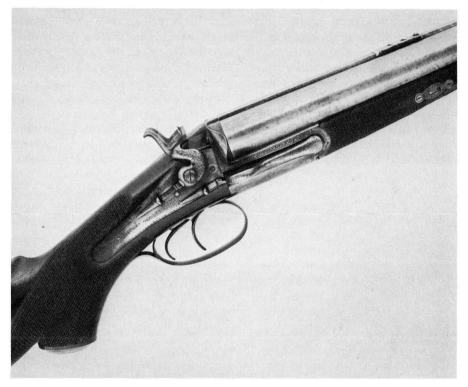

Dougal's "Lockfast" hammer gun retaining the styling characteristics of a pinfire. The bolt to lock the hammer can be seen; also the unusual reinforce on the hammer and the additional bolt to lock the sidelever. This example is a rifle.

Dougal had a sound product and he exploited it with energy and skill. If the same success had attended his desire to dispense with the word "cartridge" for breechloading guns we might today be asking across the counter of our local gunshop for a box of 50 *douilles*, though what a hundred years would have done to the pronunciation of that word I hesitate to guess.

THE GUNMAKING EGGS

One of the most famous names in British gunmaking is that of Egg. One of my most pleasant recollections is of a flintlock duelling pistol which belonged to a friend of mine. The pistol, by Durs Egg, was used to illustrate how accurate these pistols were. It shot exactly where it was pointed and I never had a misfire! Although it is many years since I have seen and handled this pistol, it still remains one of the most delightful and desirable pistols I have ever used. Perhaps time has lent enchantment but I doubt it; I have the feeling that if I held this pistol in my hands again it would arouse the same feelings of satisfaction and delight that it did all those years ago.

The maker of this pistol, Durs Egg, was a truly remarkable man. Not a great many of his best works have survived but a glorious double-barrelled flintlock shotgun made by him in 1791 can be seen in the Royal Collection at Windsor. This gun was made for the Prince of Wales and the brown twist barrels bear the Prince of Wales' arms in gold. There is a fine photograph of the gun in H. L. Blackmore's book *Royal Sporting Guns at Windsor* (published in 1968).

Durs Egg was of Swiss origin, setting up in business in London in 1772. He became "Gunmaker to His Majesty", the Prince of Wales having become George IV in 1820. Durs Egg died in 1831, but the name did not die out. Durs Egg had been in business at

Sliding barrel shotgun signed Henry Egg but made by L. Ghaye of Liège.

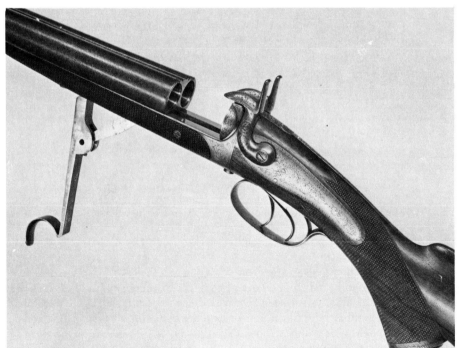

No. 1 Pall Mall, Colonade, at the corner of the Haymarket, and the business continued in Pall Mall until about 1865.

Joseph Egg, the nephew of Durs, was in business at No. 1 Piccadilly, and here he made splendid duelling pistols, first of all in partnership with Henry Tatham and then, later on, on his own. Joseph Egg, incidentally, was one of the several claimants for the honour of having invented the copper percussion cap and this claim was, in fact, stated on his trade label, "Inventor of the Copper Cap". Joseph Egg died only six years after his uncle and the subsequent history of the Eggs becomes somewhat obscure.

Charles and Henry Egg appear on the scene in 1838, when they bought the business of Joseph Manton. By 1850 the brothers Charles and Henry were in business at No. 1 Piccadilly and from 1851 to 1869 the business appears to have been run by Henry alone. In 1870 Henry William Egg first appears. Unlike his illustrious forebears Henry William does not appear to have taken out any patents nor does he seem to have made any technical advances. Such guns as I have seen have been finished to the best London standards but they are conservative in design.

Although the Henry Egg gun illustrated bears the name "EGG" on the lockplate and "1, Piccadilly, London" on the top rib of the barrel, this unusual gun was not made by Egg in London but by L. Ghaye of Liège. It is finished in the best London style and one cannot help but wonder if it was made entirely in Liège to Henry Egg's "pattern" or sent, "in the white", from Liège to London to be finished there.

As far as I can discover, Henry William Egg continued in business until 1880. The gun illustrated is certainly not the last he made but it would be of interest to discover how many other Egg guns there are. This was a most interesting family of gunmakers and, although today we tend to stress the pace of life as we move into the last quarter of the twentieth century, most of us who shoot have seen little change in the guns or ammunition we use for sporting purposes. Many of us are using guns made a hundred years ago. Certainly, Henry William could not do this since, in 1870, there would have been few sportsmen using flint-guns, so, in at least one respect, the pace of life must have seemed to be quite fast; from flint through percussion to patent ignition, then to pinfire and finally central-fire. Some things at least moved apace in those far-off days.

JAMES ERSKINE, NEWTON STEWART

I have referred to James Erskine once or twice in the past and recently requested information on him. I mentioned that I had known of this man for many years and had made efforts to find out more about him since, by any standards, he was a quite remarkable man. Enquiries in Dumfries had produced several promising leads which when followed up had suddenly come to nothing. I had become resigned to being unable to produce anything more on the Erskines and finally resolved to put down on paper what was available. I had spent time on research and talked to a number of people in Dumfries and Kirkcudbright; I had little expectation of anything more coming to light. I was wrong: once again I underestimated the "power of the press" and, in particular, of the sporting press.

At the end of September 1973 I received a letter from Mrs. Mann. She told me that

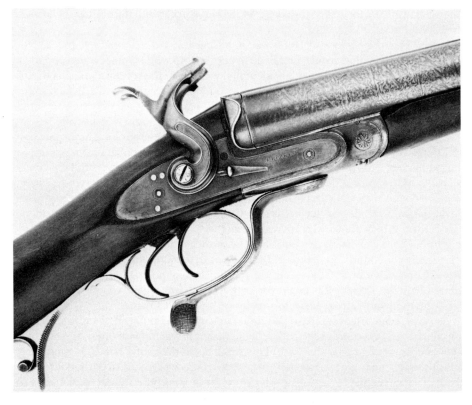

This remarkable pinfire double rifle was sold by Erskine, although it was made by Wilkes. Minimum engraving serves to increase the classic beauty of the line of this rifle.

she had just seen my request for information in *The Shooting Times* and, as one of the surviving grandchildren of James Erskine, she felt that I might be interested in having some more information on the gunmaking Erskines. The story is a truly fascinating one, because the Erskines can trace their family back to Charles Erskine, who, with his brother Robert, was with the Jacobite army of 1716. Charles went to live in Minnigaff, Galloway, where he married the locksmith's daughter and in due course acquired the business. His eldest son, Thomas, moved across the River Cree and set himself up in business as a gunmaker in Newton Stewart. Thomas's eldest son, James, left home and worked with Williams of Pool Lane, Liverpool, as a gun finisher. I think it likely that this Williams later became Williams & Powell in about 1840. James returned to Newton Stewart in 1830 and his younger brother John went to work for Williams in Liverpool in his brother's place. John stayed in Liverpool for 17 years finally rejoining the business in Newton Stewart.

James Erskine, on the death of his father, continued the business and with the help of his brother, who was accounted a first-class gun filer, began to build up a reputation

Today Erskine is best known for his loading "machines". This is an example to load 100 pin or central-fire cartridges.

which was to be recognised by the award of a bronze medal at the famous Great Exhibition of 1851. The award was for a pair of muzzle-loading shotguns with recessed hammers which were apparently given close examination by both Queen Victoria and Prince Albert. James Erskine was complimented on the high quality of the workmanship – it is to be regretted that the whereabouts of these guns is now unknown.

James Erskine is perhaps best known for the cartridge-loading machine which bears his name, later to be improved by his son William so that the output of finished cartridges could reach 1,000 per hour. Later James invented a machine for loading military ball cartridges. This was tested at Woolwich Arsenal, approved and then rejected because it might cause a strike by workmen who were still loading by hand. Guns were made for H.R.H. the Duke of Saxe-Coburg-Gotha, Prince Henry of Taxis and many other eminent people. The business in Newton Stewart was at 62 Victoria Street, where, under the direction of the last male descendant of the Erskines, William, it remained until 1907, James having died in 1891.

William Erskine, who had joined the business in 1877 when he was 13, transferred it to Dumfries, buying up the old-established business of George Hume at 6 Loreburn Street, where he remained until 1946. Then, the lease expired and the property was sold. William Erskine was unable to obtain another shop and, at the grand old age of 80, William, the third son of James Erskine, retired. I am indebted to Mrs. Eleanor M. Mann, the daughter of William Erskine. She tells me that she can remember filling the wad boards of the Erskine loading machine and that her father made these machines for export all over the world. In answer to my comment based on the opinion of the period "that the Erskine machine was wholly unsuited to the private gunroom" Mrs. Mann, as one who used the machine, tells me that her recollection is "that it was not bulky and that it could be easily operated". Her father and grandfather would be proud of her!

WILLIAM FORD, BIRMINGHAM

The earliest copy I have seen of *The Shooting Times* bears the title *Wildfowler's Illustrated, Shooting Times, Sports and Kennel News*. The date is April 1884 and the price 2d. The front page has advertisements and it is these that roused my interest. At the top left is one for "William Ford, Gun barrel borer and Maker, (New and Special System of Boring)" and we are told that this is the firm which bored the barrels of the winning guns at the Field trials. The address of the firm is given as 4½ Weaman Row, St. Mary's, Birmingham and perhaps the most significant fact about this advertisement is that in spite of changes of address, if you look at the back of recent issues you will still find one for William Ford!

I say "significant"; I could have used "interesting" or even "remarkable", and probably the last word would spring to mind when you consider the following facts. On the first page of that issue nearly 100 years ago there are five gunmakers and one ammunition-maker. The other gunmakers are Charles Lancaster, J. & W. Tolley, Thomas Turner, Charles Boswell and W. W. Greener. Of the total of six advertising only Ford is still in business! The ammunition manufacturer is Kynoch & Co., and although Lion Works, Witton, Birmingham is still there, the ammunition it sells is now under an old rival's name: Eley.

If we then move on some 50 years or so to 1930 we find in the issue for 16 August a William Ford advertisement offering their special "Goose & Duck Gun". This gun was made on "Dr. Heath's Chamberless system" to shoot brass cases and $2\frac{1}{2}$ oz. of shot. Ford now describes himself as "Practical Gun Maker, Gun Fitter and Barrel Borer". The address is now 15 St. Mary's Row, Birmingham and the works is described as the "Eclipse Gun Works". We also learn that the firm has shooting schools at Birmingham and Manchester. By 1930 the magazine has changed its style to *The Shooting Times & British Sportsman* and for the 32 pages it now boasts, the reader is charged 6d.

Let us now move on through the Second World War to 1948, nearly 20 years on. The paper has increased in price to 9d., the style remains the same but the effect of austerity can be plainly seen in the size of the paper, which is now down to eight pages! One thing remains the same: William Ford still advertise guns, repairs, reboring, new barrels and new stocks fitted. The address has changed again, however, the firm now being at Price Street but so that their former customers will not be puzzled by this change of address they are informed "late of 15 St. Mary's Row".

Ford had in fact moved about quite a lot and some of the moves are not recorded. The earliest address is the $4\frac{1}{2}$ Weaman Row one in 1884 and very probably this address is not recorded earlier in the classified directories since the firm describe themselves not as gunmakers but as barrel-borers. The year 1885 sees them at 23 Loveday Street, moving to 15 St. Mary's Row in 1889. Gunmaking appears to have commenced in 1888 on a "named" basis. In 1948 the firm had moved to Price Street, where they stayed until

Page from William Ford's catalogue, c. 1920.

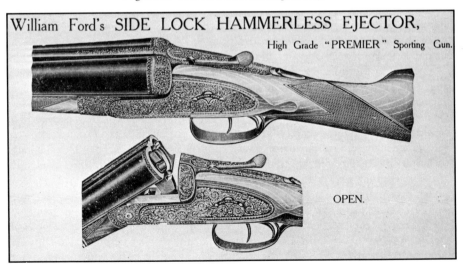

109

Ford's trade label.

1953 when they moved back to St. Mary's Row, except that this time it was No. 10, not No. 15.

The last William Ford died in 1946 and the move to St. Mary's Row was probably dictated by an amalgamation with James Carr & Sons, who were then in business at 10/11 St. Mary's Row. In 1954 the firm became a limited company and in 1965 the virtual destruction of the old Gun Quarter saw the move of Ford's out to Potter's Hill, Aston. In spite of moving well out of the way of the "developers", Ford's were again obliged to move to their present address at 352 Moseley Road, Birmingham, where it is hoped they will not be "re-developed" again.

I did not have the pleasure of visiting Ford's at their 15 St. Mary's Row address. This would have been in the great days of the Birmingham gun trade and Fords made a very wide range of sporting guns, many of which must have survived. Their best sidelocks, with Brazier or Chilton locks, could be had with double or single triggers, and at the turn of the century such a gun cost 50 guineas. A wide range of engraving was available and at the same cost you could have a best quality A & D ejector with sunk side-panels and with intercepting sears.

An extensive range of A & D guns was available, with prices down to 12 guineas and the Ford "Pigeon or Trap Gun" at 35 guineas, with cross-bolt, side-clips and intercepting safety sears. Ford's also offered a fine hammer-gun for pigeon or wildfowling together with single-barrel guns and rook and rabbit rifles. Of particular interest was the availability of double hammerless cordite rifles in all bores up to .600. The range included a 1¼ in.-bore screw-breech punt gun and a hammerless "Ball Shot Gun". To give some idea of the prices compared with today's, a Browning 5-shot automatic cost £9.

Today *The Shooting Times* averages about 52 pages, has a full-colour cover and is very different from the magazine of 30 or more years ago. However, over the years one thing has remained unchanging – William Ford still advertise "overhauls, fitting and storage, new barrels and new stocks". Quite a remarkable achievement. I only wish that I could put the clock back and visit their Eclipse Gun Works and order myself a double .600 hammerless express rifle and at the same time see the St. Mary's Row of half a century ago. You will note that I am not greedy: I did say half a century ago – it could, as you now know, be a whole century ago!

W. J. GEORGE, DOVER

One thing which I have tried to do over the years is to collect catalogues. To my intense regret I did not start doing this until the late 1940s, when already the attrition of the gunmakers had speeded up owing to the changed economic and social conditions, and the former magnificence of the catalogues of more lordly gunmakers had degenerated into a typed listing of second-hand guns.

One of my early post-war visits to London resulted in my receiving one of Henry Atkin's last independent catalogues, which whetted my appetite for more. I then tried to acquire older catalogues and I was fortunate enough to be given some by readers and later to receive photocopies.

One development was the introduction of facsimile catalogues. Possibly one of the finest of these reprints was that issued by Holland & Holland in July 1976. The original was issued 1910–12. It was 8 in. × 11 in. and had 72 pages. The H & H Royal Hammerless ejector with detachable locks was 75 guineas and over half the catalogue was devoted to rifles and cartridges for rifles and the Paradox ball-and-shot gun.

Such pristine catalogues as the H & H reprint make one look very carefully at any "mint" catalogue from the period before 1914. So it was when some years ago I received a copy of a catalogue issued by W. J. George of 181 Snargate Street, Dover. The catalogue was the same size as the H & H one but with fewer pages – 24 instead of 72. The covers were in an attractive green with gold lettering and the whole was, as they say, "got up in a fine manner". The catalogue was in pristine condition but there was no indication that it was a reprint, but on the other hand there was no evidence of use. It appeared to be unopened. I have seen one or two catalogues bearing the same name and from the same period and in the same condition.

A feeling of curiosity had been aroused but it wasn't until I received the offer of a reprint of this catalogue from Larry Barnes of Gunnerman Books, Auburn Heights, U.S.A. that I was motivated to delve more deeply. How best to do this? A search through the literature had not produced any useful leads and the only mention of the

THE ECLIPSE HAMMERLESS GUNS.

These Guns I confidently recommend to those who require a Gun to use, and not to look at, the price has been kept as low as possible, without doing away with the very best workmanship and material. I am aware that there are plenty of Foreign and Carret-made Guns advertised at a lower figure, but is it policy to buy at a few shillings less and pay pounds to keep the same in working order?

No. 121.

No. 119.—Top Lever, Side Lock, Hammerless, Double Bolt Action, with Stirling Steel Extended Doll's Head Rib, Very Fine Twist Barrels, Choke Bore, Automatic Safety Bolt, Pistol Grip, Selected Walnut Stock, £7 : 7 : 0.

No. 120.—Ditto, Damascus Barrels. £8 : 8 : 0.

No. 121.—Ditto, but with Greener's Treble Cross Bolt, Superior Finish, and Locks Nicely Engraved, £9 : 9 : 0.

No. 124.

No. 122.—Top Lever, Anson and Deeley's System Action, Damascus Barrels, Choked Bored, or order, Greener's Treble Cross Bolt, Selected Walnut Stock, Pistol Hand, and Fitted with my Automatic Safety Bolt, Plain Finish, £10 : 10 : 0.

No. 123.—Ditto, Fine Damascus, or Steel Barrels, Shooting Carefully Regulated, £12 : 12 : 0.

No. 124.—Ditto, Ditto, but Extra Finish, and can be had as a Trap Gun, if required, to fire very heavy charge, £15 : 15 : 0.

ECLIPSE EJECTOR GUNS.

To meet the wishes of numerous Customers, I am prepared to supply either No. 122, 123, 124, Hammerless, Fitted with Patent Automatic Ejector, which ejects exploded Case only, at the extra charge of £5 : 5 : 0.

Any Goods not approved of I shall be pleased to exchange if returned in good order three days from receipt of same.

W. J. GEORGE, GUNSMITH, DOVER.

7

A page from a catalogue issued by W. J. George of 181 Snargate Street, Dover.

firm I was able to find was in a list of 1908 which was given to me by Peter J. Wilson. However, a clue was given in the catalogue itself. In the introduction one reads "W. J. George, Cycle and Gun Manufacturer" and the clue lies in the word "cycle". The local newspaper, the "Dover Standard of 19 December 1896 refers to the firm and to the fact that guns and ammunition are stocked and that cycles by all the best makers can be obtained together with repairs and the "riding is taught by experienced instructors".

Very possibly, then, Mr. George had started in business selling and repairing cycles and was so listed in the directories. This would account for his absence in the current literature, which is based largely on trade directories. Mr. George offers for sale the "Excelsior Gun" at 50/– (i.e. £2.50) and a similar top-lever hammer-gun but with bar-action locks at £3 5s. od. This is the "Eclipse" keeper's gun. The top of the range is an A & D-action gun with ejectors at £21. The potential customer is warned to "Beware of Foreign Rubbish" but later in the catalogue customers are told that a few foreign-made guns can be supplied at £1 17s. 6d., which have been tested "but no further guarantee can be given". At even lower prices were the bolt-action military rifles converted to 12-bore and for about £1 one could buy such a gun, carefully selected, "which would not go off unawares". One cannot help wondering who bought the rejects!

"Collector's Guns and Rook and Rabbit Rifles" were listed along with "Saloon and Garden Guns" at less than 50p. Walking-stick guns in .320-bore and up to .410 could be had, along with "Air Canes" complete with shot and rifle barrels, pump, wad cutters, bullet moulds and shot measures. Both single and double percussion muzzle-loading guns were still available, together with several revolvers and some rather appalling single-shot pistols, loading tools, game bags and a range of cartridges.

At the end of the catalogue the reader is advised that George manufactures the "Dover" cycles. The office and showroom was at 181 Snargate, the works at 11 Snargate and cartridges were held at 3 Five Post Lane. I wonder if any W. J. George guns have survived and how long George remained in business?

R. W. GLANVILLE, WOOLWICH

My search for information on old gunmakers more often than not starts with an example of a gun they made or, perhaps, sold. We may have a gun, rifle or pistol with a maker's name and, perhaps, the location of the business. This can be quite simply London or even a small town which, today, one would hardly think could support a gunmaker or even an ironmonger (many guns and cartridges were sold by iron-mongers until the increasing weight of legislation turned them away from this bureaucracy-ridden trade).

The cartridges may also have been a clue to the one-time existence of a gunmaker, since on the paper tube would be the name and address of the loader or vendor with, perhaps, his own special name for the cartridge. A very considerable amount of valuable information has now been put together by the members of the British Cartridge Collector's Club on this aspect of the gun trade, and many gunmakers long since forgotten have been rescued from total oblivion by the efforts of the members of this organisation.

Yet another source of information on old gunmakers is in advertisements in the sporting press of long ago and also in the advertisement pages of sporting books. From such advertisements a considerable amount of very useful information can be obtained; each item is perhaps small in itself, but, when they are all added up, one often gets a remarkably clear picture of the whole.

Closely allied to the gunmakers' advertisements in the sporting press are those in the trade directories. I have just had a letter from Alan and Ann Jerrard in New Zealand and enclosed was a photocopy of an advertisement in a Lancashire Trade Directory dated 1880. It is extremely interesting: it advises potential customers that Best Powder is to be had at 2s. per lb, and revolvers can be had from 8s. each (or 40p and no firearms certificate). The name of the gunmakers was Jones of Blackburn, Lancashire and nowhere have I been able to find out anything about him – no guns to examine, no mention in the lists of gunmakers and no mention in the most up-to-date directories of the gun trade.

Other potential sources of information are invoices, letter-headings, trade cards and printed material. One of the rarest sources is old photographs. An example is shown here of the shop of R. W. Glanville, Woolwich. We know the number but not the street, and all the information we have about Mr. R. W. Glanville is that he left this country shortly after the First World War and went to Sydney, Australia. If there is still a Glanville in business as a gunsmith in Sydney or elsewhere in Australia I should like to hear about the history of the firm.

Now, what can we learn from the photograph? The first interesting and, to me, slightly puzzling thing is mention of the "South African Miniature Rifle Range". One can assume that the premises housed a rifle range and that customers could either shoot for fun or try out the stock on the premises. Was Glanville's the only gunmaker who offered such delights or were there others? I am familiar with the "Winchester Rifle Range" and the fact that years before Glanville shooting galleries were being run by Lang in London. Perhaps the South African Rifle Range had something to do with the Boer War?

The original photograph is sepia-toned and, as you can see, cracked across the middle. Despite this we can see that the window contains four double-barrelled hammer shotguns and one hammerless double-barrelled shotgun. There are three single-shot hammer rifles and Mr. Glanville is holding a fourth. These could be rook rifles, but also there is a possibility that they were chambered for the Morris Aiming Tube cartridge. This was .297/.230 centre-fire and available in both "long" and "short" case lengths. In the front of the windows are the usual 100 boxes of empty primed cases and on the top are several revolvers of the "Bulldog" type and a single-shot pistol. There are several boxes of Kynoch cartridges and on the right of the window is a fine cased revolver. Altogether quite fascinating and I only wish I had a time machine and could walk through the door of the shop and find out what was for sale inside the shop. Photographs of premises are usually to be found in catalogues; there can be few actual photographs such as this, and that is what makes it all the more interesting.

A gun shop in the early years of the twentieth century.

WILLIAM GOLDEN, HUDDERSFIELD

Previously I have used a photograph of a W. & C. Scott shotgun to illustrate a feature of early hammerless shotguns, namely cocking indicators. I had hoped to be able to show an earlier Scott shotgun, since they were of importance in the development of the sporting shotgun in Britain, representing as they did an alternative to the Anson & Deeley action. In addition to being made by Scott themselves in Birmingham, guns employing the Scott action were made by Holland & Holland as the "Climax", and by several other makers both in London and the provinces.

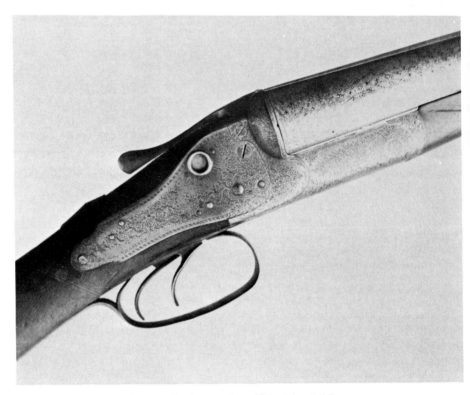

Best quality hammerless sidelock by Golden.

When I was shown an early hammerless gun recently, I noticed the "Patent Crystal Indicator" set into each of the lockplates. This gave the first clue; the second was that when the barrels were removed, the distinctive Scott cocking rods could be seen through rectangular slots in the action flats. The name on the lockplate of this gun was Wm. Golden, 6–12 Cross Church St., Huddersfield; this checks with the address given in White's Directory of the Borough of Huddersfield for 1894. In this Directory will also be found Chas. Golden, 53 Tyrrel St. and the firm of Carr Bros., 4 Cloth Hall St., who bought the business of Golden in 1914 and who continued in business themselves as Ironmongers until 1949.

The hammerless gun by Golden, illustrated here, presents several problems. It was made after 1879 but whether it was made by Scott or by Golden under licence from Scott, is difficult to tell, and only someone with knowledge of the facilities of Wm. Golden would be able to give any indication of whether or not they had the capability to manufacture it themselves. From an examination of the gun I would be of the opinion that Golden made it themselves in Huddersfield. As a Yorkshireman by ancestry I should certainly like to think that this was the case. There are other problems requiring a solution. What was the relationship between Charles and William Golden? What was the respective size of the two businesses? And did this Charles Golden have any connection with a C. Golden who took out several patents relating to firearms between 1860 and 1870?

I have also been able to see a slightly earlier Wm. Golden hammergun. This one is marked on the top rib "Maker to His Majesty, the late King of Prussia". This, of course, poses even more problems! How on earth did a relatively obscure Huddersfield gunmaker become "Hofrustmeister" to the Prussian Court and to which King of Prussia does the legend proudly borne on the top rib refer? Questions and yet more questions. It could have been Frederick William IV but this is unlikely, since he became totally mad and on his death in 1861 the crown passed to his brother William I. William became German Emperor in 1871 and it is quite likely that the subtle difference between Konig and Kaiser may have escaped the attention of the engraver. If we disregard this possibility the gun could have been made at any time, since the inscription states "to ... the *late* King of Prussia" and this, of course, takes us back to Frederick William IV, since William I would have been the late German Emperor!

The Golden family appear to have begun their gunmaking in Bradford, since the patents taken out by Charles Golden give his address as Bradford, so we can assume that the William Golden and Charles Golden in the Directory of 1894 were the sons of Charles Golden of Bradford. Much of this, of course, is conjecture. I would be most interested to learn of any other Golden guns and, in particular, the reason for the inscriptions on the top rib. Did the King of Prussia visit Yorkshire during the mid-nineteenth century? If not, how did Golden get his appointment? It is all very interesting, and I hope that with the help of readers we may be able to add some fact to the fiction of Golden, the Gunmaker of Huddersfield.

MORE ABOUT WILLIAM GOLDEN

The response to my request for further information on the guns of William Golden of Huddersfield has been most heartening and a quite surprising range of weapons seems to have survived bearing the name of this maker. It will be recalled that it all started with Colin Booth's William Golden gun built on Scott's Patent Action. For purely personal reasons I was interested in this maker and I hope to build up a picture of the type of business which was carried out by Golden in Huddersfield.

In any study of this nature we have to rely on the guns themselves to a great extent, since their survival rate is fairly good and rather better than, for example, gunsmiths' catalogues, which have a very bad habit of getting thrown out with the rubbish. Written evidence is usually confined to the immediate locality and is often preserved in local museums or libraries. However, the guns first. From A. L. Lyall of Snainton near Scarborough I received a letter which told me about a William Golden box-lock No. 2099. This gun has Damascus barrels and is proved for $2\frac{3}{4}$ in. cartridges and according to Mr. Lyall's sketch, this was, in fact, a re-proof post-1925.

Further information in the form of a long letter and several very clear sketches came from D. Smith of Clowne near Chesterfield. Mr. Smith's Golden gun is a sidelock ejector, and from the markings this gun is based on Perkes' patents of 1886. Perkes, a London gunsmith, took out a number of patents covering ejector mechanisms and it is likely that this gun still employs modified Perkes ejectors. Although the action bears London marks, the barrels of this gun carry marks which indicate that it was re-proved after 1954. The proof marks also indicate that new barrels have been fitted, and it is not unlikely that the original gun had Damascus barrels.

Damascus barrels are fitted to Mr. John Hill's Golden bar-action hammer-gun. John Hill of Penistone near Sheffield also tells me that his gun bears the following legend, "W.M.S. Patent No. 2752". This gun No. 9422 may still have "loaded" indicators since these were included in Scott's Patent No. 2752 of 1865, but the patent also covers a bolting system. I can't give Mr. Hill much help on the quality of his gun without seeing it and now is as good a time as any to advise readers that I cannot, under any circumstances, value guns. A little thought will indicate the reason for this! My old friend John Allwork, a contributor to *The Shooting Times*, also wrote to tell me that he had a Golden gun, being a .410 double hammer-gun, and this is more likely a Belgian gun retailed by Golden.

Lastly we have a stranger in the camp: E. R. Herniman of South Molton, Devon wrote to tell me that he has a C. Golden gun marked "Tyrrel St., Bradford". This is a 2 in. chambered 12-bore hammerless ejector, No. 1225, and has Whitworth's Fluid Compressed Steel barrels. Mr. Herniman's gun was re-proved in the post-1954 period and bears Deeley's patent numbers.

As can be seen, quite a bit of additional information is to hand. All of these guns were made before the First World War and most have been re-proved for modern powders and have passed this stringent test satisfactorily. What we now need are some Golden catalogues or trade advertisements, cartridge cases bearing the name Golden or, indeed, any shooting accessories.

I shall retain all the letters on Golden in a special file in the hope that more information is forthcoming. If any readers live in Huddersfield they might be persuaded to visit the library to see if any facts regarding this firm have been kept.

W. GREENER, GUNMAKER

Very few gunmakers receive the ultimate accolade, the use of their name to describe a type of gun or part of a gun. One thinks of the Purdey "bolt", the "Anson & Deeley" system, Holland & Holland "Side-locks", Greener "Cross-bolt" and Greener

The Golden hammer gun which on the rib bears the legend, "Maker to His Majesty, the Late King of Prussia".

"Safety". Greener, who was he? Why should a French catalogue still describe a shotgun of German manufacture as having a system of locking "Fermeture Greener" and why should a German catalogue state "mit Greenerverschluss"?

We have to go back quite a long way to discover the beginning. The story can be said to start in the year 1806, when W. Greener was born in the village of Felling near Newcastle upon Tyne. Now, two-thirds of the way through the twentieth century, Felling is *in* Newcastle upon Tyne, between Hebburn and Gateshead. The younger Greener was apprenticed to Burnand (*The Shooting Times*, 8 January 1972), and unfortunately I still know little about this maker other than that by 1848 the style was Richard Burnand and the address Pilgrim Street.

Greener did not stay long with Burnand; he moved to London, where he worked for the famous John Manton. William Greener had an extremely high opinion of both the Manton brothers; he extolled the benefits of the "top rib" and was later to write: "Joseph Manton is entitled to the gratitude, not only of the present generation of the gun-making fraternity, but of all succeeding ones; for this reason – he not only gave a character to English guns . . . he raised the English artisan with himself and left them the acme of mechanics."

One has only to look at a William Greener gun to appreciate that the time spent in London had not been wasted. By 1829 William was back in Newcastle, where he set up

A truly magnificent 16 bore double-barrel, percussion muzzle-loader by William Greener.

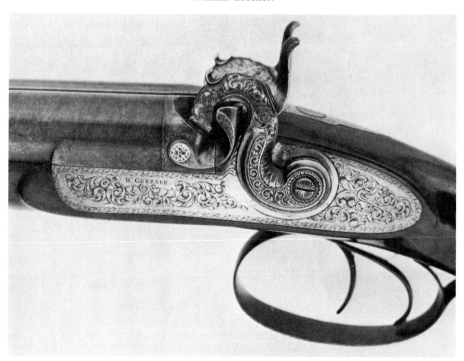

in a small way as a gunmaker. As with many "country" and also London gunmakers Greener had to travel to Birmingham, the home of gunmaking, both to get work done and for material. The time spent in travel was begrudged, and in 1844 Greener decided to establish himself in the Birmingham area where he was able to engrave on the top rib of his muzzle-loading percussion guns "W. Greener, maker (By Appointment) to HRH Prince Albert". Not content with gunmaking he invented and used one of the earliest types of electric light, improved the miners' safety lamp and invented a self-righting lifeboat.

One of the reasons why William Greener is still remembered is because of his writings, otherwise it is very possible that he would have been overshadowed by his son W. W. Greener. His first book, *The Gun*, was published in 1834, his second, *The Science of Gunnery*, in 1842, to be followed by *Gunnery in 1858* in that year.

Perhaps his greatest contribution was the invention of the first "expansive" rifle bullet. It was rejected by the British government, which later paid £20,000 to a Frenchman, Minie, for a bullet designed on similar principles. Greener petitioned that he had a prior claim and was granted £1,000 in 1857, "for the first public suggestion of the principle of the expansive bullet". To the last, William Greener was firmly convinced of the superiority of the muzzle-loader. I have used the gun illustrated here, and can well understand his feelings, for this is a truly excellent sporting gun regardless of whether "it is loaded in front or behind".

In his *Gunnery in 1858* Greener states, "Notwithstanding all the skill and ingenuity brought to bear upon it, it is, we think, sufficient to prove that breechloading guns cannot be made sufficiently durable to yield any reasonable return for the extra expense and trouble attending their fabrication." Greener died in 1869, still firmly convinced of the superiority of the muzzle-loader, so it was left to his son W. W. Greener to exploit the benefits of breechloaders and his patent, the first in his name, was for a pinfire with half-cocking facility and pinfire extractors.

W. W. GREENER, GUNMAKER

William Wellington Greener was the second of four sons born to William Greener, his birth, in 1834 at Newcastle, coinciding with the publication of his father's first book, *The Gun*. The book was dedicated to the Duke of Wellington and his admiration for the Noble Duke was also shown by christening his son Wellington.

As a boy, "W.W." was occupied with his father's business, then in Newcastle, and pistols, powder and equipment were delivered on board whaling-ships and East Indiamen which were being fitted out on the Tyne. With the transfer of business to Birmingham "W.W." became responsible for the outworkers, craftsmen who worked at home instead of in a factory or communal workshop and who, at that time, formed a large proportion of the Birmingham gun trade. Although handicapped by defective eyesight, he worked for some time on the boring bench and it was because of this type of work that he developed a very fine sense of touch which was to prove of value in later years. A good gunmaker was often said to have "eyes in his fingertips" and it is quite remarkable how imperfections can be detected by "feel" alone.

In 1851 a new factory was erected at Rifle Hill, Aston, and son and father appear to have parted company. Certainly there were differences: the father viewed the introduction of the breechloader with scarcely concealed derision and the son would have nothing to do with the old-fashioned muzzle-loader. In 1864 W.W. Greener patented and started to manufacture an underlever, pinfire, half-cocking breechloader, and it is interesting to note that such was the rift that W.W. Greener was at pains to advertise that he had no business connection with his father. With the death of W. Greener in 1869, the Rifle Hill and St. Mary's Works were again brought under one management. In the mean time, however, the son had patented a self-acting striker and in the same year, 1868, protection was sought for an over-and-under gun with laterally opening barrels, similar in concept to the later Dickson and Britte guns.

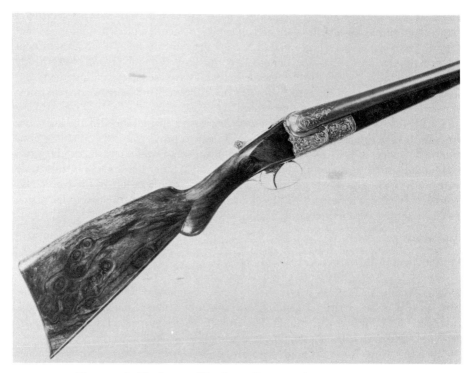

The remarkable Greener "St. George" gun. Built as an exercise in gunmaking, this superb shotgun features Greener's "Rational" stock.

I have never seen a Greener side-opener but no doubt one was made. The famous Greener "cross-bolt" appeared, and was combined with bottom holding-down bolts in 1873 and in future years was to be widely employed, not only by gunmakers in Britain but also abroad, particularly in Germany and Belgium.

W. W. Greener followed in his father's footsteps, exchanging the tools of gun-making for a pen: his first book, *The Modern Breechloader*, was published in 1871. *The Modern Breechloader* appeared in answer to numerous enquiries by sportsmen for the book *Gunnery in 1868*, which had been promised by W. Greener and whose death occurred before the book could be completed. Encouraged by the reception given to his first book, W. W. Greener wrote a second, *Choke Bore Guns* in 1876, and then in 1881 his *magnum opus* was published: *The Gun and its Development*. This book passed through nine editions and has recently been reprinted in facsimile. Greener's later books include *Modern Shotguns, The Breechloader and How to Use It* and books on rifle shooting.

Greener's name will always be associated with choke-boring, although he did not, according to present scholarship, invent this system of barrel-boring. Shades of Manton v. Manton were evoked, following the appearance of the Greener "Facile Princeps" gun. In 1880 a famous lawsuit took place, in which the firm of Westley Richards claimed that Greener's invention was an infringement of their patent; Greener won his case.

By 1890 Greener claimed, with some justification, that his factory, which fronted on St. Mary's Row and had spread along Loveday Street to Bath Street, was the largest in Britain; and by 1923 the firm of W. W. Greener Ltd. was to claim that the factory was the largest sporting gun factory in the world. W. W. Greener died at the age of 87 in 1921. The business was continued by his sons, Harry and Charles E. Greener, the firm having been made into a private limited company in the previous year. With the death of Charles Greener in 1951 the business was under the direction of H. Leyton Greener until it was sold in 1965 to Webley & Scott Ltd. The workmen, tools and expertise were subsequently dissipated and the factory pulled down, thus ending a business which made a truly great contribution to the art of making sporting guns.

W. GRIFFITHS' HAMMER-GUN

Every now and again I come across a new maker – new, that is, to me, since most are now long-since dead and gone. It is of particular interest to encounter a gun of superb quality by what is to me an "unknown".

Earlier in the year I received some prints of a gun by Griffiths from a gunsmith friend in America, Bill McGuire. I later asked for a loan of the negatives and Bill kindly sent me a set which I developed myself. Apart from the fact that the negatives were of a very high quality, it was obvious that here was a very fine gun by a maker whose work could stand comparison with that of the London trade. My readers will be familiar with the names of the provincial gunmakers whose work could stand alongside that of any gunmaker in the kingdom. Griffiths appears to be one of this select band of cunning craftsmen.

According to Bill McGuire, the barrels are marked "William Griffiths, late J. W. Edge". Bill wanted to know what Edge had to do with the gun and I was able to tell him that it was common practice for someone who had served his time or who had worked for a maker of repute to mention this fact on his own products, at least in those

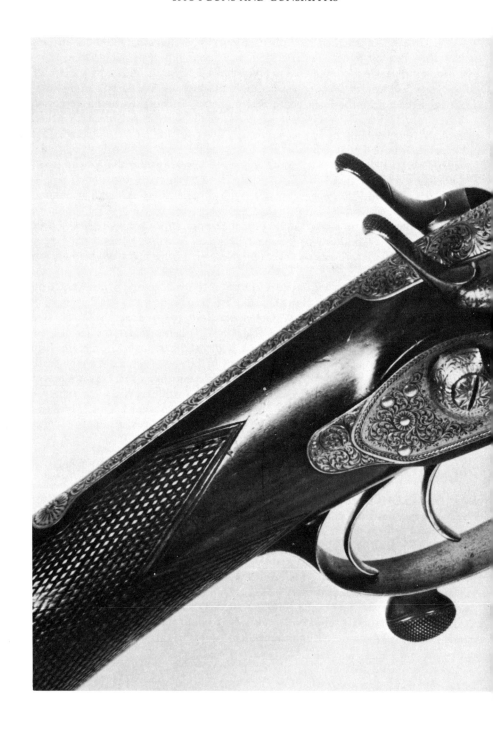

This gun by W. Griffiths shows the typical grace and elegance of the
"Manchester Makers".

early years before his own reputation was fully established. J. W. Edge was to be found at 24 Ridgefield St., Manchester in 1848; certainly by the end of the century he was no longer in business and he was not listed in 1828. I have seen a very fine percussion shotgun by John William Edge and it is obvious where Griffiths learned his skills and perfected his craft. Edge had several patents to his credit but none has been discovered by Griffiths.

If Griffiths did not have the necessary technical innovative capacity to think up new ideas he was certainly a skilled and artistic craftsman. One has only to cast an eye over the lockplate of this gun to see that here is a maker whose sense of line, form and shape is beyond criticism. It would be very interesting to see how many other hammer-guns are still in existence with this same style of lockplate. One can also see that the quality of the barrels is of a very high order and the engraving on lockplate and action leaves nothing to be desired.

Technical innovations? Yes, there is one. Take a closer look at the hammers and strikers. The strikers have a specially shaped head and the inside of the hammer is flat, with an inclined slot which engages with the projecting piece on the head of the striker or firing pin. There are, in fact, a number of systems of a similar nature, most dating from the mid-1860s since, of course, the locks on this gun are not rebounding.

If we were to ask where Griffiths worked we have a slight problem since there were three makers with the name Griffiths and all had the initial "W". One worked in Birmingham, one in Worcester and one in Manchester. It seems likely that the Manchester Griffiths would be the man, but he is listed as W. J. Griffiths. This may have been a son of W. Griffiths or there may be some other explanation. Perhaps a reader in the Manchester area can come up with some answers. Certainly W. Griffiths was a maker of very high-quality guns and we ought to know a little more about him if at all possible.

MORE ABOUT WILLIAM GRIFFITHS

In December 1976 I wrote about a superb shotgun made by William Griffiths of Manchester and owned by Bill McGuire of Wenatchee, WA, U.S.A. Not only did Bill McGuire's letter start me off on a search for more information about Griffiths but the excellence of Bill's photographs started me off on a complete revamping of my photographic equipment and technique, the cost of which could have bought me quite a good British shotgun! However, both the research and the new equipment have paid dividends, some of which I can share with you.

One other major benefit was the valuable co-operation I received from readers who sent me details and photographs of their Griffiths guns. One such correspondent was Captain P. T. Owen, who has an A. & D. Griffiths gun, cased and complete with Griffiths' label. A copy of the label is reproduced here through the kindness of Captain Owen. Of further interest is the fact that the gun bears an escutcheon which records the presentation of this gun from "F.C.W." and the date 1888. We can also see from the label that the address of the firm in 1888 is 70 Bridge St., Manchester, and again we see reference to "successor to the late J. W. Edge". We also have the statement "By Her

Griffiths' trade label.

Majesty's Royal Letters Patent", a somewhat grandiloquent and rather misleading suggestion often employed by Victorian gunmakers. In support, however, we do learn that Griffiths was a "Gun and Patent Rifle Maker".

As mentioned in the earlier article, no patents attributable to Griffiths have yet come to light. One is, therefore, forced to accept the proposition that Griffiths may very possibly have manufactured someone else's patent firearms. Only a study of surviving Griffiths guns will demonstrate the truth or otherwise of this assertion. We do know that Griffiths certainly sold and very probably made the A & D-actioned gun dated 1888. I doubt very much whether the manufacture of A & D-actioned guns, patented though they were by Anson and Deeley, was sufficient to justify the claim on the trade label, and it is possible that somewhere or other we may yet discover another Griffiths gun or rifle with unusual patent features. In the earlier article I asked if a reader in the Manchester area could come up with some information on Griffiths. Readers of *The Shooting Times* being what they are, I am happy to say that the response was splendid.

Quite apart from Captain Owen, who sent me details and photographs, my attention was drawn to Christie's sale of 8 December 1976, where Lot 113 was described as a "composed pair of 12-bore hammer-guns by W. Griffiths, Nos. 1905 and 1933". Then came a series of letters from Roy Jacob with a mass of details about Manchester gunmakers, including the mysterious Mr. J. W. Edge, to whom reference is made on the Griffiths label. Edge appears first of all in 1828 and, according to Mr.

Jacobs, the firm became Griffiths and Worsley in 1863. However, the situation is rather complicated by the fact that William Griffiths is recorded as being in business on his own in 1855. Then there is William J. Griffiths who is to be found at St. Mary's Gate in 1870 and, from 1874 to 1899 at 70 Bridge Street (this is also the address for William Griffiths). Griffiths is last recorded in 1906. We certainly now have more information on several Griffithses and time will tell exactly how they are all interrelated.

More photographs of guns by Griffiths came from Mr. Hodgson, and details of a hammerless 12-bore (with similar engraving to the original hammer-gun) owned by Mr. Pretty. Christie's Lot 163, although later, is very similar to the gun owned by Bill McGuire, even to the pheasants on the lockplate (Bill McGuire's gun is No. 1823). From Mr. Jubb came details of his Griffiths gun, which is marked W. Griffiths & Son, Haymarket. The rib has "London Fine Twist" engraved on it.

Not only has the exercise turned up some information on Griffiths, I now have some very useful photographs of Griffiths' guns which will help identify other guns and also may well serve to establish what one might be tempted to call "The Manchester School of Gunmaking". If we can come across some guns by Edge this may well help further to display the evolution of a style of gunmaking and engraving which appears to have been peculiar to the Manchester area. Certainly, William Greener established a school of gunmaking that owed nothing to London, and it seems likely that, although far less well-known, Griffiths, in his own way, did much to develop and foster high-quality gunmaking in the North-West.

JOSEPH HARKOM & SON, EDINBURGH

Often, when buying something, the choice can become quite agonising, even causing sleepless nights. This is particularly so when you know that having made the choice there is no chance of changing your mind – you are stuck with the decision or at any rate the very real possibility of having to make the best of a bad job and cut your losses.

To many of us, buying a shotgun represents a considerable capital expenditure and it is not something that is done without considerable thought. To ease the task a checklist can be made out which shows all the things that you need in a gun. Sooner or later, however, you come down to facts which cannot be listed. Here you have to decide on the basis of past experience, the experience of others or just the feeling of "that's what I want". Often this feeling cannot be justified by any means known to science, and quite often, too, it is right.

One or two barrels, bore size, chamber lengths, British or foreign, new or second-hand? Then, the difficult one: does it need repair? Hammer or hammerless, ejector or non-ejector? The list can go on and on.

Have a look at the gun illustrated here. The maker was Joseph Harkom & Son of Edinburgh. The founder of the firm was born in London in 1807 and set up in business in Edinburgh towards the end of the first half of the nineteenth century. As you can see, the gun is a double 12-bore hammer sidelock with top lever and the fore-end secured by a cross-bolt. If you look along the barrels you will also see that this gun has been sleeved and from this you can assume that it has also been "overhauled", "renovated",

Very high quality double hammer gun by Harkom of Edinburgh.

"rebuilt" or whatever the current phrase is. The important point about the work is that it has been done by a gunmaker, Wiseman of Birmingham and not by a back-street part-time amateur.

I haven't a Harkom catalogue of the period, say 1870–90, when this gun was made. I do not know what the price would be when new. At a guess I would say about £18–£20. In 1900 a specially-built hammer pigeon gun with top-lever snap action and rebounding locks cost between £30 and £45. What has to be remembered is that this gun was made during the period when many people bought hammer-guns from choice and not because the hammer-gun was a cheaper alternative to the more expensive hammerless gun. The quality is obvious and was seen by the present owner, who paid £70 for it. After some use the barrels were found to be bulged and the decision had to be made: scrap it, keep it as a non-shooting gun or spend money on it and keep it in service. The actual work needed was a resleeve and tightening up of the action. This work cost in the region of £125 so, in effect, we now have a gun costing £200. This is four times the current (1976) price of a new hammer-gun, double the cost of a new Spanish double and about equal to a newly advertised Spanish O/U gun.

A little more time was spent on the gun by the owner, the wood was refinished by him and the chequering brightened. I have handled the gun myself, though I haven't used it in the field, and the quality is apparent. Certainly the gun conveys that feeling of

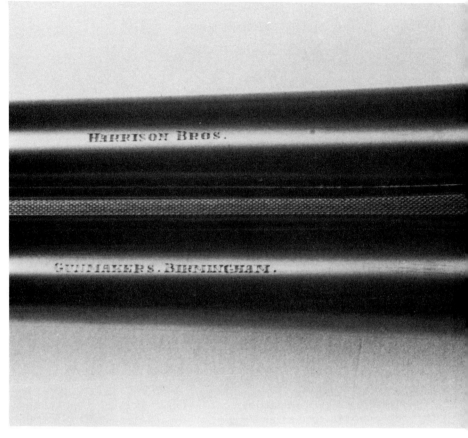

The name "Harrison Bros." is clearly seen on the barrels of this 12-bore box-lock ejector gun. The invoice for the gun shows that the quality scroll engraving, by Mr. Harry Morris, cost an extra £2 10s. od!

breeding; it shoots well and it suits the owner. His only comment is that he would not use it when shooting in company, since people today do feel that a hammer-gun is not as safe as a hammerless gun because of the need to let down the hammers on loaded chambers. With cold and wet hands the hammer can slip from the thumb and, even if the muzzles are pointed in the right direction, the safe direction, one's companions still don't like an accidental discharge no matter how safe!

The question remains, was it a wise decision to spend £200 or so on a hammer-gun? Certainly, a hammer-gun of this quality would today cost considerably more than £200 if it could be bought new. The wisdom of the decision must rest with the owner; the gun is an efficient weapon and he shoots well with it. We cannot put a price on the pleasure and satisfaction gained from owning, handling and using this gun – or can we? Say £200?

JOHN HARRISON

This is a long story and a rather special one. John Harrison was born on 26 October 1905 and he died in April 1981. I met John but once, in 1969 when I was gathering material for a series of articles on the Birmingham gun trade which were published in *The Shooting Times*.

When I had a long letter from another Mr. Harrison, a reader, I thought I should try and put together as much information as possible on the working life of a man I had liked and admired. The letter followed our recent meeting at the 1982 Game Fair, where I had learned that Mr. F. Harrison had bought a gun carrying the name "Harrison Bros., Birmingham". Mr. Harrison was in a position to tell me quite a lot about his Harrison Bros. shotgun and after our meeting letters flowed between us and I received some photographs and historical data of immense interest and value.

The first item we should look at is the invoice for this gun. It was made for a Mr. R. S. Morley and is described as a 12-bore box-lock ejector gun No. 9487 with 28 in. barrels and $2\frac{1}{2}$ in. chambers. It is proofed for $1\frac{1}{4}$ oz. of shot and the barrels are bored:

right – $\frac{1}{4}$ choke, left – $\frac{3}{4}$ choke. A Churchill-type top rib is fitted with a secret head extension. The gun has an automatic rocker safety and an Anson push-down fore-end rod and is decorated with "Best" engraving. A half pistol-grip and a horn tip finish the gun, with the exception of an oval engraved with the owner's initials. The gun cost £62 with a further £2 10s. od. (i.e. £2.50) for the extra-quality engraving. This, remember, was in 1954. The gun case cost an additional £6 10s. od.

We now lose sight of the gun, until it was bought by Mr. F. Harrison in 1978. He was so impressed by the gun that he wrote to John Harrison to ask if details could be provided. The letter he received was from 32b Lower Loveday Street, not from the Price Street address of the original invoice, and advised Mr. Harrison that the gun had been made by the Harrisons, Albert and John, but Albert had retired, though John being "much younger at 72 is still going". John went on to say that the barrels for the gun were made up from the tubes by W. Pearce (now deceased). I had met Mr. Pearce in 1969 when he told me that he had started work with Webley's when he was 14 years old and had set up on his own in 1956. The barrels were bored by Mr. T. Yates, now retired. I had also met this gentleman on more than one occasion; he was quite remarkable, with a very odd sense of humour.

After they had been bored, the barrels came back to John Harrison, where they were jointed to the action, filed-up and finished. John was an action filer and he produced the action body on the "Regal Pattern", which was a copy of the box-lock then sold by Churchills. All this inside work – tumblers, sears, springs, etc. – was fitted by John, as was the Scott lever-work and secret head. Triggers, guard, etc. were made by Mr. H. Jones. This was yet another member of the gun trade I met in 1969. He had started by taking his father's dinner to him and running errands, way back in 1912, working, as was often the practice, "half time". The automatic ejector work had been made, fitted and timed by Mr. E. Smith, Mr. J. Mallen fitted the rough stock to the body of the action – "heading up" as it is called – and it was then finished to measurements and polished by Mr. Eastwood.

We now are coming to the completion of the work. The gun was polished for engraving by the renowned Mr. Woodward and it was then engraved by my very dear old friend Mr. Harry Morris. After engraving it was then hardened by Mr. Woodward. At this point it came back to John Harrison for the last time. The gun was sent to proof before stocking and, as can be seen from the invoice, it was then proofed for $1\frac{1}{4}$ oz. rather than the more usual $1\frac{1}{8}$ oz. The last job before the gun was ready to send to its new owner was to free, assemble and test the gun. This was done by John Harrison.

We don't know what the original owner thought of his new gun but we do know that when the second owner, Mr. F. Harrison, acquired the gun he was delighted. He went to see John Harrison in Birmingham in 1978 and spent the day in his workshop. This was a memorable experience and was evidently a great pleasure to Mr. John Harrison, who was delighted that one of his guns had come to light and was now in the hands of a man who very obviously appreciated it.

Let us just briefly go back over the chronology. The gun was made in 1954. We have

Mr. John Harrison at work.

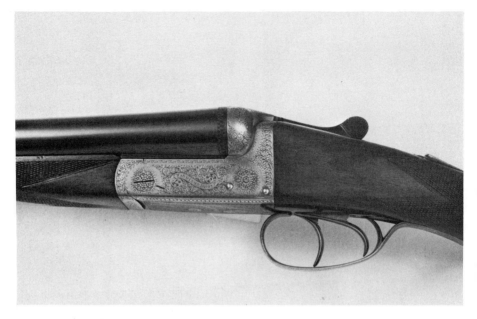

The end product. A good quality A & D double signed on the bar of the action, Harrison Bros.

seen *how* it was made and the people who did the work have been named. I then saw Mr. John Harrison in 1969 and also I was able to meet quite a few of the men who had had a hand in the creation of gun No. 9487. Even after such a short time some had either retired or died and by the time Mr. F. Harrison bought the gun in 1978 very few of the original makers of the gun were still in business and those that were, were in the evening of their lives! What might appear to be a fairly straightforward A & D-type shotgun turns out to have quite a history: one which reflects much of the past of the Birmingham gun trade and which, on close examination, tells us something about the practices and the people who were once part of that close-knit and rather special community.

CHARLES HELLIS & SONS, LONDON

The gun illustrated captured my attention when I saw it at the Churchill, Atkin, Grant & Lang "open day" in Birmingham. I had not seen this type of treatment on an Anson & Deeley-type box-lock gun before. I thought that I had at one time or another encountered most of the ways that the timeless A & D action could be styled. "Styled" is, I think, the only word that could be used in this context – I am still slightly shy of using the American "crafted".

If we think about it, the basic A & D is a box-like action, and the simple but effective limbs of the action are best so accommodated. Just to jog the odd memory, this action

Once inside the back court this is the door through which one gained access to the workshop of the Harrison brothers. In the old days their names would be chalked on the door.

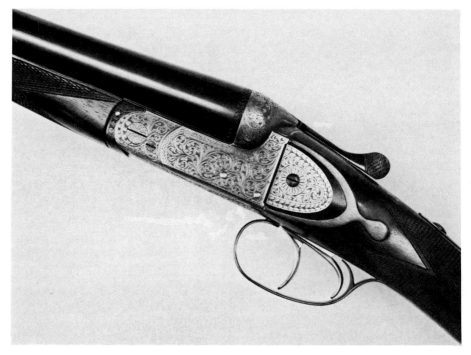

A truly delightful A & D action gun by Hellis, with sunk side panels and
unusual engraving.

dates back to 1875. Today, it is still being built, in all sorts of variants and in many
countries other than the one of its origin; these nowadays are neither replicas nor
reproductions but repetitions of a soundly designed and truly great shotgun action.

Within the confines of the mechanism and excluding the numerous "improved" A
& D-type actions which have appeared over the years it might at first be thought that
there is very little that can be done to make one A & D-actioned gun different from
another. Let us have a look at what can be altered – and, of course, what cannot: the
barrels, two in number and side-by-side, top-lever operation, and a fairly well-defined
position for the triggers and guard in relation to the action body. So, what is left? Well,
first of all there is the type of fence. The fences fitted to the Hellis gun are, in fact,
amongst the commonest employed. They are known as "Webley pattern" fences and
they are encountered on guns of high quality like the Hellis, as well as those of the
lowest quality. They are quite simple and straightforward, and this pattern of fence
was also to be found on sidelocks, especially when not jointed up to the action face.
(An alternative type of fence was known as the "ball fence", with a quite distinct ball
shape, and when this was a "flattened ball" one could describe it as a "Purdey pattern"
fence.)

Next we come to the action body itself. This could be quite square in shape, with flat
sides and a quite abrupt shoulder behind the fences. Any change would involve

rounding the body as much as possible without causing what we might call "internal problems"; but in such a case it was almost essential that the shape of the hand of the stock be also changed to suit the rounded action.

In the Hellis gun the action sides are quite flat and it could well have been finished with a side-panel and drop-point. An alternative would be for the side-panel to be sunk and decorated. This was quite common practice on the best A & D guns in the years following the turn of the century. What is unusual about the Hellis is the fact that the sunk panels have inlet metal plates. Such plates are sometimes encountered. They do not have anything to do with the mechanism but are there as decoration. In the Hellis these sunken metal sideplates are slightly inset into the back of the action. The sideplates are also provided with a quite distinct border and a well defined drop-point. The panels are well engraved and the whole presents quite a challenging appearance which is unique in my experience. One way of treating the back of the action body is to have what was known in the Birmingham trade as a "fancy back", the back of the action body having scroll work which, of course, requires careful fitting of the stock.

The Hellis gun takes its unusual appearance from the metal sideplates and is, I think you will agree, one way of making an A & D gun that is different from the competition. I know little about Charles Hellis & Sons and lack a catalogue from which to gain further information. However, I know that they commenced work in 1894 and that this gun has the 61 Pall Mall address. I would guess that it was made after 1908 but exactly when I cannot say. Three generations worked in the business until it was taken over by Henry Atkin in 1956 and thence it was incorporated into the present (1979) "House of Churchill". This gun is a very good example of the best work of the smaller independent London maker and I hope that we may learn more about Charles Hellis & Sons and the guns made by this firm.

THOMAS HORSLEY OF YORK

The names of certain gunmakers immediately arouse my interest and stimulate my curiosity. One such name is Thomas Horsley of York, a man of considerable ingenuity and the maker of shotguns of extremely high quality. By the mid-nineteenth century York boasted five gunmakers: Bates, Hook, Wilson & Wood and Thomas Horsley at 48 Coney Street.

Horsley's most active period, from the innovative aspect, was from 1862 to 1868. Two of his best-known patents date from this period, No. 2410 of 1863 and No. 1138 of 1867. The first covers his sliding, spring-locking bolt. Easily seen in the illustration is the rather odd (at least to modern eyes) top lever. This is not pushed to one side but drawn to the rear by thumb pressure on the raised tang. The thumb-piece is connected to a vertical lever pivoted at the lower end. This pivot can, in fact, just be seen in front of the trigger guard. When the thumb-piece is drawn back this withdraws a locking bolt, which, when the barrel is closed, enters a recess in the barrel lump (which can also be seen in the illustration). As with most makers of his period, Horsley was not content with the original idea. An examination of his output will show variations in the design features which, for the most part, were not patented.

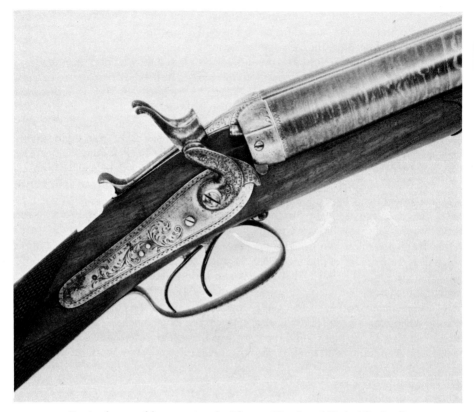

Bar-in-the-wood hammer gun by Thomas Horsley of York. The "pull back" top lever and striker retraction system can be seen. Note also the lockplates, marked "Burnett".

Regrettably, this example is not numbered and, as we shall see, presents a problem with regard to the locks. We can, however, compare this gun with one Horsley made in 1877, which bears the same patent numbers and the serial number 2439. This gun, discussed in *The Shooting Times*, 5 June 1971, is different in a number of details not the least of which is the fact that the rear lump of the barrel passes through the bar of the action and protrudes slightly underneath the gun. It is, like the gun illustrated, bar-in-the-wood, but not as completely bar-in-the-wood, and this is but one of the reasons why I feel that the *un*numbered Horsley is the earlier example.

The gun illustrated has back-action locks but the later Horsley has bar-action lockwork. The odd feature of the earlier gun is the fact that the lockplates are externally marked "Burnett". There are no other marks on the locks other than the name Burnett and this maker is listed as being in business in Southampton. One wonders if this is the famous "Bloody Burnett", maker of Colonel Hawker's renowned "cripple stopper". As to why an early Thomas Horsley gun has Burnett locks fitted I cannot find an adequate answer. One possibility is that the gun was originally a

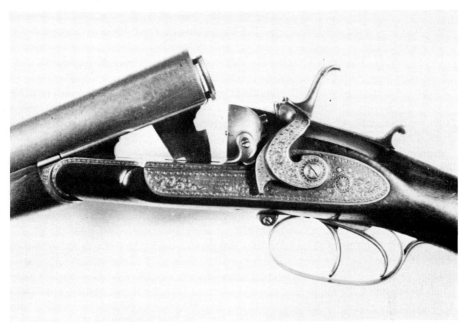

Horsley gun with bar-locks Number 2439 made in 1877.

muzzle-loader and was subsequently converted to breechloading, or that the purchaser of this gun had a particular pair of locks which he wanted fitted to the gun. In studying the locks you will notice that in front of the hammer there is a slight projection marked "Patent 1138". As Horsley states in his patent, "the strikers for exploding central-fire cartridges are brought back, when the hammers are raised, by means of two small levers joined to the breech plate and acted upon by inclines on the neck of the hammer". The "inclines" can be seen also at the bottom of the levers. This system was of value until the appearance of rebounding locks and spring strikers.

All in all, a very interesting gun and as with all good stories there is just that hint of mystery about it – why Burnett locks?

ONE OF THE FINEST HORSLEYS

This piece was prompted by the illustration of Coney Street, York and the chance to see and photograph one of the finest Horsley shotguns it has been my pleasure to come across.

First, a brief "recap" on the firm of Horsley. Records available at the North Yorkshire County Library, York state that the firm started in business in Stonegate about 1830. They then moved to 48 Coney Street on 1 January 1834. In April 1856 the firm moved to 10 Coney Street adjoining the George Hotel, where they remained until

1915 before moving to Blossom Street; there they stayed until just before the Second World War. The firm was last at 102 Micklegate, closing down, after over a century in business, in 1954.

The founder of the firm, Thomas Horsley, died in 1882, being followed by his only son Thomas Jnr. With the death of Mr. Horsley Jnr in 1915 the business remained in the hands of his four sons until the death of the eldest son, also called Thomas, in 1954. Horsley's was one of the few truly famous provincial gunmakers and one who, moreover, did not seek further fame and fortune in London or Birmingham as did many of his contemporaries.

Regrettably, we cannot accurately date the shotgun which is the subject of the illustration but I feel that it can be attributed to the 1870s and was certainly made when the business was still in Coney Street. This gun employs only one of Horsley's several patents, that dating from 1863 and covering the unusual sliding lever, which is pulled back with the thumb to open the gun. Prior to this patent Horsley had taken out a patent to protect a breech closure based on a lever operated from inside the trigger guard, and it is interesting to note that this patent was taken out in the name of Thomas Horsley Jnr. The breech closure used for the gun illustrated does not disclose whether or not it is Horsley Snr or Jnr who was responsible, and many of the guns which have been built using this action have also been fitted with Horsley's patent

Mechanical retraction of the strikers is no longer needed with rebounding locks and spring strikers. The Horsley top lever is retained, however, and this example of Horsley's work is engraved in an arresting and unusual manner.

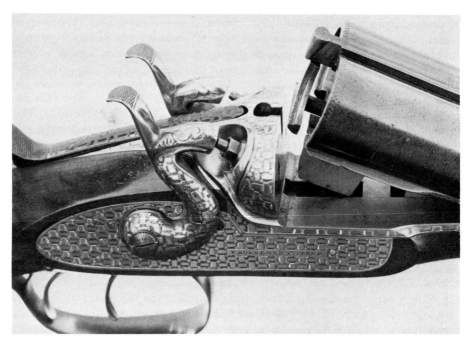

"retracting strikers" and have informed the owners as to whether or not the chambers were loaded by means of Horsley's patented "loaded" indicators.

Illustrations of guns with both these features, patented in 1867 and 1868 respectively, have featured in my articles, but it is interesting to note that the present Horsley gun lacks both, since rebounding locks are fitted and "loaded" indicators enjoyed but a brief popularity in this country although they can still be found as "cocking" indicators on some Continental guns. What did survive was the Horsley sliding top lever. This must have enjoyed a degree of popularity in the county of its birth in a manner similar to the Powell "lift-up" lever in the Midlands. The treatment of the hammers and fences is almost "turn-of-the-century" but the use of a "bar-in-the-wood" action may well have been a sop to the stylistic conservatism of his clientele. Who knows?

However, even to the person unacquainted with the peculiarities of Victorian shotgun actions, the style of the engraving arouses immediate interest and delighted comment. This is where I have to confess to total ignorance of who might have done this work, since I have not seen engraving of this style on any other gun. The Horsley is without doubt one of the most interesting guns I had the pleasure of seeing during 1980 and I cannot help wondering if there are any more.

W. HORTON OF GLASGOW

One of my readers, Mr. John Mullins, wrote to me saying that he had just bought a 12-bore shotgun by a W. Horton of Buchanan St., Glasgow and that he was not able to find out anything about this firm. I was told that the gun was a box-lock ejector with an Anson-type fore-end and carried Birmingham proof marks. Mr. Mullins went on to say that the gun handled nicely and that it had all the characteristics of an expensive gun. He also gave me a list of things he wanted to know; this is my attempt to answer some of his questions.

The first thing to strike me was how little I knew about Horton. I had heard of him for nearly 30 years but although I had seen a 12-bore cartridge with the name "Horton, Glasgow", I had not seen a gun or a catalogue of the firm and must admit that despite living in Glasgow I had not even looked for any evidence of the firm "on its home ground".

Mr. Mullins' letter was to change all this. First of all I remembered that I had a little bit of literature on Horton contained in a very early issue of *The Badminton Magazine of Sports and Pastimes* of November 1903. This was given to me by one of my oldest shooting friends, D. R. Pickup, the man indeed who might almost be said to have started me off on my long love affair with firearms. This magazine he gave to me when I visited him in 1980 to renew an acquaintance disturbed by the passage of all too many years. However, that is another story for another time – back to the magazine! I recalled that it had an advertisement of the "Perfect Gun" by Horton: it is shown in the photograph here. Except for Holland & Holland's it was the largest advertisement in the magazine and gave me a slightly different outlook on the importance of W. Horton.

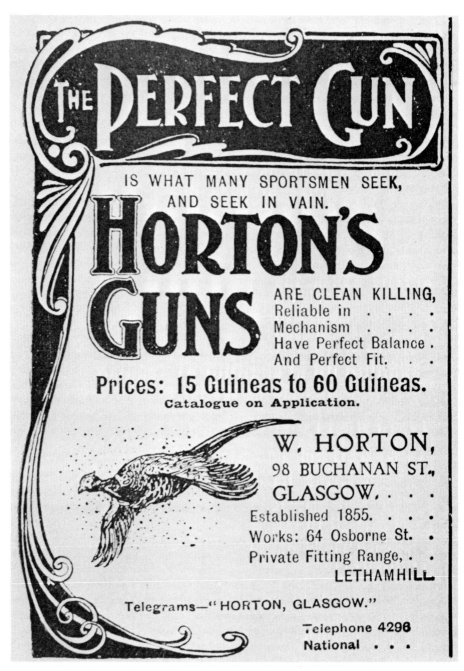

Horton's advertisement in *The Badminton Magazine* for November 1903.

I then put together the information I already had from various sources. From the researches into Glasgow gunmakers which I carried out a quarter of a century ago, I knew that William Horton was English and a gun-stocker to trade. The firm had been founded at 29 Union Street, Glasgow in 1864 and the only information prior to this was a patent by a W. Horton of 1855 which dealt with improvements in percussion muzzle-loading guns. The firm moved to Royal Exchange Square, where they advertised as agents for Colt. By 1900 we find them at 98 Buchanan Street, Glasgow, one of the foremost shopping streets in the city. Today, this address belongs to the Royal Bank of Scotland, and though the staff were most helpful and polite, my enquiries at the Bank about gunmakers did not bring forth any useful information. The firm moved to 199 Buchanan Street but this was only the works, and today, although the building still stands, no evidence of a gunsmith's workshop remains; but ample space and suitable buildings still exist at the back of the shop frontages.

The factory was interesting. One reason was that the firm was large enough to have a factory and another that while the shop remained in Buchanan Street for many years it was the factory that changed its location. The first and earliest information is that it was located at 11 Princes Square. This I found to be off Buchanan Street and convenient to the shop. The place itself is of interest since I was told that it had been a barracks, but no remains of No. 11 were to be found; the building is there, but no No. 11. I then found that the works had moved to 64 Osborne Street near the Saltmarket. This was an area of Glasgow that had been completely rebuilt, and No. 64 was a purpose-built "flatted" factory so designed as to harmonise with the tenement dwellings round about. By some quirk of fate the whole of the building which houses No. 64 is still standing, though many around it have been pulled down in yet another "city development plan", this one of recent origin. A thorough search through the building and its inhabitants brought to light no trace of Horton and so this avenue to further knowledge remains blocked.

Now about the shop: no one remembers this, either. I knew that the stock had been bought by the old-established firm of Arthur Allan at some time in the 1920s and the present manager of the shop, John, had told me something of the takeover. A further call at Allan's produced the information that they had Horton's "try gun" but on examination, although it might well have been used by Horton at their "private fitting range" mentioned in the advertisement, I found a minor problem, in that the gun is marked "Harkom", the famous Edinburgh gunmaker. (It is, in itself, a very interesting gun.) John told me that Mrs. Anderson, the former manager of the shop, was with Arthur Allan's when they bought the stock from Horton but from her I learned but little; as far as she had been concerned the takeover of Horton's had "just been a lot of hard work". I felt a bit upset at this; here was someone "on the spot" who might well have been able to tell me much about the Horton shop. Then I remembered that when I was a young man I lived in Birmingham; to this day I regret that I did not use my time properly in going round old gunmakers instead of drinking beer or chasing girls, or both!

The "private fitting range" at Lethamhill also appears to have disappeared – what we have now is a motorway and a golf course. However, all is not lost; I am heartened by the fact that Horton's advertisement tells me that "a catalogue can be had on application", and although it's now far too late for me to write for one, somewhere, someone may have one, and more information will come my way. Also, of course, where are the Horton guns? How many are still in use, and what do their owners think of them? What started with a reader's query, and the valued gift of a 1903 magazine, has led to all sorts of things, including forays into parts of Glasgow I did not even know existed.

CHARLES LANCASTER

Just behind Grocers (Wholesale) and in front of Gun Carriage Makers will be found the names of Gun Barrel Makers. Heading the list in "Pigot & Co.'s" *Directory* for 1821 is the name of Wm. Fullerd, who is to be found at 56 Compton Street, Clerkenwell. Next comes the subject of this article, Chas. Lancaster, Coach & Horse Yard, Great Titchfield Street.

Whether Coach and Horse Yard still exists I cannot say, but certainly many best-quality sporting guns still exist which proudly bear the name Charles Lancaster, and, something unusual amongst gunmakers, there is a quite extraordinary book *The Art of Shooting* which bears the same name. I have a first edition, 1889 and a 13th edition of 1962 and any book with a span of over 70 years is remarkable if only for that reason.

That celebrated sportsman and author Colonel Hawker refers to Lancaster in his *Young Sportsmen* and tells us that it was on his advice that Lancaster "came forward to the west end of the town to produce with his own name" and that if the rest of the gun was as good as his barrels "he need not fear as to standing one of the first on the list and making a fortune". Lancaster did set up in business as a gunmaker at 151 New Bond Street in the year 1826. Charles Lancaster died in 1847 and the business continued under his two sons Charles William and Alfred; both contributed to the art of gunmaking and their names appear on many patents.

One of the more unusual patents was that taken out by Charles William in 1850 which covered the use of oval boring for rifle barrels. The specification also described the system being used for cannon and Lancaster devoted much of his time to the development of his "elliptical" cannon. It is a wonder that Gilbert and Sullivan made no mention of him!

In 1859 Alfred set up on his own account; but after the death of both Charles William in 1878 and Alfred in 1890 the businesses were again combined under the direction of Henry Alfred Alexander Thorn, who, in effect, became "Mr Lancaster". Thorn was an even more prolific inventor than the Lancasters. Today he is remembered for his multi-barrel pistols and long guns (*The Shooting Times*, 16 May 1970) but he also made popular his best guns with back-action locks, which featured the distinctive lockplate seen in the illustration. Later this gun, which was Lancaster's Grade "A" was to be fitted with their "detachable and attachable" sidelocks "at no extra charge". "East Sussex", writing in 1914 in *The Shotgun and its Uses*, doubted whether it was wise to permit the amateur to "squint at the machinery", and one is left with the impression that no *gentleman* would inspect the lockwork of his gun!

The year 1897 saw the introduction of the "Pygmy" cartridge, a development which

Charles Lancaster's Grade "A" sidelock with the distinctive lockplates.

anticipated the 2 in. cartridge of 30 years later. The Pygmies were loaded in Joyce's or Eley's Pegamoid cases and were $2\frac{1}{8}$ in. long and $1\frac{7}{8}$ in. when loaded. The standard load was 28 grains of Walsrode powder and 1 oz. of shot. Made in 12-bore only, the Pygmies were not a success but they did pave the way for the later light game gun, the famous Lancaster "Twelve-Twenty". Lancaster as a separate entity ceased to exist in 1932 when the firm was bought by Stephen Grant and Joseph Lang.

JOSEPH LANG, LONDON (1)

My readers will by now be well aware of my constant plea for data and information on gunmakers, no matter how trivial the information may at first appear. Let us take as an example one of the oldest and most respected names of the London trade, Joseph Lang.

We know, for example, from their published catalogues and also from their letter-heading that the firm was established in 1821. From other sources we know that Joseph Lang served his time with Wilson of Vigo Lane. His reasons for leaving and setting up on his own are not known, but there is evidence to show that his business prospered, since five years later we are able to read in the *Morning Chronicle* of 13 September that "Gentlemen sportsmen are respectfully invited to inspect J. Lang's extensive stock of New and Second-hand Detonating and Flint Lock Guns, by all the

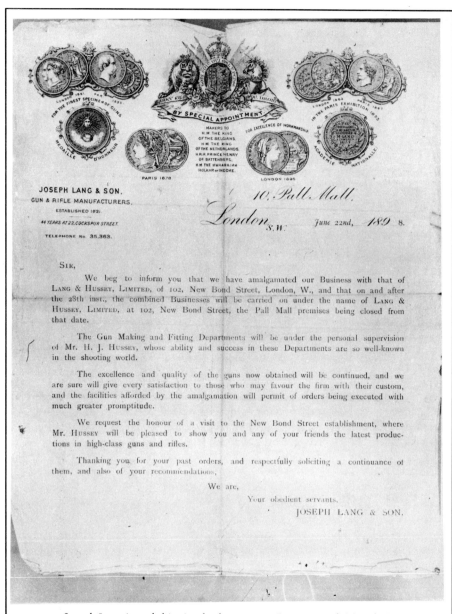

Joseph Lang issued this circular letter on 22 June 1898 advising their customers of the forthcoming amalgamation with Lang & Hussey.

first rate Town Makers, at his repository, 7 Haymarket. J.L. has just had the whole of Joseph Manton's valuable stock of highly-finished Guns, in cases complete, consigned to him, which he is now selling at reduced prices." Joseph Lang married the daughter of James Purdey, and by 1853 had moved to 22 Cockspur St. In 1875 the firm changed its style to Joseph Lang & Son and shortly afterwards the two brothers, Edward and James, established separate businesses. Edward traded as Joseph Lang at 10 Pall Mall, whilst James Lang traded from New Bond Street.

By 1898 a number of changes had taken place and the firm of Joseph Lang & Son issued the circular letter reproduced above to their customers, dated 22 June. First of all we note that the style of the firm is still Joseph Lang and Son and that the address is given as 10 Pall Mall. We can also see from the letter that the Pall Mall premises are to be closed as from 28 June 1898, and that the business is to be carried on from 102 New Bond Street. This, of course, was the address of James Lang & Co., in 1894.

However, in 1895, James Lang had become Lang & Hussey Ltd., Mr. H. J. Hussey having been the "late assistant manager" of Holland & Holland Ltd. In addition to moving to new premises the name of the firm was to be changed to Lang & Hussey Ltd. and the combined firms were to be under the personal supervision of Mr. H. J. Hussey; he became the managing director of the combined firm with Henry Webley as chairman, but such was the importance of the name of Joseph Lang that the style was again changed in 1901 back to Joseph Lang & Son and so it remained until the firm became Stephen Grant & Joseph Lang Ltd. in 1925.

From the foregoing you can see how many of the great London makers had histories of quite astonishing complexity. The power of old, respected and important names was too great to be discarded easily and the sight of such names on top rib and lockplate had an effect which could not be lightly ignored. The wish of Mr. Hussey to see *his* name on a best London gun can well be appreciated but pride had to succumb to business sense.

The difficulty of untangling the takeovers, mergers and just simple changes of style and address can be appreciated, and the importance of saving every little scrap of paper, of noting each change of style and address should be evident. Look at what we have been able to discover from a simple circular sent out by a London gunmaker on that day in June 1898. Even today the name of Lang still carries weight, for although a century and a half has passed the name Lang is still (1977) borne by a London gunmaker – Churchill, Atkin, Grant and Lang. We also learn that this firm was established in 1821, but we know better. The firm of Joseph Lang was established in 1821, and I for one can't help wondering what Joseph Lang would have thought about it all if he could have foreseen the future that day in 1821 when he left to set up on his own in the Haymarket.

JOSEPH LANG, LONDON (2)

The gun illustrated in this article might appear at first sight to be a simple underlever bar-lock hammer gun of the final quarter of the nineteenth century. However, certain things permit an estimate of the quality of the gun: the shape and style of the triggers, the shape of the hammers and the treatment of the fences. These things, easily visible from a photograph, will tell you that, without knowing who made this gun, it was *well* made and, in spite of its obvious age, it is a gun which was valued.

Now for the things which we can't see from the illustration. It is possible to read the name on the lockplate: "J. Lang & Sons, Patent". Even this style is important because of the use of the word "Sons", in the plural. Also of interest is the Continental style of engraving the name in a curve around the hammer instead of in a straight line along the lockplate as was more common. A look at the barrel gives us the address – 22 Cockspur Street, London – and we have the number of the gun, 5688, and on the flats or table of the action body the mark "J.P. Patent" enclosed in a diamond, and that is all. In handling the gun the first unusual feature becomes apparent; as the rather long underlever is *pushed* forward, the hammers are brought to half cock.

The photograph was taken without a tripod in natural light, and with the press of the people around me at the Tayside Field Sports Fair in August 1980 I was not able to achieve anything more satisfactory.

It was not possible to take the gun apart nor was it possible to give the gun the degree of careful attention that it undoubtedly merits, but this is one of the problems of looking at guns at this type of event. One is in the position of being a greedy boy in a cake shop which is on the point of closing and one has to stuff as much away as possible and devil take the tummy-ache! Also, of course, there is the passage of time. This is being written several months after having seen the gun and my camera has to be my memory, along with a few barely legible, scribbled notes.

The gun bears the initials of a patentee who does not appear to have been the maker or vendor. Who then do we have with initials "J.P." who might fit the bill? A look through the patents of the period brings to mind one person, James Purdey. The patent could be a Purdey's of 1870 which blocked the triggers until the barrels were securely locked. It is unlikely to be any of the other patents taken out by Purdey during the period and, of course, without the gun itself I cannot verify whether or not it is the 1870 Purdey safety patent. Certainly the last quarter of the nineteenth century was a hothouse of ideas, many of which were concerned with safety, and the Lang gun may have been fitted with Purdey's trigger-locking device at the request of a customer.

When we look at some of the other aspects of this gun we again come up with some unanswered questions. A point noted while the gun was in my hands was the size and shape of the strikers or firing pins. These, as you may be able to see from the photograph, are quite large, and the reason why this feature is not protected by patent is because the patent which Lang took out afforded provisional protection only. The feature is not the size of the striking pin but the fact that it is retracted to permit the gun to close by means of an extension on the extractor which pushes it back without the need for an internal spring. Today the problems caused by having the protruding firing pin tie up the gun are largely forgotten, but at one time a great deal of effort was expended by gunmakers to ensure that the firing pins were withdrawn after firing.

Another very interesting feature of this gun is the self-cocking facility. Lang did patent a self-cocking system in 1878 which was used on some of his hammerless guns and which provided for the system to be used on hammer-guns as well. However, on the gun, Lang does not mention anywhere which patent he was using other than the

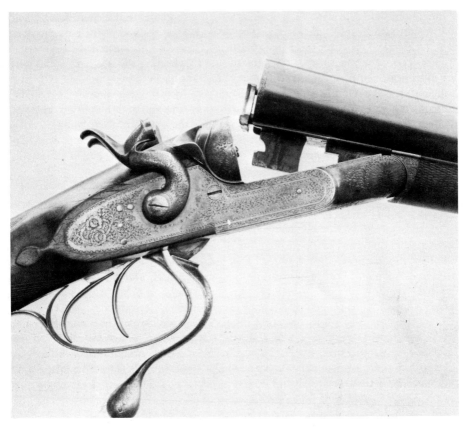

This Lang central-fire gun has an underlever which moves forwards; note
also the shape of the "bite" on the rear lump.

one we presume to be Purdey's.

As you can imagine, here we have a gun with a self-cocking feature, striker
retraction and possibly a trigger-blocking safety as well as a type of snap action; what
do I now want? A chance to have another look at the gun and take it apart.

The maker, Lang, occupies a very important position in the firmament of those
bright shining stars which were the London makers of the nineteenth century. He
established himself at 7 Haymarket in 1821, describing himself as a "Gun & Pistol
Maker". He then moved to 22 Cockspur St in 1853 and this is the address *our* Lang gun
bears. In 1869 his son Edward was taken into partnership and we find the Company
style changed to "Joseph Lang and Son, Gun, Rifle & Pistol Manufacturers, 22
Cockspur St, London". Besides Edward there was another brother, James, who was
also a partner in the firm of Joseph Lang for many years before setting up on his own as
James Lang at 33 New Bond St. It was James who appears to have inherited the spirit
of inventive genius, because his mother was a daughter of James Purdey, the founder

of that famous firm. Edward Lang appears to have eventually sold the business, which continued to trade under the management of H. J. Harris while James Lang became Lang & Hussey Ltd. After this things because extremely complicated.

Throughout the 1890s there was a great deal of "wheeling and dealing" and it was not until after the First World War that the situation became simplified with the formation of the Company, Stephen Grant & Joseph Lang Ltd in 1925. The subsequent history of the firm was dealt with some time ago and there is no doubt in my mind that one could get a very good book out of the history of Joseph Lang, even a television series that would rival Dallas if all the documents could be obtained! I do hope that someone has saved what papers there were following the end of Churchill, Atkin, Grant & Lang.

LANG'S PINFIRE

The name engraved on the top rib or action of a shotgun is to many just a name and, all too often, the attrition of time has destroyed records and erased memories and all that is left to us is a name. Fortunately this is not always the case and the name on a gun or above the window of a gun shop can re-create history and bring to life some of the people whose actions shaped or altered the course of past events.

One such shop is at 7 Bury Street, St. James's, London, SW1. The name above the window is that of Atkin, Grant & Lang Ltd. Fairly common names, but the three together mean something, for behind them lies a wealth of gunmaking history, a century and a half of commercial and technical endeavour. It would be abortive to attempt to trace the fascinating and exceedingly complex background as to how and

The "first" British breechloader, Lang's pinfire of 1852.

why these three names appear today above a shop in a London street. So instead let us take one name, that of Lang, and one gun, on the top rib of which is engraved "Joseph Lang, 22 Cockspur St., London".

The Lefaucheux pinfire breechloader, or as it was then known, the French "crutch gun" made its impact at the time of the Great Exhibition of 1851. Joseph Lang himself is listed as an exhibitor and one assumes that he showed an example of his percussion muzzle-loader. In 1852, a few months after the close of the Exhibition, Lang was marketing his own version which, as can be seen from the illustrations, was far neater than the original Lefaucheux.

The example shown bears London proof marks and employs a single-bite underlever lock. The barrels are Damascus, 27 inches long and are nominal 12-bore. The method of bolting can be seen from the illustration where the action is open: the single bite at the rear of the lump is, of course, locked by the rotary underbolt. Later improvements to the pinfire included the double-grip rotary lever over-guard action exemplified by Stephen Grant's pinfire of 1861.

The Lang pinfire open to illustrate the short operating lever and the single "bite" on the barrel lump.

JAMES LAWSON AND OTHERS: GIVE ME A CLUE!

"James Lawson, Gun Maker, Cutler & Ironmonger, Fishing Rod & Tackle Manufacturer": this information is culled from the receipted invoice dated 19 October 1900 (see illustration). The invoice was given to me by my old friend Allan Paton, but regrettably it does not tell us anything about the goods which Mr. Robert Paton purchased in that first year of the twentieth century. We have what might be James Lawson's signature and an indication of how business was conducted – "many thanks, most humbly" (all very Dickensian!)

In over 30 years I have encountered just one firearm which bore the name of Lawson. This was a Royal Irish Constabulary revolver from the Kater Collection, and, although not *made* by Lawson, it was sold by him and so engraved on the top strap.

Records tell us that the firm was established in 1872. Then Lawson was described as a "Gunmaker, Cutler, Edge Tool and Mathematical Instrument Maker". From my own records I know the firm was still in business when the First World War broke out. But did Lawson make guns? The answer, very probably, is that he did not. So, at this stage of our enquiries what do we know about the firm? Very little, I'm afraid. All we have is one revolver, one entry in *Scottish Arms Makers* by Charles E. Whitelaw, a number of notes taken from the Glasgow Directories by me over the years, and, of course, the invoice.

James Lawson was but one of a number of similar businesses which did not restrict themselves to selling firearms and ammunition but sold quite a selection of other items as well. Not far away was the firm of William Landell, which lasted well into my lifetime and where I spent a very happy day with the old retainers of the firm who told me stirring tales of riot and insurrection in Glasgow, of the militia being called out and the mob being pursued across the bridge into the then warren of the Gorbals.

Arthur Allan, too, was described in 1855 as a "Gunmaker, Cutler and Edge Tool Maker", whereas Hugh Brown, also to be found in Argyle St. spread his net even wider: "Sawmaker, Ironmonger, Cutler, Plane, Edge Tool and Gunmaker". Thomas Camp bell reminds me of the Birmingham trade, where gunmaking and dealing in spirits so often went together. By 1857 Thomas Campbell had a shooting saloon in Glasgow's Saltmarket and I wonder if this was a shooting saloon or gallery or a saloon bar with shooting instead of, perhaps, darts! The famous John Dougal started his business life as a fishing and fowling tackle maker, later to specialise in needles and fishing hooks. The business was established in 1808 and recorded as a gunmaker in 1837.

From the list of ventures described, which merely scratches the surface, we get a picture of a busy, bustling commercial life, where opportunities come and go and where the people are ready to seize an opportunity whenever it is presented. Also it can explain how at times a gunmaker's name on a gun cannot be located in the records. Only this week I have had to tell two readers that I couldn't help with their queries. One was about a gun by Cufflyn of Folkestone, the other J. Carr & Son, Gun & Rifle Makers, London. The latter might be the London retail outlet of a Birmingham firm but with regard to Cufflyn the only recourse is to local records in Folkestone. This is why any scrap of paper that has anything to do with guns or gunmaking is important.

James Lawson was just a name in the directories, two lines on a Birmingham-made revolver, until that important bit of paper appeared and then, to me at least, he came to life, momentarily, the obscuring mists of time swirling aside to let us see, briefly, a little of the business life of Glasgow and of John Lawson.

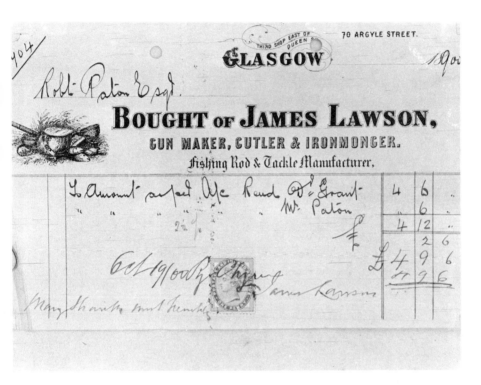

James Lawson's invoice dated 1900.

Guns themselves are fairly robust; their chief enemies are rust and politicians. Trade labels in guncases, as we have seen in several earlier articles, also tend to tell us quite a bit, but here oil, physical damage and various nibbling creatures which eat paper have taken their toll over the years. Next of course we have catalogues and adverts. The latter can be single sheets or printed material in newspapers, magazines, books etc. In later years cartridges and cartridge boxes can also help, as can entries in trade directories. Lastly, we come to the most neglected source of information of all, business correspondence, letter-headings, invoices, bills, etc. Where these have survived all sorts of items of interest are likely to be uncovered.

So when you are clearing things out of the attic and come to a pile of old papers, look through them please. There might be an old bill or invoice that could answer some questions. Don't forget, will you?

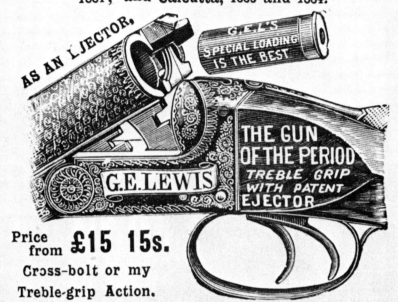

G. E. LEWIS'
"THE GUN OF THE PERIOD."
Has taken Honours wherever shown.
Paris, 1878; Sydney, 1879 and 1880; Melbourne, 1880 and 1881; and Calcutta, 1883 and 1884.

AS AN EJECTOR,

G.E.L'S SPECIAL LOADING IS THE BEST

THE GUN OF THE PERIOD TREBLE GRIP WITH PATENT EJECTOR

G.E.LEWIS

Price from **£15 15s.**

Cross-bolt or my Treble-grip Action.

The above is the latest development of **"The Gun of the Period,"** fitted with the newest and best Patent Ejector, combined with G. E. Lewis' Treble Grip.

We also make this Gun as a Non-Ejector, with treble-grip or cross-bolt action, at **12 Guineas** and upwards, or with top-lever and double-bolt, from **10 Guineas.**

Our stock of Sporting Guns and Rifles, Ready for Delivery, is the largest in England. Send for 200-page Illustrated Catalogue of finished Stock, giving bend, weight, and full description of every gun. We invite Sportsmen to come and inspect our Stock. Any Gun or Rifle may be Tested at our Range before purchase.

REPAIRS.—All kinds of Repairs by a Staff of the most Skilled Workmen in the Trade. Quotations Free.

Secondhand Guns by other Makers taken in exchange.

G. E. LEWIS, Gun and Rifle Works,
32 & 33, LOWER LOVEDAY ST., BIRMINGHAM.
ESTABLISHED 1850.

Advertisement for G. E. Lewis at the turn of the century.

G. E. LEWIS & SONS, BIRMINGHAM

Readers of this series will be aware of my constant plea for old catalogues. One reader who has most kindly responded in a very practical way is Mr. Shepherdson, who sent me the Lewis catalogue for 1926–7.

A word about Lewis. The firm was founded by G. E. Lewis in 1850 and the address given on their 1926 catalogue is still the same today, 32–33 Lower Loveday Street, Birmingham. This is in the traditional gunmaking quarter of Birmingham, around the old church of St. Mary's, where in the days before the ring road the streets were full of gunmakers: Weaman Street, Whittall Street, Sand Street, Bath Street, Price Street, St. Mary's Row.

But, back to Lewis & Sons, makers of the renowned "Gun of the Period". Looking through the catalogue we turn over the pages of a past history. An ordinary gun in a stout cardboard box could be sent to any part of the British Isles for 2s. 6d. and this included the box! A gun could be sent to most parts of the world for 10s. including packing and insurance.

Lewis produced their best-quality sidelock hammerless ejector for £60. If Whitworth steel barrels were requested, this cost an extra £10, as did a single trigger. Best-quality locks with intercepting sears were used and the action body had carved fences, scroll and game engraving and all in the best of taste. A best quality A & D gun with Southgate ejector and treble top-lever action was just £10 cheaper, but all the extras could be had for the same price. A slightly cheaper sidelock was available at £50, but here the stock was not jointed up to the fences; but when we turn the page again we see another best sidelock with concealed extension and side-clips at £60 and this would be a gun to be very proud of. Coming down the scale, a sidelock ejector was to be had for £45 and here the purchaser had the option of a cross-bolt action, either square or round, instead of the normal extension. Some of the very wide range of guns offered were "named". The "Ariel", for example, was a best-quality A & D-action gun in a lightweight action with prices from £50 to a third quality at £35.

It is of interest to read that the new model "Gun of the Period" which was a registered trade name, was offered with high-grade steel barrels at £30 and with "Superior Damascus" barrels at £2 extra. A double 12-bore of A & D pattern with top-lever treble grip and steel barrels could be had for £8; this gun was, of course, of "Continental Make", but the prospective purchaser was assured that "These are well made and reliable weapons."

Looking through the pages one comes across the helpful remark "that if you want to get within range of the wily duck and geese – order a Magnum at once". Lewis built a magnum firing the 3 in. 1½ oz. load for as little as £18, and if you were prepared to have hammers on your gun then you could buy one at £10. Three-inch 12-bore cartridges were then selling for 25s. per 100. The magnum was tested to give 85 per cent patterns at 40 yards and was well reviewed by the sporting press of the time.

Pigeon guns were also offered, firing the 2¾ in. case with 1¼ oz. of shot. Both hammer and hammerless styles were available and, as usual, a wide range of prices suitable for all pockets could be had. The Lewis top-lever treble-bolt hammer gun was a very handsome weapon and, at £18, appears to have been good value. A cheaper version was available, the "Keepers' Hammer Gun" at £9 10s., but with side-clips and a percussion fence the price went up to £12. Slightly cheaper was the "New Model Keepers' Gun" at £9, but this model had back-action locks instead of the bar-locks of the gun costing 10s. more.

The range of guns offered in the 1926 catalogue is truly amazing, and it makes me annoyed that I was still in my pram at the time! A single-barrel hammerless 12-bore magnum wild-fowling gun was £16. To give you some idea of values the 5-shot Browning automatic 12-bore shotgun was £9. Ball-and-shot guns were offered, double Express rifles from .303 to .600 bore and a range of bolt-action sporting rifles based both on Mauser and Lee Enfield military rifles. An interesting item is the Lewis "Cape Gun" with a rifle barrel and smooth-bore shot barrel, the shot barrel on the right. Gun cases, cleaning equipment and a wide range of sportsmen's knives complete the range that was on offer to the sporting man in 1926. Cartridges are shown on the inside back cover, best-quality, with deep brass heads at 21s. per 100 and reliable smokeless at 14s. per 100. If you bought 500 they could be sent carriage paid to any station in England and Wales. An interesting exercise in nostalgia, if nothing else, and for me a most useful mine of information on guns which were being made in the mid-1920s.

THE LIVERPOOL GUNMAKERS (1)

Gunmakers in the United Kingdom can be classified in any one of a number of different ways. One is simple: London makers and provincial makers. If we then take the provincial makers we have to leave out those in Birmingham who occupied a special place as suppliers of guns and gun parts to the rest of the country (including the great London makers).

In the assessment of the importance of a city or town one factor would be the number of gunmakers it contained over a period of time, and here, according to DeWitt Bailey and Douglas Nie in their book *English Gunmakers* (published in 1968), Liverpool comes out top of the league, with 125 makers.

Apart from numbers, another factor could be the contribution made to the art and craft of gunmaking by a provincial maker, and here Newcastle upon Tyne would have a claim, along with William Greener (who later moved to Birmingham) and William Rochester Pape. The city of York would also claim recognition for one of its sons, Thomas Horsley. Across the Border, as befits a capital city, Edinburgh could lay claim to a number of important makers: John Dickson, Alexander Henry, Mortimer, Harkom, MacNaughton and Dan'l Fraser, while Glasgow had James D. Dougall. I have earlier written, at some length, on the Manchester makers, and, in particular on the excellence of guns made by John William Edge and William Griffiths.

Not far away from Manchester lies the great seaport of Liverpool, and it was very probably the vast export business of the city that resulted in the number of gunmakers it supported, four times that of Manchester. However, when you come to examine the gunmakers individually you are, at first, inclined to rate Liverpool purely by the number of makers and not by their contribution, either artistic or technical, to gunmaking. The earliest gunmaker who comes to mind when thinking about

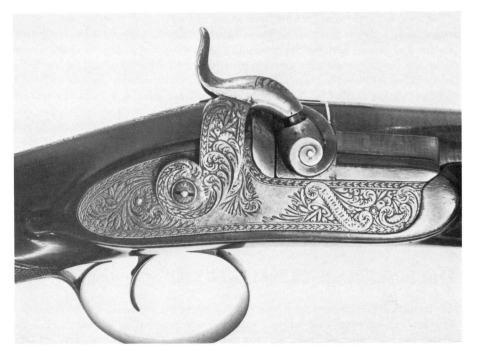

Single-barrel percussion gun by Holden of Liverpool. It features an
interesting and unusual styling of percussioning.

Liverpool is a woman, Ann Patrick, whose name is to be found on splendid duelling
pistols. The business was established by Jeremiah Patrick, who was first recorded in
1795 at 36 Lombard Street. This firm is important since it was later succeeded by
Williams & Powell.

My interest in Liverpool makers was stimulated by talks with Colin Haygarth of the
Cottage Gun Shop in Dunnet, Caithness. Colin, in his younger days, worked for
Summers, and when looking through his stock of guns we found two by Liverpool
makers, W. Cook and J. C. Collins. Neither of these makers is listed and, in fact, both
are more likely to be vendors of guns than makers.

Not all the makers listed from the late eighteenth century were mere vendors or
exporters of cheap trade arms. We know from the examples of work by Ann Patrick
that quality guns were made in Liverpool and throughout the nineteenth century one
or more makers would have undoubtedly seen that a market for high-quality sporting
arms was on his (or her) doorstep and, like Edge and Griffiths of Manchester, set out to
capture some of the business available from the rich merchants and manufacturers of
Liverpool. Such is the perversity of human nature that among the sporting gentlemen
of Liverpool with their "best" London guns there must have been a few who relied on
the native product and were, perhaps, excessively proud in using (and praising) the
Liverpool-made gun.

Unfortunately, there is little written about the provincial trade. Contemporary accounts refer, in the main, to the great London makers, with the odd reference to Westley Richards of Birmingham as being a maker worthy of notice. Since the writers of the day did not favourably mention provincial gunmakers it would be left to the individual to pit his knowledge and assessment of quality against the tide of fashion and have the courage of his convictions to carry a gun bearing a locus "Liverpool" instead of "London".

If such guns of quality were made, it is to be hoped that some have survived past neglect and the attentions of the amateur restorer. Do you have a gun with a Liverpool address? If so I would like to hear about it. A full description and a drawing or a good photograph would be a great help. Let us see what we can discover about the Liverpool makers. Were guns made in that city the equal of those made in Manchester? In the last analysis our comments are likely to be highly subjective, but making allowances for partisan feelings the task of assessment is not all that difficult; quality speaks for itself and, if necessary, I would suggest we use Griffiths of Manchester as the criterion.

THE LIVERPOOL GUNMAKERS (2)

I am continually receiving information on the Liverpool gunmakers and no doubt will do so for some time, but I think I have enough now to warrant my writing more on the subject and further whetting the appetite of those whose interest lies in guns made or sold from this famous seaport. A number of anomalies have come to light during the research and, in addition, I am slightly at a loss to know how to present the information so far garnered. This is because, unlike the exercise on Manchester, we do not yet have one outstanding maker or one outstanding gun. However, we have to start somewhere, so let's start with the oldest gun that has come to light.

This was a 16-bore double percussion shotgun by T. Wilson & Co. with 28 in. Damascus barrels and back-action locks. Details and two colour prints (not suitable for reproduction) were sent to me by Mr. Westbrook and, from the records, we know that Wilson was in business from 1850 to 1871, with premises in London as well as Liverpool. This information comes from Carey, *Firearms Makers*, but oddly enough T. Wilson & Co. do not appear in Bailey and Nie's book, *English Gunmakers*, nor do they appear in my own listing in Liverpool, but they are shown in the London directories up to 1871. No other Wilson gun has come to light as a result of the present enquiry.

Mr. Ward sent me a photograph of a rather fine pinfire 13-bore double shotgun by John Sampson of North John St., Liverpool. This firm is recorded as being in 13 Castle St. from 1836 and at the address given from 1846 to 1860. This gun has a gold escutcheon bearing a crest consisting of a bird with another in its beak over three horizontal arrows. My copy of Fairbairn's *Crests* was loaned some years ago and never returned so I cannot, at present, make even a guess at the identity of the original owner.

We then move forward in time to the firm of Hooton & Jones who I know were in business at 60 Dale St. in 1908. The book *English Gunmakers* is silent about Hooton &

Hooton and Jones trade label.

Jones, although a Hooton is mentioned as being in business in Cambridge in 1852. A Robert Jones is listed as being in Liverpool in 1852 and Slater's *Directory* shows the same firm in business in 1848. At present I have no information as to when they were founded or went out of business but it must have been after the First World War.

I was, of course, waiting for a trade label inside a gun case to tell me more about Hooton & Jones, and sure enough one turned up! This was owned by Mr. J. Harrison, who told me it bore, inside the lid, a gold-embossed leather label with the legend "Hooton & Jones, Gun, Rifle and Pistol Manufacturers, 60 Dale St, Liverpool". To my regret and, as you can imagine, to Mr. Harrison's, too, the case lacked that important item, a gun. The label lacked the important date – that when the firm was founded – but from almost nothing, the firm of Hooton & Jones was slowly taking shape. Then along came Mr. Clark who has a Hooton & Jones 12-bore box-lock ejector. He had no case for the gun until the 1979 Game Fair, when he was able to buy a case label which he kindly photographed for me and which is reproduced here.

Another maker who was unknown to me was E. & G. Higham. Mr. Stones told me his gun had the address Ranelagh St., from which one authority dates the gun to between 1857 and 1869. From this source we learn that the firm was established in 1795 in Warrington, Lancashire and it seems likely that they moved to Liverpool to take advantage of the rise to prosperity of this port during the nineteenth century.

Then things took an interesting turn. I received a photocopy of a trade label which cannot be reproduced but it is clear enough to see that it is "E. & G. Higham, Gun Manufacturers, Est. 1795, No. 4 Chapel Street, Liverpool". There is a truly delightful engraving of a sporting scene which I would like to show you, but this would need to be photographed under special conditions to gain full benefit. The sender, who has contributed to our knowledge of the Liverpool makers, wishes to remain anonymous. Another Higham gun is owned by Mr. R. R. Baxter; and from Mr. Stamp I learned that he has a 12-bore Magnum non-ejector with the 4 Chapel Street address.

Most letters were about two makers: William Richards, founded in 1801 in London, and Williams & Powell, founded in 1780 and bought by William Richards in 1905. Williams & Powell were established in Liverpool in 1849. This information will already be known to readers who keep a close watch on "Letters to the Editor", since it was to be found in a letter from Mr. B. Watson Hughes in *The Shooting Times*, the issue of 10–16 January 1980. John Matthews told me about his Williams & Powell double muzzle-loader which, from the address, 25 South Castle Street, dates from 1860–70. Another Williams & Powell, No. 8190, was described to me by Mr. Barnes, who also gave me a sketch of the crest which so far, for the reasons explained above, I have not been able to identify. Several W. Richards guns were also reported, one of which, a breechloading carbine with the address 51 Old Hall Street, Liverpool, was particularly interesting.

A great deal of information was provided by Mr. W. S. Mealor, including mention of Blisset & Son of South Castle St., and, from Mr. Parry, along with a lot of useful information, came mention of a rifle by T. Bland with the address 62 South Castle St., Liverpool as well as their better-known London Strand address. Mr. Greenfield and Miss Hollingdale both described their W. Richards guns, one of which also bore the Preston address.

Last, but by no means least, came information on W. C. Carswell, Exchange Buildings, Chapel St., Liverpool with the added information from Mr. W. H. Mealor that this firm is still in business. I find that they are now at Old Hall St., but Mr. Borthwick provided interesting information concerning the locks on his gun, which will now stimulate me to do some more research since I had not encountered any guns with locks of the type described. I did in fact earlier illustrate a detached lock, and was delighted to find that locks of this type were still being used – although, since the gun is only just in proof, Mr. Borthwick tells me he rarely uses it.

So, in short, no rare outstanding guns, but a lot of useful information collected, a lot of interesting facts which now need to be further investigated and my thanks to readers who, once again, came up with the answers!

MACLAUGHLAN OF EDINBURGH

It is now over a quarter of a century since I added a percussion muzzle-loading double rifle by MacLaughlan of Edinburgh to what was then my small collection of rifles and shotguns. It was a red-letter day for several reasons. First, this was the beginning of a collection of Scottish nineteenth-century firearms and it was also my first example of the product of that gunmaker of the Scottish capital. As I was to discover in the years that followed, the Edinburgh makers need acknowledge none as their superior.

The second reason was that this was the first truly "mint" example of a percussion double rifle that had ever come my way. To be able to handle something that had survived the neglect of the years was a new experience and this was all the more remarkable since the rifle lacked a case. The reason for the preservation of pristine newness was the fact that the rifle had probably never been used and had been in store for most of its uneventful life.

Bullet moulds were available to cast round ball. Well patched, the rifle performed as well as could be expected since it was, of course, a weapon intended for close-quarters shooting. The chief pleasure was in the glorious finish of the rifle. The barrels were twist steel, not Damascus, and had been most delightfully browned, showing the figure to perfection. The lustrous dark blue of the trigger guard was a delight to behold as was the full-colour case hardening of the hammers and lockplates. All in all something quite delightful to have and to enjoy. All too sad that it now languishes back in store, but that is a sign of the times we now live in, I'm afraid.

With a rifle like this my chief interest was to find out something about the maker. Here I was to come up against a blank wall. Some years later I was able to establish that "M'Lauchlone" was first of all to be found at 8 Lothian Street, Edinburgh in 1808. By 1817 the business had moved to 39 Nicolson Street, and in 1831 moved to 24 Frederick Street, where it remained until last listed in 1848.

From the style of the rifle I would put it towards the end of the first half of the century – perhaps one of the last made. No name or address is to be found on the rib,

A very early MacLaughlan trade label.

merely "MacLaughlan, Edinburgh" on the lockplates. There is no crest on the silver escutcheon and one gets the impression that the rifle is unsold stock. However, this is mere conjecture and nothing else happened as the years rolled by, except that I was given a splendid MacLaughlan percussion target pistol – but again no address.

I found nothing more about this maker of truly superb weapons until recently, when I received a small (3½ in. × 2½ in.) gunmaker's label through the post. This was sent by a reader, Mr. D. Elliott, who told me the label had come from a mahogany, brass-cornered case which he had rebuilt for a double-barrelled percussion shotgun. The original gun, according to Mr. Elliott, may have been a single-barrel weapon with a 40 in. barrel. The condition of the case was such that little else could be discovered from the worm- and moth-eaten remnants of the partitions and furnishings. But one thing had survived remarkably well – the label. From this we can see that the business was at 8 Lothian St., so the label is dated between 1808 and 1817 and as such is the oldest one in my small collection. We are also told that William MacLaughlan can provide superfine and common gun powder, patent shot and flints "with every other article necessary for a shooting sportsman". Also to be obtained were fowling pieces and pistols "on the latest and best constructions" and we learn that military arms can be cleaned and repaired. With this label, MacLaughlan comes a little more to life and I can certainly testify that the MacLaughlan rifle and pistol I have are undoubtedly of the "best construction".

MANCHESTER MAKERS

My interest in Manchester gunmakers can be traced back to the receipt of a set of fine photographs from an American friend, Bill McGuire. Bill had sent me some prints of a W. Griffiths hammer-gun in almost mint condition and the quality of this gun was sufficient to make me want to learn something more about the maker and also about the background and influence on Griffiths, working in Manchester away from the centres of gunmaking – Birmingham and London.

One thing I had learned, however, was that good gunmakers in nineteenth-century Britain were *not* confined to the traditional centres of gunmaking. Gunmakers of high quality were to be found in Edinburgh, Glasgow, Newcastle, York and elsewhere – so why not Manchester?

If we go back to the 1820s the gunmakers of Manchester are W. Aston, T. Conway, Richardson, Wm. Shaw and T. Styan. Just one more than Liverpool supported. Thirty years later the position was as follows: Thomas Conway was still in business, not only making pistols but also crossbows, and we have a new maker, John William Edge. New, also, is the firm of Gascoigne and Dyson and John Kaye of Shude Hill. William Steel has also appeared, while still in business is Robert Stensby of the oddly named Hanging Ditch. You may disagree with that last statement. However, from the firm of Robert Stensby & Co. Ltd. of Manchester I learn that Robert Stensby married into the firm of Thomas Styan and the firm changed its name to Stensby about 1832, moving from 48 Hanging Ditch to No. 11. Whether or not this was a physical move, or just a change in street numbering as often happens, I cannot say, but the present firm of

Robert Stensby can trace its ancestry back to 1804.

The other interesting name is that of John William Edge. We find them first of all, in 1828, at 68 King Street, and by 1863 they are established at 2 St. Mary's Gate. According to Mr. Roy Jacob, who has done some research into the firm, the name changes to that of Griffiths & Worsley at the St. Mary's Gate address, indicating perhaps a takeover on the original business of Edge, though by what circumstances this occurred is at present a mystery. However, there is a problem with the name Griffiths, since there is also a William Griffiths as well as the William J. Griffiths who appears to have taken over the business of Edge. One possible solution is that the Griffithses were brothers and that both worked for Edge before setting up in separate businesses, one in the old premises of Edge at St. Mary's Gate, the other slightly earlier in 1855 at 17 Erskine St., Stretford New Road.

There were other makers and retailers of firearms in Manchester during the period under review, the best estimate so far being in the order of about 75. How many others made guns of the quality of Griffiths I cannot at present say; much depends on whether or not Griffiths trained enough men to produce high-quality work and whether or not there was the market in Manchester for work of high quality. If not, the "best"

Newton's trade label.

workmen would leave to work for gunmakers elsewhere. The way that a craft flourishes and then dies is influenced by a number of rather complicated factors.

In my search for other makers I have come up with the name of T. Newton. Newton was one of the later Manchester gunmakers and at present little is known of him except for his one top-lever, back-action double gun. This gun was brought to my notice by Mr. Ward and later the owner, Mr. B. C. Brown, very kindly sent me the photograph of the label reproduced here. The Newton gun does not compare in any way with the Griffiths gun which started the "Manchester exercise" but it is a good quality top-lever back-action hammer-gun of the classic type. Without examination I cannot tell whether or not it was made by Newton himself or in Birmingham for retail sale by Newton. However, it *is* another Manchester gun and, as such, extends our knowledge of this area and its gunmakers.

MANTON & CO., CALCUTTA

Few people would dispute that the most famous name in the history of British gunmaking is that of Manton. The two brothers, John, the elder and Joseph, made an extraordinary contribution to the development of the modern shotgun and, although John died in 1834 and Joseph a year later, the name Manton remains undimmed by the passing of the years and the artistry of their craftsmanship still has the power to delight and amaze.

Less well-known, perhaps, is the fact that the firm of Manton set up a business in India in 1825. Frederick Manton left England for Calcutta and the business was established at 10 Lall Bazaar, Calcutta. The firm passed out of the hands of the Manton family in 1846 and, prior to moving to 13 Old Court House St., the firm was in business at 63 Cossitollah, Calcutta.

The first Manton & Co. Calcutta catalogue that I have seen was shown to me by Gron and Chris Edwards during a recent visit to them. I have known both for many years and have learned a great deal from Gron Edwards' experience in gun collecting, which goes back to the years before the Second World War when one could not pick up a book to find the answers since there were hardly any relevant books then written! Gron told me of his delight in reading the books written by J. N. George which, for the first time, gave the gun collector an indication of the great scope of his subject.

The two illustrations here are from the Manton catalogue which Gron kindly loaned me. Gron's own comments are of interest. The catalogue is 9 in. × 11 in. with 111 pages. Guns, cartridges and associated equipment take up 75 pages, the remainder being devoted to hog spears, knives, tennis, cricket, football, fishing and other pastimes. Manton's address was then "The Pioneer Gun & Rifle Works" and in the early days the firm sent guns abroad.

The 1909 catalogue identifies certain guns as being made by U.K. firms: for example, the "Standard" A & D 12-bore for use "with shot, ball or shell" was made by and bears the name of B. Woodward & Sons, London. Other guns in the very extensive range offered (with the exception of Holland & Holland and the products of gun factories such as Winchester, FN, and Mauser) are unnamed and one is left with the

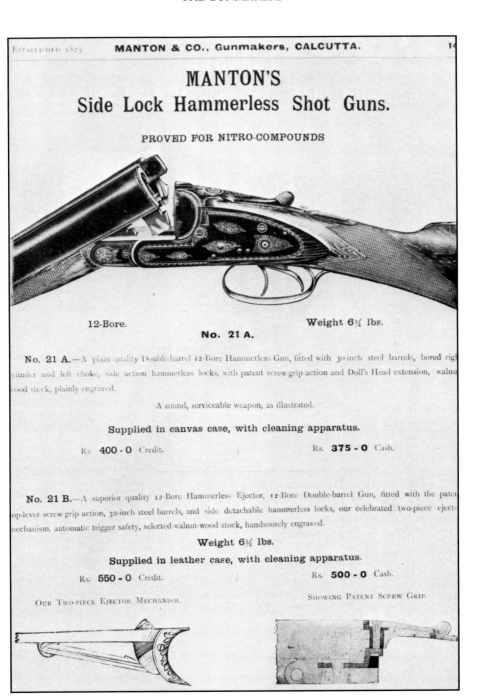

ESTABLISHED 1825.   MANTON & CO., Gunmakers, CALCUTTA.   14

MANTON'S
Side Lock Hammerless Shot Guns.

PROVED FOR NITRO-COMPOUNDS

12-Bore.   Weight 6¼ lbs.
No. 21 A.

No. 21 A.—A plain quality Double-barrel 12-Bore Hammerless Gun, fitted with 30-inch steel barrels, bored right cylinder and left choke, side action hammerless locks, with patent screw-grip action and Doll's Head extension, walnut wood stock, plainly engraved.

A sound, serviceable weapon, as illustrated.

Supplied in canvas case, with cleaning apparatus.

Rs **400 - 0** Credit.   Rs. **375 - 0** Cash.

No. 21 B.—A superior quality 12-Bore Hammerless Ejector, 12-Bore Double-barrel Gun, fitted with the patent top-lever screw-grip action, 30-inch steel barrels, and side detachable hammerless locks, our celebrated two-piece ejector mechanism, automatic trigger safety, selected walnut-wood stock, handsomely engraved.

Weight 6¼ lbs.

Supplied in leather case, with cleaning apparatus.

Rs. **550 - 0** Credit.   Rs. **500 - 0** Cash.

OUR TWO-PIECE EJECTOR MECHANISM.   SHOWING PATENT SCREW GRIP.

A page from Manton's Calcutta catalogue.

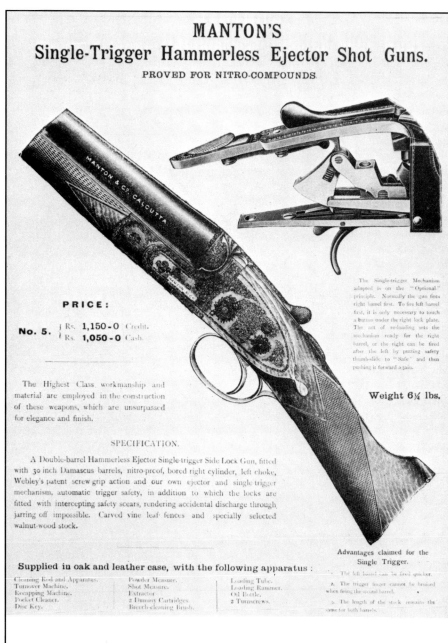

MANTON'S
Single-Trigger Hammerless Ejector Shot Guns.
PROVED FOR NITRO-COMPOUNDS.

The Single-trigger Mechanism adopted is on the "Optional" principle. Normally the gun fires right barrel first. To fire left barrel first, it is only necessary to touch a button under the right lock plate. The act of re-loading sets the mechanism ready for the right barrel, or the right can be fired after the left by putting safety thumb-slide to "Safe" and then pushing it forward again.

PRICE:

No. 5. { Rs. **1,150-0** Credit.
{ Rs. **1,050-0** Cash.

Weight 6¼ lbs.

The Highest Class workmanship and material are employed in the construction of these weapons, which are unsurpassed for elegance and finish.

SPECIFICATION.

A Double-barrel Hammerless Ejector Single-trigger Side Lock Gun, fitted with 30 inch Damascus barrels, nitro-proof, bored right cylinder, left choke, Webley's patent screw grip action and our own ejector and single trigger mechanism, automatic trigger safety, in addition to which the locks are fitted with intercepting safety scears, rendering accidental discharge through jarring off impossible. Carved vine leaf fences and specially selected walnut-wood stock.

Supplied in oak and leather case, with the following apparatus :

Cleaning Rod and Apparatus.	Powder Measure.	Loading Tube.
Turnover Machine.	Shot Measure.	Loading Rammer.
Recapping Machine.	Extractor	Oil Bottle.
Pocket Cleaner.	2 Dummy Cartridges	2 Turnscrews.
Disc Key.	Breech-cleaning Brush.	

Advantages claimed for the Single Trigger.

1. The left barrel can be fired quicker.
2. The trigger finger cannot be bruised when firing the second barrel.
3. The length of the stock remains the same for both barrels.

Manton's "best" sidelock advertised in his Calcutta catalogue.

question: "Were any guns or rifles actually manufactured in Calcutta?" I think not, and am of the opinion that the guns bearing the name Manton were probably made by firms in Birmingham. It would be interesting to see what sort of proof marks the Manton guns and rifles of the pre-1914 era bear.

The terminology used by the firm is interesting. "Big Game" rifles are the 8-, 10- and 12-bores; the .450, .500 and .577 rifles are described as "Express Rifles" and the .400 and .470 rifles are known as "High Velocity". Mention of "shot, ball and shell" is made above. The shell was the "Mead" shell which consisted of a hollow spherical core cast inside a spherical bullet. Other types of shells could be had, including the "Forsyth" and the "Calvert". Rotary bullets were also advertised and I understand this term to mean the type of "vaned", cylindrical bullet such as the "Brenneke" or "Stendenbach". Duck guns in single 8-bore and guns for 3¼ in. paper- or metal-covered 12-bore are also advertised, and in addition to the Browning 5-shot automatic shotgun the Swedish Sjogren was also offered. Double-hammer and hammerless rifles are shown, together with the .275 and .350 bore "Mauser-Rigby" magazine rifles. A "Farquharson action" rifle for the .450–.400 cartridge is advertised but this is the Webley falling-block action of 1902, and this lends further weight to my belief that Webley & Scott made most of the rifles and shotguns in the Manton catalogue.

BSA air rifles with both "Adder" and Lane's "Rotary" air gun pellets are the only air weapons to be seen in the pages of the catalogue but there is no lack of variety with the pistols. Colt, Webley, Browning and Mauser automatic pistols are illustrated, together with a range of Webley revolvers including the "WG" Target Model, the Army Model and the "WP" hammerless .32 revolver. Webley Mark IV .455 revolvers as well as the Mark III .38 are to be had and, at less cost, the solid frame RIC and "British Bull Dog" revolvers, together with the short-barrel "Metropolitan Police Model" and the interesting .360 No. 5 Webley "Express". Smith & Wessen and "other American makes" complete the handgun section. A very wide range of shotgun cartridges, rifle cartridges, rook rifles and revolver and automatic pistol cartridges were also offered, a range wide enough to deal with most enquiries and a treasure house for the collector.

One comes to the end of the arms' section of the catalogue with the feeling that a very full and magnificent meal has been enjoyed, and that for a brief period something of the grandeur that was Imperial India has lived again.

ALEXANDER MARTIN, GLASGOW

The traditional gunmaker occupies a unique place in the scale of relationships between the shopkeeper and the customer. "Shopkeeper?" you may say with some justifiable surprise, since *your* gunsmith is certainly more than a shopkeeper, a mere vendor of packaged goods. For many of us the gunshop from which we purchased our first air pistol and supply of pellets was a magical place, and with the passing of time a warm and close relationship grew up, a relationship that transcended the shopkeeper-customer involvement; one in fact became a friend, for the transactions were no longer restricted to goods and money. I have, throughout my life, had the pleasure of knowing many gunmakers, gunsmiths and gun vendors and my life was enriched by

A fine "Celtic" engraved sidelock by Alex. Martin of Glasgow. Beasts, knotwork and strapwork are featured in this unusual style of engraving which is to be found on guns by several Scottish makers.

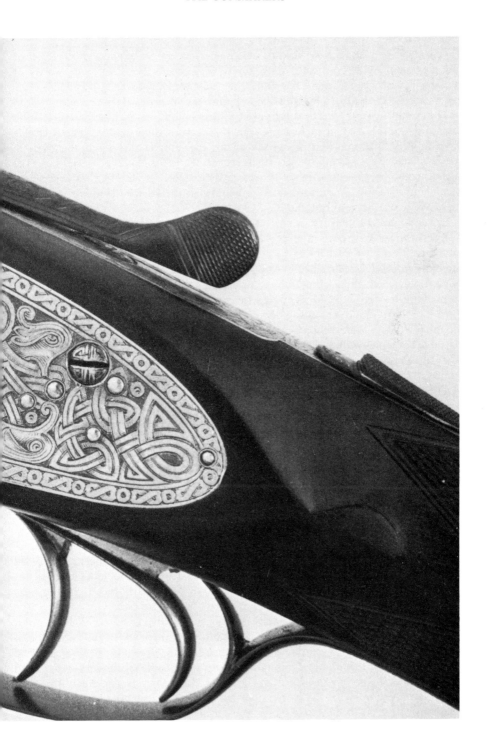

their knowledge, their wit and their concern for my welfare.

One such man was Sandy Martin, who had taken over a business in the heart of Glasgow that had been in the family for several generations. Most gunmakers of renown had something special for which they were well known and upon which their reputation was founded. This could be a special type of gun; a classic example would be the Powell with the vertical top lever, Dougal with his "lockfast" action, John Dickson with the "Round Action", Greener's special actions, and Westley Richards with the A & D action. Martin's produced one special type of shotgun, the "Martin Rib-less" which saved a quarter of a pound of metal and removed a potential source of rusting under the ribs. Martin's also offered their sidelocks with "Celtic" engraving but for most people the firm was pre-eminently concerned for the major part of its existence with rifles and rifle shooting.

It was founded in Paisley in 1837. I well remember a story told to me by Sandy Martin of those early days. Attempts had been made by Dougal to produce tubes for gun barrels and from what can be gleaned of gunmaking in those far-off days, the attempts to produce tubes had not been successful. Sandy told me of a letter in his possession written by his grandfather: the letter had been sent from the Black Country to the family in Paisley and recounted the trials and tribulations of a journey from Paisley to Port Glasgow by coach, then to Liverpool by ship and then on to the Black Country where a sack of horse-shoe nails collected in Scotland was made into gun barrel tubes which would then be brought back to Scotland and used to build guns. This letter now seems to be lost but it is an important document, since it does tell us something about the gun trade in the first half of the nineteenth century.

The firm prospered and moved to Glasgow. They were first established in the old Trongate, then moved to Argyle Street, and finally to Exchange Square. In the 1880s the firm laid the foundations for its pre-eminence in regulating rifles for full-bore target shooting. Members of the firm had many successes at Bisley and produced Lee-Metford and Lee-Enfield target rifles and special Breech Loading Match rifles in .256 calibre. These rifles were built on Farquharson actions and also on the less well-known Field action. The firm offered sporting rifles of all types, including Colt and Winchester rifles and a wide range of Colt and Webley target revolvers.

Yet another speciality was the range of sights and sight protectors. Even in the days before the First World War novelty items could be bought, and for a shilling (5p) penknives made from .303 cartridge cases could be bought, and for a little extra, interesting pencils were also to be had. One of the most intriguing items that one could buy three-quarters of a century ago was a "Burn's Patent Barrel Cooler" used for softening the fouling inside the barrel on hot and dry days. I have yet to meet anyone who used one of these devices or even anyone who ever saw one.

One of my last memories of Sandy Martin was of being taken by him into a warehouse, not far from the shop, which was filled to the roof with guns and rifles of all sorts. An Aladdin's Cave of treasure. In those days I had no money to buy and had to be content with just looking; this in itself was a treat, for few outsiders ever crossed the threshold. To my regret I learned that all the contents were sold to an American dealer, although many of the more important items had been gifted to the Glasgow Museum where, as the "Martin Collection" it delights the firearms enthusiasts and serves to commemorate the name of one of the important Glasgow gunmakers, now incorporated in the firm of John Dickson & Son.

THOMAS MARTIN AND THE MANCHESTER GUNMAKERS

The gunmakers of Manchester continue to provide much that is of interest to readers and a great deal of speculative data. If I may refresh memories once again the list of makers in 1823 was W. Aston, T. Conway, Richardson, Wm. Shaw and T. Styan. I was indebted to Mr. Peart for information on Thomas Styan which showed that the firm

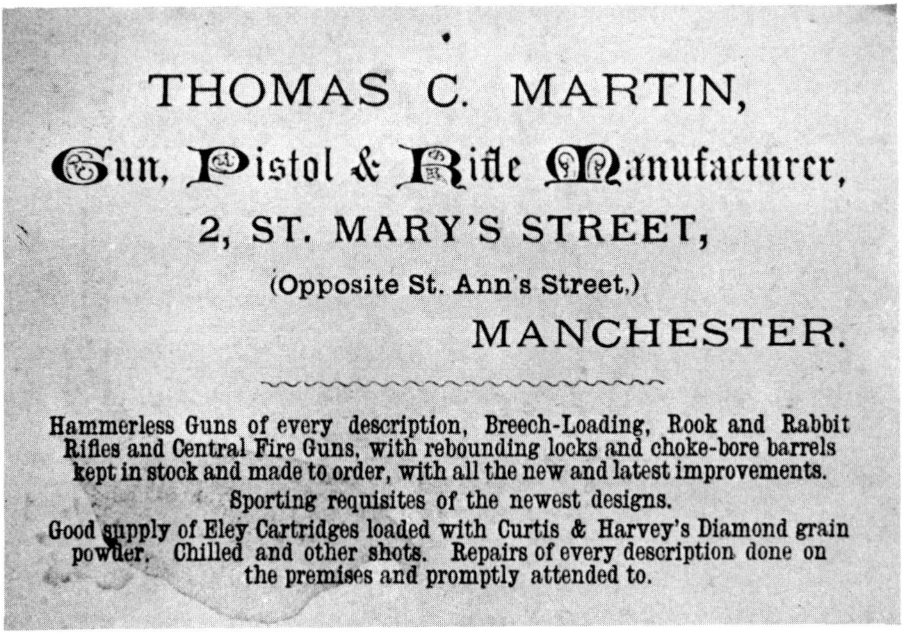

THOMAS C. MARTIN,

Gun, Pistol & Rifle Manufacturer,

2, ST. MARY'S STREET,

(Opposite St. Ann's Street,)

MANCHESTER.

Hammerless Guns of every description, Breech-Loading, Rook and Rabbit Rifles and Central Fire Guns, with rebounding locks and choke-bore barrels kept in stock and made to order, with all the new and latest improvements.
Sporting requisites of the newest designs.
Good supply of Eley Cartridges loaded with Curtis & Harvey's Diamond grain powder. Chilled and other shots. Repairs of every description done on the premises and promptly attended to.

Thomas Martin's trade card.

did, in fact, go back to 1804. I mentioned earlier that the firm of Styan become Robert Stensby in 1832, and Mr. Peart of that firm gave me a reproduction of one of Thomas Stensby's original business cards. Such cards are quite rare, rarer even than the trade labels one finds inside gun cases.

Gun cases are a bit harder to lose than are business cards and the fact that the labels were glued inside the lids of gun cases probably accounts for the survival rate. The card illustrated is 3½ in. × 2½ in. I was given it by Mr. W. T. C. Smith, late of the firm of E. Chilton, lockmakers. I have not been able to trace Martin, for he is not in any of my lists nor has he turned up as a result of correspondence generated by the articles on William Griffiths.

Griffiths, it will be recalled, started the whole affair. I have now seen several guns by this maker, or photographs, and all appear to be of the same high quality. At the 1977 Game Fair I was able to see where Griffiths had acquired his sense of line and appreciation of quality. On his trade label it states "Successor to the late J. W. Edge" and an Edge gun turned up at the Fair. This was brought by Mr. Jacobs, who has done much to bring some sense of reason to the history of the rather complex relationships of several of the Manchester gunmakers. The Edge gun was percussion and the case bore the address Russell St., Stretford Rd., Manchester. This was a truly superb gun and once I have a little more information on Edge I hope to be able to devote an entire article to this gun.

Besides Griffiths, Edge, Styan and Stensby I have mentioned Newton, and following this mention Mr. Baxter wrote to me to let me know that he had a Newton 12-bore pinfire gun. Again we have to presume that this is the same Newton since, somewhat oddly for a pinfire, this gun has been rebarrelled. I say "oddly", for I have encountered few pinfire guns which have been rebarrelled as pinfires. Most of the pinfire guns I have seen have had rather badly pitted barrels owing, possibly, to the very corrosive nature of the pinfire caps.

The Newton gun was rebarrelled by Chas. Osborne of London and the 30 in. steel barrels are so marked. Mr. Baxter tells me that he has used his Newton pinfire with home-loaded pinfire cases, black powder of course, and has had some success at his local black-powder clay shoots even against central-fire black-powder guns.

Another of the Manchester makers who appears to have had a long and involved history is the firm of Thomas Conway, listed as gun and pistol makers in 1848 at 6 Blackfriars. Conway is also described as a crossbow maker. According to Mr. Jacob's researches Thomas Conway first appears in 1804 and the firm and its successors last until 1884, although in the closing years the firm is under the name of James Shannon.

Yet another maker was Thomas Hepplestone of 25 Shudehill, who is listed about 1900. Mr. Richard Green, who has a Hepplestone gun, told me he bought it from Thomas Newton around 1935 and that Newton ceased to trade about 1940.

So, as you can see, the data on Manchester makers continues to build up, based on the survival of the guns themselves – the best evidence of all, for we can tell something of the quality of the makers and perhaps make a good guess as to whether a gun was made "in house" or for the trade by Birmingham makers. If the gun is cased then perhaps more evidence is to be found on the trade label and there may even be some additional material in the gun case itself; old invoices, a letter or a bill of sale. Then we have the trade directories. Full of valuable information but not entirely trustworthy, since gunmakers did not *have* to be listed and, indeed many were not. Then there is the evidence from contemporary literature, advertisements and so on, less to be gained here on provincial makers perhaps but every now and again some little gem of sparkling information does turn up. Lastly there is the business card. This is what

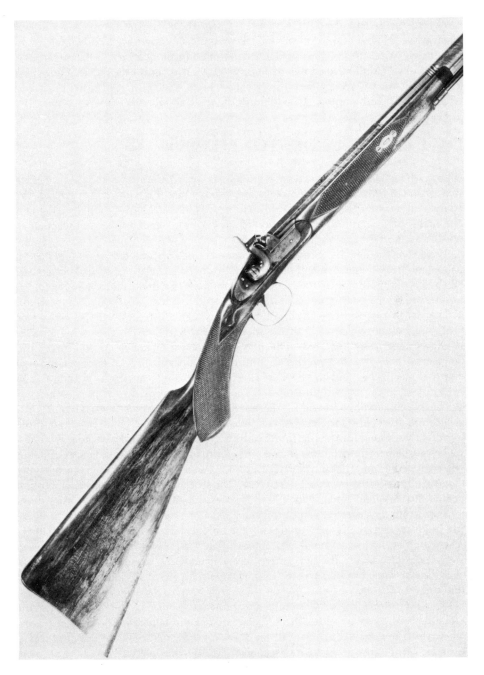

A truly delightful little .410 muzzle-loading percussion shotgun by
Murray of Stonehaven.

prompted the article, the little card of Thomas C. Martin of 2 St. Mary's Street, Manchester. Not mentioned in any list I have, but, as a certain well-known television personality used to say "rather late, certainly fourth quarter of the nineteenth century". I wouldn't have known of Thomas C. Martin but for the fact that goodness knows how many years ago his business card was left with the firm of either Brazier or Chilton of Wolverhampton. An odd quirk of fate, undoubtedly.

DAVID MURRAY OF STONEHAVEN

All too often when I am asked by a reader for information on a shotgun or other weapon I can only echo what he tells me, usually just the name and, perhaps, the address on the gun, as no further information is available. With a good drawing or a reasonable photograph some indication of age can be given and an idea of whether or not the weapon is "run of the mill" or rare.

In spite of the valiant efforts of the compilers of lists, the gatherers-together of names and data, many, many gunmakers and gun vendors are unrecorded both in the gun books of the past and in the meticulously researched works of today. For example, nowhere in my personal records or in the latest published works is there any mention of David Murray of Stonehaven. Stonehaven is a small town on the east coast of Scotland about 15 miles south of Aberdeen. On the barrel of the percussion muzzle-loading 50-bore gun illustrated on the previous page is the name of David Murray and the name of the town, Stonehaven. The gun is truly delightful. A 50-bore gun is bored just over .45 inches and this example has a barrel 24 inches from muzzle to the breeching, and overall the gun is just under 40 inches long.

The barrel is stubb twist and for the first 6 inches from the breech is octagonal; then it becomes 16-sided, there is a convex followed by a concave baluster turn and the barrel is then round for the remainder of its length. Not seen in the photograph is the rib below the barrel, with two ramrod pipes for the brass-tipped wooden ramrod, but you can see the single flat pin which secures the barrel to the stock, the breech having the usual hook fitting into the false breech. The stock is well made with a drop-point behind the lockplate, and the lock itself is secured by a single side nail.

Apart from the engraving on the barrel, maker's name and town, and the name on the lockplate the gun is quite plain, except for the rear of the bar-action sidelock. There are two figures stamped into the lockplate, "54", and this might be the bore. Despite being very plain the gun is extremely well made and, according to the man who gave it to me some 15 years ago, it was made by David Murray. Note, I said *made* and not sold by Murray.

Some time after this gun was made, the gunmaking business of David Murray left Stonehaven and moved a little further south and slightly inland to Brechin in Angus, where the firm remained until the death of the last proprietor, a descendant of David Murray, Mr. Fitzroy Murray. He was one of the many people I have had the pleasure of knowing in the gun trade over the past 35 years or so. I had enormous enjoyment from his company, although he admitted that he was not a gunmaker and had, in fact, been destined for other things.

So, for many years, the only thing I had to remind me of Fitzroy Murray was this little muzzle-loader, light enough for my young son to use and long enough for me to use also. Then, some years later, from Bob Duncan, also of Brechin, I was given a double 12-bore top-lever hammer-gun signed "D. Murray, Brechin". This gun was not of Murray's manufacture but had been made in Birmingham but it was, once again, a very solid reminder of the fact that the firm of D. Murray had been in business in Brechin. But for the personal reminiscences of Fitzroy Murray and the two Murray shotguns I would never have known of the existence of the gunshops in Stonehaven and Brechin for, to the best of my knowledge, neither is included in any list of gunmakers in the British Isles. The Murrays, so far as I know, did not contribute to any advances in the art and science of gunmaking and I have not been able to trace any patents in their name, but on the evidence of the little percussion muzzle-loader, the sportsmen in and around Stonehaven must have had the opportunity of buying some rather nice muzzle-loaders and maybe some of them have survived. I should hate to think that my little gun is the sole example of country gunmaking from this part of the world.

PAPE OF NEWCASTLE

One of the more intriguing aspects of the British gun trade is the indisputable fact that not all the brains, skills and ingenuity were concentrated in Birmingham and London. Provincial towns also boasted some outstanding gunmakers, and Newcastle upon Tyne had its share of master craftsmen. One of her sons, William Greener, would have rated Newcastle highly for the gunmaking skills there, even though he was for most of his life associated with Birmingham. Another son of Newcastle was William Rochester Pape and he did not desert his home town for London or Birmingham.

Although I have written about Pape before, when the opportunity to examine a Pape hammer-gun of quite remarkable quality was offered to me not long ago, I felt that it was high time that this unusual man was granted space again.

William Rochester Pape, the son of James Pape and Dorothy Rochester, was born in 1831 at Amble. He started work with his father, who had a business of game dealer and fishing-tackle vendor in Collingwood Street, Newcastle. In 1857, a year after his marriage to Dorothy Crawford, he set up in business on his own account at 44 Westgate Street. He was granted the first in a long series of patents in 1866, and to many it is the first patent that is the most important – it states "The muzzle end of the bore is tapered inwards".

It appears that Pape did not fully exploit the idea and, either independently or otherwise, a number of gunmakers – Scott, Greener and Dougall – all vied to produce the tightest and most consistent patterns by a painful process of trial and error. A great deal of research on the "invention" of choke boring has been done by Dr. G. G. Oberfell of Oklahoma. In his book *The Mystery of Shotgun Patterns* (1982), he refers to the detailed investigation he carried out in this country in connection with choke boring, and it was his contention that "choke boring might have been invented prior to Pape but we have failed to find any satisfactory reference in this connection". Dr.

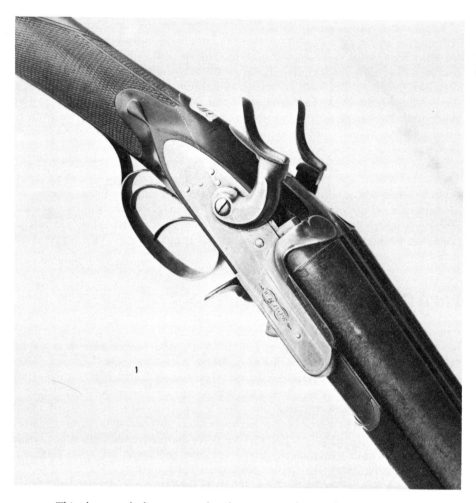

This photograph shows unusual strikers on one of Pape's hammer-guns. At
the rear of the striker an extension enters a depression on the inside of the
hammer so that when the hammer is drawn back it also retracts the striker.

Oberfell went on to say "by winning the London Gun Trials in 1858, 1859 and 1866 it
placed Pape in the forefront of the world's gunmakers".

The Pape hammer-gun which is the subject of this article is inscribed "Winner of the
London Gun Trials 1858, 1859 and 1866" on the top rib. The results of these trials
serve to indicate the success of the Pape guns under the conditions of the trials but it is
to the more obvious details of his guns that the modern collector turns his interest.

There are three aspects of the Pape gun illustrated which are notable. Under the bar
of the gun can be seen the first – a tooth-like projection which is an extension of the
lump and provides a "snap-action" closure of the breech. Closure is by the vertical-
spindle breech lock operated by a short tap-like lever in front of the trigger guard, and

this is pushed forward to disengage a plate from the bite in the rear lump. Without the "tooth", earlier actions had to be closed by pushing forwards on the lever. The system for withdrawing the striker is shown in the patent; this differs from that shown in the illustration of gun No. 2003. The system shown in the patent is similar to that on an earlier gun, No. 1652, depicted in *The Shooting Times*, 24 May 1969. The earlier gun was heavily and tastefully engraved; this later example, as you can see, is free from engraving but relies on the shape and form of the metal for effect. Engraving was omitted, not because the owner would not pay for it, but because he did not wish it. Just take a look at the fences, the hammers and the chequering of the stock.

Of particular interest is the design of the strikers, which are drawn to the rear when the hammers are cocked. The system is very much neater than the earlier design and probably would not be noticed unless specially looked for. The locks themselves appear to have been made by Pape (or, if not, for him) since they are internally marked with the Pape trade mark. This can be clearly seen on the trigger guard and it is also impressed on the flats of the action bar.

In a period when engraving was the norm, this gun stands out because, except for a border round the breech end of the barrels, it lacks engraving. That it would be a pleasant gun to use (with the right cartridge) I have no doubt whatsoever, and certainly it would grace any gun cabinet, no matter what gun it was placed alongside.

A final point: the third of Pape's patents that we find incorporated in this gun is the patent extractor. Extraction is accomplished by having an extension to the extractor which engages a slot in the standing breech and, as the barrels are opened, the extractor is withdrawn, so withdrawing the cases for removal.

William Rochester Pape retired from active business in 1888, leaving it to his son Victor. He died in April 1923 following a road accident; he was 91 and was rightly described as Newcastle's veteran gunsmith.

PLAYFAIR, ABERDEEN

The craft of gunmaking appears to have reached its peak in Aberdeen in the seventeenth century. One of the earliest entries in the records of the town is for "Thomas Gordone, Gunmaker", who is noted for "keiping of the thre knok the zair bygane". This entry is for 30 April 1591, and translated into modern English tells us that "Gordon had looked after the three town clocks during the past year". Some seven years later Gordon is mentioned in the town accounts for "mending the quheills of the towbuithe knok, and finding the oyle thairto". Gunmakers in Scottish towns appear to have had a virtual monopoly on the "rewling of the knokis of the burght" or the mending and regulating of the town clocks.

One of the later entries in the Aberdeen records is for Charles Playfair, who is recorded as being elected Deacon of the Incorporation of Hammermen in 1841. The number of gunmakers had fallen severely by the opening of the nineteenth century and Playfair is the sole survivor of the trade recorded in the old manner.

Playfair was, however, a remarkable representative of what had become an almost extinct craft and had, in fact, in 1821 founded the firm which was to bear his name for well over a century. Little is known of the early years of the founder but we know that in 1842 the firm, with premises at 94 Union St., was offering a wide range of fishing tackle, bows and arrows, cricket bats and balls and other sporting goods. By this time the second Charles Playfair must have joined the firm, for in 1845 the younger Playfair left Aberdeen for Birmingham and in 1846 entered into partnership with Mr. Thomas Bentley.

The firm of Bentley & Playfair of Summer Lane manufactured all types of arms, and one of the several mysteries which surround their activities is whether the name of Charles Playfair's partner was Thomas or Joseph Bentley. Certainly the establishment was one of some importance and a London office was opened at 60 Queen Victoria St. Charles Playfair the elder remained in Aberdeen and died there in 1876. The original firm appears to have been taken over by Messrs Robb, who continued the business. Charles the younger became Chairman of the Birmingham Proof House and he became a director of the Birmingham Small Arms Company, of which he was also an original shareholder, on the formation of BSA in 1861. Charles Playfair II died in 1898 aged 75 years and it is difficult to assess what contact, if any, he had with Aberdeen, where the company, founded by his father, continued to trade.

Business in Aberdeen must have been good at the turn of the century since the firm adopted the style "Gunmaker to Prince Albert", and by 1876 it had become a private company at 138 Union Street, a move enforced by the acquisition of the original premises by the Town & Country Bank Company.

In Birmingham the third Charles Playfair, later Lt. Col. Playfair, presided over the amalgamation of Bentley & Playfair with Isaac Hollis & Sons and, continuing the family association with the Birmingham Proof House, Lt. Col. Playfair established the laboratory facilities in 1912 and two years later he was appointed Proof Master, a post he held until his death in 1941.

Meanwhile, in Aberdeen, the firm of Charles Playfair & Company continued to be patronised by the sporting fraternity until, in 1955, the business was sold to the firm of William Garden Ltd., who continued to carry on the business until reorganisation had been completed.

No patents have been traced to members of the family nor, indeed, was the contribution to gunmaking such that the name of Playfair was widely known, yet a contribution was made and it would merit further work if only to bring to light the activities of but one of the many Birmingham gunmakers, Bentley & Playfair, since, as with many of their contemporaries, recognition of their role in the industrial life of Birmingham has been neglected.

WILLIAM POWELL & SON (GUNMAKERS) LTD. (1)

When, last year, I had the pleasure of handling a pair of Powell sidelock guns belonging to Alan Richardson, little did I think that this would start a chain reaction which would involve David Powell, a director of this long-established Birmingham firm, and quite a large number of readers of *The Shooting Times*. These were people who, in response to my request, sent me details of their Powell guns. The replies which

I received are tabulated here, together with additional material furnished by David Powell.

As you can see, the period covered is from 1865 to 1909. Mr. Moore has the oldest Powell, which is a pinfire. Like my own Powell, which was made in 1867, the hammers on Mr. Moore's gun are missing and the gun in between, that owned by Mr. Harman, has been converted from pinfire to central-fire. Gun No. 4498 is of interest since, like the firm of Powell, it is still in the hands of the family. This is a central-fire hammer-gun and three years ago it was overhauled by Powells. The gun went through nitro proof at the Birmingham Proof House and is still being used by the present owner, Mr. G. R. Greaves!

I have little information on gun No. 6378, other than that originally it would have had Powell's patent strikers which, as I have learned from a contemporary advertisement, showed the word "Loaded" and "a casual glance informs one of the fact whether a cartridge is in the gun or not". Mr. Moore also owns No. 6563 and again this is central-fire, with Powell's patent strikers. This system was, in fact, patented in 1869. Yet another vintage Powell gun still in use is that owned by Mr. R. P. Filbee, originally bought in 1879, which is highly regarded and used in preference to Mr. Filbee's other guns.

A rather unusual situation has arisen with the Powell guns owned by Mr. Spiller. He has No. 8241, which was one of a pair made in 1886, and he also owns No. 8572, again one of a pair, made in 1888. One is No. 1 and the other No. 2 of a pair but regrettably not a matching pair. Mr. J. G. Fleming kindly wrote to me on behalf of his father, who owns gun No. 8958. This gun is described as one of a pair but in fact it was not so made, and it would be interesting to find out what was the number of the second gun of this "pair".

Mr. Phillips acquired his Powell gun in rather poor condition as a gift and has spent time and money on bringing it back to useful life. Apparently made as a ten-bore, it was subsequently fitted with 12-bore barrels around 1894. These barrels were scrapped and new barrels – 26 in. 12-bore 2¾ in. – have now been fitted, and the gun is in active service once again.

I have been able to discover little about No. 9491 other than from the number – which places it around 1892.

We now move into five figures and with gun No. 10009 we also come across our first hammerless sidelock ejector. This will be similar to Alan Richardson's gun and from the information given by Mr. P. G. Wilson it is likely that this was a "No. 1 style" gun.

Still in the ten thousands, Dr. Bright told me that he uses a Powell box-lock ejector No. 10088, but here adverse comment is directed against the vertical lever, Dr. Bright being of the opinion that the top lever, pushing sideways, is more convenient. Powell's literature of some 70 years ago accepted this possibility and identical guns were offered, one with the Powell vertical lever, the other with the treble bolt and lateral lever. Another sidelock ejector with a number in the same range is that owned by Sean White, dating from 1896. Here, the gun was supplied in a best leather case with the initials of the original owner, "E.W.B." Alan Richardson's Powell guns were, of course, the ones which started the entire exercise (illustrated later). Not far removed in the number sequence is 10334 owned by "Leicestershire", who asked that his name be

Guns by William Powell & Son (Gunmakers) Ltd.

Number	Bore	Ignition	Date of Manufacture	Original owner
3577	12	pf conv. to cf	1865	Rev. E. Lane
3710	12	cf originally pf	1866	George Hall
3850	12	pf	1867	Edward P. Wolferdham
4498	12	cf	1870	E. Greaves
6378	12	cf	1876	W. R. P. Jervis
6563	12	cf patent strikers	1877	Owen S. Wynne
6938	12	cf A & D action	1879	T. W. Watson
8241	12	cf A & D action	1886	U. Charlton
8572	12	cf A & D action	1888	Col. F. C. Manley
8958	12	cf h/less ejector Deeley system	1890	William Sayer
9206	10	cf box lock	1891	Charles Eley
9859	12	cf barrels only		
9491			c1892	Not known
10009	12	cf sidelock ejector	1895	Not known
10088	12	cf boxlock ejector	c1895	Not known
10200	12	cf sidelock	1896	Col. E. E. Broderick
10249/50	12	cf sidelock	1897	J. Evans
10334	12	cf sidelock	1897	C. G. Rose
12168	12	cf h/less ejector	1909	A. Powlett

withheld. There is some reason behind this, because gun No. 10334 was the most expensive, i.e. original first cost. Again, this is another Powell still in frequent use, and highly regarded by the present owner. Last of all we have No. 12168 made in 1909. This is interesting since it has gold-engraved "1" on the lever, rib and pipe and it was not one of a pair. Was this truly one-upmanship or did Mr. Powlett, the original owner, intend to buy a second gun later on? We shall never know!

Present owner	Comments
Richard Moore	Marked Powell's patent No. 122. Bolted foreend, hammers missing
Michael Harman	Double gun with steel Damascus brls, bar locks, 30 in. brls
Author	Plain quality patent snap action Damascus brls. 30 in. Hammers missing
G. R. Greaves	Damascus brls, nitro-proof, snap action. Still being used. Original cost £20
Not known	Mint condition, nitro-proof. Originally one of a pair
Richard Moore	Rebounding locks, best quality, original cost £30
R. P. Filbee	Still in use
W. G. Spiller	One of a pair of best h/less guns with best Damascus brls, automatic safety, in best double, oak and leather case
W. G. Spiller	One of a pair of best h/less guns with best Damascus brls. Powell No. 1. Patent action
J. G. Fleming	30 in. Damascus brls. Cost £37 incl. leather case
H. Trefor Phillips	Originally Patent Snap action gun rescued from the scrap heap and subsequently re-barrelled for 26 in. 12, 2¾ in. chambers. Gun now in use and lever system liked
T. G. F. Wilson	
P. G. Wilson	Deep scroll engraving, one of a pair
P. H. Bright	Brls renewed, still in use
Sean White	Damascus brls. 28 in. In best leather case. Powder charges given on label in case.
Alan Richardson	This was the pair of Powell guns which started this exercise! S.T. 7 July, 1973.
"Leicestershire"	Best h/less ejector with 29 in. Damascus brls. Deeley ejector. Regularly in use in the field and on clays
J. A. Walker	30 in steel brls. A & D ejector. Engraved No. 1 in gold on lever, rib and pipe

Finally, Messrs A. Vero, D. H. Mills, M. Manley and W. Young did not tell me the number on their guns. From the list above they should be able to date their guns quite closely but a further letter with the additional information – the number – will help to complete the series. There is, of course, more work to be done on the data we have managed to collect between us, but for now, a warm "Thank you" to those who helped make the survey a success.

Powell's trade label.

WILLIAM POWELL & SON (GUNMAKERS) LTD. (2)

The year is 1802. The place, Birmingham. Possibly the most important event in the lives of most of the inhabitants that year was the signing of the Peace of Amiens in March. So important an event was it that William Murdock illuminated the Soho Foundry of the world-famous firm of Boulton and Watt. "What was so special about that?", you might ask. Well it was done with illuminating gas, not oil lamps or candles!

Certainly not as spectacular, but of importance to our story was the founding of the firm of Powell & Simmons. Joseph Simmons died in 1812 and some time after this William Powell appears to have moved to No. 3 Bartholomew St., from the original premises in the High Street. At Bartholomew Street the firm was especially well placed, for just across the way was the Birmingham Proof House, the foundation stone of which was laid in 1813. William Powell then moved to Carrs Lane. Earlier maps refer to "Cares Lane"; although the gun trade was for many years one of the principal industries of Birmingham no complete history has ever been written. Certainly, the industry started on the south side of the city and William Powell's present premises are probably nearer to the original gunmaking quarter than those establishments still surviving in the area around St. Mary's Church. Possibly the move north was to gain easier access to the Birmingham and Fazeley Canal, or more likely to the north lay available ground for building.

Without doubt Powell's must have taken part in the manufacture of firearms for the Napoleonic Wars, for in the year following the firm's establishment war broke out

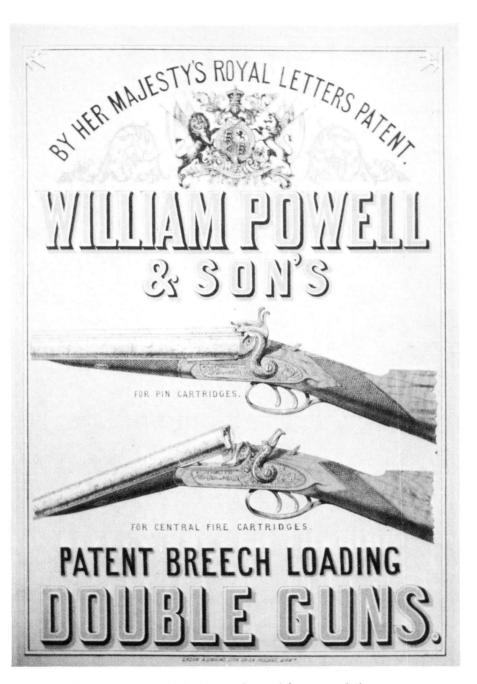

Card advertisement for both pin and central-fire guns with the patent
action.

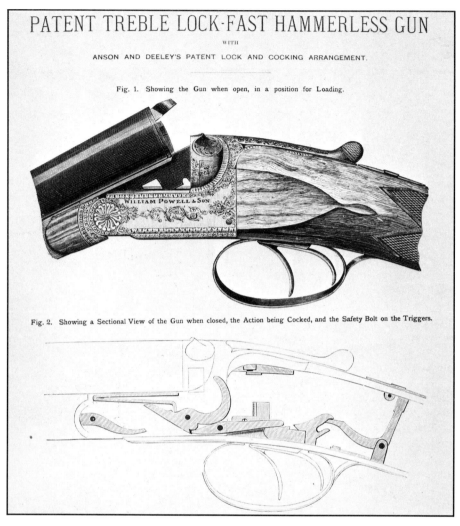

Advertisement available to potential customers showing the working of
the Patent treble lock-fast snap action.

between France and Britain, not being concluded until Napoleon's defeat at Waterloo
in 1815.

The premises at Carrs Lane must have been fairly typical of the gun trade
throughout the second half of the nineteenth century. In the aftermath of the wars in
Europe, the gun trade suffered a slight recession, but business picked up with the
enormous demand for arms as a result of the American Civil War. Powell's were not,
however, solely concerned with warlike weapons since, even if they didn't manufacture military weapons during times of war they would nevertheless be affected by

shortages of skilled labour and materials. Before the end of this conflict, however, Powell patented the first of the inventions which formed part of their contribution to British gunmaking, for Powell's were not merely "makers of guns".

In 1864 the Powell Patent Snap Action appeared, at first on hammer pin-fire guns, then on hammer-guns and finally on both A & D and sidelock hammerless guns. The Powell snap action enjoyed a long period of popularity and many guns employing this system are still in use, as readers of *The Shooting Times* will know from our past surveys. The distinctive feature of the Powell system is that the top lever is lifted instead of being pushed to the side and the locking quadrant which it actuates bears securely against the top of the barrel lump. The system has the merit of simplicity and security and I would not be at all surprised to see it reintroduced.

In 1866 an ingenious half-cocking mechanism was patented and three years later, in common with other progressive makers, Powell's invented a system to indicate when the gun was loaded. This may seem a little odd today but most shooting men had only just got used to pinfire guns where the pin protruding from the breech could tell you whether or not there was a cartridge in the chamber and whether or not it had been fired. The ingenious gunmaker did away with pins and introduced central-fire guns and, "Damn me – you couldn't tell whether the gun was loaded or not without opening the blasted thing." So, for many, until they got used to the idea, to have a device which told you whether cartridges were in the chamber or not was quite the vogue. Then, of course, people just got into the habit of opening the guns when they were not shooting them; this was quite simple with Mr. Powell's patent snap action!

Another little problem was the removal of the fore-end to get the gun into these new-fangled short cases. For this the fore-end had to be removed to take off the barrels and in 1873 a spring-bolt fore-end fastening was introduced. In 1876 a transverse-bolt locking system was patented and, of course, Powell's continued to build high-quality "treble bolt top-lever A & D system guns" for "those sportsmen who may not find our Patent Action with Vertical Lever convenient to manipulate".

No further patents were taken out after 1876 but by this time there were enough well proven ideas to ensure that guns of the highest quality could be built; and sportsmen on the whole are a pretty conservative lot. By the end of the century it must also have become apparent that the guns bearing the name Powell which left the Carrs Lane premises possessed an important quality which must have pleased the owners but which may have given the makers' pause for thought – they lasted rather a long time if well looked after!

Even now, 77 years later, this is still the case and among the lists of Powell guns which still survive, a surprising number remain in use in spite of Damascus barrels and rebounding locks. One such hammer-gun made in 1896 has a bar-in-the-wood action and the present owner told me that "it had fired many, many shots and is as good as ever". Other Powell guns have quite fascinating histories, guns made in 1893 being bought in 1922 as a 21st birthday present and still in use today. One comment made against the vertical-lever action was that the user of a loaned Powell "eased springs" by holding back on the lever instead of the hammer, fortunately nothing dreadful happened but the man got quite a fright.

Throughout the whole of the correspondence which followed the survey into surviving Powell guns one fact emerged time and time again – the affection and high regard that the owners had for their guns.

For any firm to have survived for a century and three quarters is remarkable enough in these days of constant and never-ending change but that it should still be run by the same family is even more remarkable. In 1977 David and Peter Powell completed the expansion of the premises and a thorough renovation of the outside of the building, which has restored it to its former glory and provided a focal point of interest for the citizens of Birmingham, many of whom must be slightly tired of never-ending concrete. That these changes have also provided ample facilities for new sales areas for both shooting and fishing equipment should do much to ensure the survival of the firm for the next 175 years.

WILLIAM POWELL'S SINGLE SNAP ACTION

Until 1880 gunmakers in Britain were prevented from using what was to become the most widely accepted method of breech closure for double guns, by virtue of patent protection. When the patents protecting the Purdey bolt expired, many of the patent snap actions of the third quarter of the nineteenth century fell into well-deserved obscurity, with the exception of the snap action patented by William Powell.

I first came across this action on a pinfire shotgun which, in the gloom of the gunshop where I first located it, I took to be a *hammerless* pinfire! Such a peculiarity, had it existed, would have been the find of the century but, alas, gloom and a long session in the pub at lunch-time had created some confusion! The action dates back to 1869 and, as you can see from the illustration of a much later centre-fire gun, the chief peculiarity of this action is that the top lever moves vertically instead of horizontally. It was described by the maker's adverts in 1880 as "Powell's Patent Snap Action (with vertical lever)" and the reader was further informed that there were "upwards of 5,000 guns on this system now in use".

In order to meet all requirements Powell also made a "Treble Lockfast Snap Action" with a horizontally working lever. The design of this action was patented in 1876 but it is the original snap action that has always intrigued me. The lack of hammers for my pinfire and my inability to obtain any, has prevented my using this type of action in the field, even with pinfire cases and reduced black-powder loads. I had often wondered how many people got on with the vertical lift of the lever and whether or not a confirmed user of the vertical lever would alter his style of shooting or, perhaps, more precisely, his style of gun-handling to cope with a vertical lever. I have found that if I wait long enough answers to my questions have a habit of being answered!

During a recent visit to Surrey I had the pleasure of meeting Alan Richardson who very kindly showed me some of his guns, amongst which was a superb centre-fire "true" hammerless Powell with the vertical level. Not one but a pair, and cased! The photograph does not do justice to those truly magnificent guns, which have that unmistakable air of quality. My later enquiries brought to light the fact that these guns were made in 1897 and it is a comment on the value of the pound sterling that the pair cost £84. Today *one* William Powell best sidelock will cost about £2,000! "Today?",

Powell's sidelock with the Patent action which requires the lever to be lifted instead of pushed sideways. This action dates back to 1869.

you might say to yourself! Yes, today. For the firm of William Powell & Son Ltd. is still (1973) in business in Carrs Lane, Birmingham and, since the first William Powell started making guns in 1802, this is quite a record.

It is perhaps more of a record than appears at first sight. William Powell and Joseph Simmons went into business together in the High Street, Birmingham and by 1818 Joseph Simmons, "Master Gunsmith in the Borough of Birmingham", was dead. William Powell continued the business and in 1860 a move was made to new premises, those which have now been occupied by the firm for over a century in Carrs Lane.

The truly astonishing thing about William Powell & Son is that the present Directors of the company are Bernard V. Powell, David M. Powell and Peter T. Powell: the fourth and fifth generation. I think that this must be a record.

JAMES PURDEY & SONS LTD.

This is not a history of the firm of Purdey since I wrote about that some time ago. It is rather more a privileged peep behind the scenes, similar to being allowed into the workroom of a "bespoke" tailor where some of the secrets of his craft are revealed and there can be seen the expensive suit covered in chalk marks and with the lining hanging out.

It all started when I wrote about the British over-and-under shotgun. I stated in the first article in the series on O/U shotguns (*The Shooting Times*, 5–11 February 1981) that Woodward was bought by Purdey in 1949 and that Purdey ceased to make their own O/U and made the Woodward instead. This statement was criticised by one man with whom I would not cross swords, the late Mr. Harry Lawrence, who, without intending any disrespect to the directors of this famous company, was to me, at least, "Mr. Purdey".

I am told that the true facts of the situation were that in 1947 Mr. Woodward approached Mr. Tom Purdey and offered to sell him his business. No offer could be made on the trading results which were then available and Mr. Woodward asked Tom Purdey, then the senior member of the family, whether he would build the Woodward O/U gun in the future. This was agreed, with the proviso that the Woodward side-by-side would *not* be built by Purdeys. The tooling and templates were collected from the premises of Woodward in March 1948 and the first pair of O/U Woodward guns made by Purdey were 16-bore, but subsequently the design of the original Woodward was modified quite considerably.

In defence of what I wrote, I quote a Purdey catalogue in which it is stated that "Purdey have acquired the world-famous business of James Woodward, makers of the Woodward O/U gun which has proved so successful that it may be considered the finest O/U gun that has ever been built by craftsmen in this country or wherever best guns are built by hand!" The comment continues by stating that "Mr. Purdey had

The late Harry Lawrence, O.B.E., pointing out to me some of the
features of the side-by-side Purdey shotgun.

decided to build his over-and-under guns in the future on the Woodward principle in Purdey's factory in London by Purdey craftsmen."

That there is a considerable amount of the Woodward gun in the Purdey O/U of today cannot be denied, but the building of a gun by traditional means is such that each one is individual; it is unlike those made before and those that will be made in the future. Today it is difficult to compare a hand-made gun with anything else, the nearest thing would be a sculpture in wood and metal. It is not an assembly of machine-made interchangeable components. For one thing, there are no engineering drawings, just the tooling and some metal templates and a lot of skill.

I was met at Purdeys by Harry Lawrence and then introduced by him to Richard Beaumont, Chairman of Directors and to Nigel Beaumont who had brought a Purdey O/U "in the white" from the factory. This means that the gun lacked stock and fore-end, "slave" screws were in use and the gun was neither finished nor engraved. The only marks were those impressed by the Proof House.

Before we have a look at the Purdey "in the white", let us consider a little of the history of the Purdey O/U. We have to go back to 1924, when Mr. Ernest Lawrence Snr, then works manager at the old factory, was approached by Atholl Purdey to build an O/U gun. Harry Lawrence was then in the factory and the making of the Purdey O/U which drew on the ideas of E. C. Green was entrusted to him with the instructions that this gun must be the "strongest O/U made". This gun, the first O/U Purdey, had six grips, and not many were made. It was strong, but with this strength came the penalty of weight and in the years before the Second World War, when the direction of the company was in the hands of Mr. Tom Purdey, instructions were issued to lighten the gun by eliminating two of the six grips and the top extension. This, the second Purdey, O/U, can be regarded as the "four-grip" Purdey and it was made in small numbers until 1939, when Purdey's unique talents were put to the far more serious work of winning a war.

After the War the offer by Woodward was accepted, as I have mentioned, and three types of Purdey O/U can be said to have evolved: the Woodward gun made by Purdey, the Purdey-Woodward and today's Purdey O/U built by Purdey in their own factory. More of the last gun is now made by Purdey than ever before. Owing to changes in the gun trade Purdey now make their own locks, and the O/U can be offered in .410, 28-, 20-, 16- and 12-bore.

Now it is time to examine the Purdey O/U "in the white". Let us take first the action body with the left-hand lock removed. We can see the inside of the right-hand lock, the tumbler, the bridle, back-action mainspring and the sear spring. Above, on the tang of the action, is the safety. To understand the very considerable work which has to be done to make an O/U gun of this sort we next take a look inside the bar of the action. The superimposed firing pins can be seen, also the two locking bolts. You can also see the camming surfaces on the sides of the wall of the action and the recesses on the top of the wall and inside which interlock with the intricate work which is very evident at the breech end of the barrel. Here the extractors have been removed, but the bites for the bolts can be seen and the undercut mating surfaces for the interlock between breech and action body.

The fore-end iron is attached to the barrel (but not the fore-end) and, in the

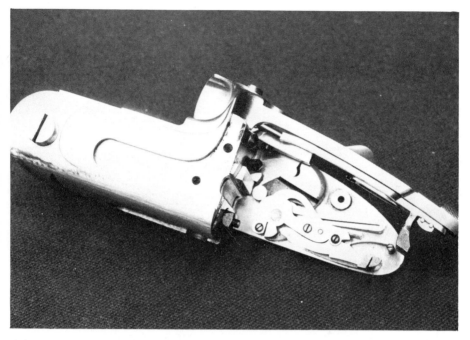

The action "in the white" looking in to the right-hand lock.

Inside the action bar. You can see how the barrel interlocks with the walls of the action and the two bolts on the face (one of which is visible).

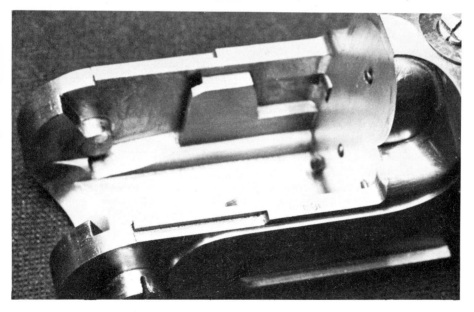

The intricate work at the breech end of the barrels of the Purdey over
and under gun.

illustration taken of the barrels from slightly above, the "wings" on each side
of the barrel can be seen. This feature prevents the ingress of water into the
areas of the ejector mechanism (not fitted) and also helps to prevent damage to
the wood of the fore-end. A solid rib is fitted to these barrels since ventilated ribs
can be dented – they will be provided if requested.

In addition, the barrels can be made "ribless", i.e. with the side ribs removed. If you
have to know the price, you can't afford one! If you *can* afford one, then the current
waiting list is two and a half to three years. If you look upon the Purdey O/U merely as
a *gun* it is too expensive and not for you anyway; it can be justified on the basis of an
investment. It should be regarded for what it is, and for what a gun of this type has
always been, a work of art. Art and craft allied to utility and beauty make each finished
gun something unique. To attempt to place an economic cost on skilled craftsmanship
of this high order is rather like equating the auction price of a work by Picasso to the
cost of paint, wood and canvas. You may not be able to own either, you may not be
able to understand the philosophy of either, but I am thankful that I live in a society
where both are possible.

I now make a plea for any information on the whereabouts of existing Purdey O/U
guns with details of their construction. I fear that there are few in this country and if

The "wings" can be seen when the barrels are viewed from above.

those with a Purdey O/U abroad can let me have drawings or a photograph for my records I would be greatly obliged. All information, without exception, will be kept in strict confidence.

A PAIR OF PURDEYS

To my regret I was unable to attend the Game Fair in 1975 and I am very sorry to have missed the opportunity of meeting the many readers who came to the stand with suggestions or queries. I value this contact highly and I was interested to receive several letters from people who had wanted to talk to me about matters dear to them.

One man in particular expressed surprise that I had never written about the firm of Purdey. I was able to tell him that I had written two articles on this famous firm but, as always, I tend to forget how quickly time passes and, it is only when I realise that there are readers who weren't born when my first article was published that the passage of time becomes all too self-evident.

The first Purdey of whom there is any record worked in the Minories, the centre of the London gun trade since the reign of Elizabeth I. His son worked for several gunmakers before joining, in about 1803, Joe Manton as a gun-stocker. Purdey then left Manton to work for Forsyth, the inventor of the percussion principle, who started

A cased pair of Purdey sidelocks with three sets of barrels.

a company to make guns with Forsyth patent locks in 1808. Purdey was employed by the Forsyth Patent Gun Company of 10 Piccadilly, as a stocker and lock-filer. In 1814 James Purdey set up in business for himself. In 1826 he took over the premises of his former master, Joe Manton, and set about making guns which were to enhance the reputation of London as a centre of gunmaking, a reputation already established by Manton. Even the early Purdey percussion guns show a distinct style of their own which was in no small way to determine the fashion for sporting guns and which still exerts a very strong influence.

The founder died in 1863 and his son carried on the business until 1909. The "house style" was restrained and totally respectable. It is indeed rare to find a flamboyant Purdey, but in this sober magnificence you will not find the smallest flaw in even the smallest screw. Superlative workmanship was not enough; to reach and maintain these heights technical innovation was also required. Here the firm introduced the famous Purdey bolt which has securely fastened the barrels of countless shotguns to the action and is still the most widely used system for side-by-side shotguns.

Purdey had built flint guns, percussion guns, pinfire and centre-fire hammer-guns, and in 1880 there appeared the Purdey with the famous Beesley self-opening action. Frederick Beesley is a somewhat neglected figure, but his invention was to secure the position of the firm of Purdey even more firmly. It now (1975) needs but five years for the Purdey action to reach the century. This is a remarkable achievement by any standards, particularly when it is enhanced by the fact that catalogues which show guns made in other countries refer again and again to the "Purdey system". This is not all, for Purdey established the traditional style and finish which has become the pattern for the side-by-side double sidelock shotgun.

There are, of course, all sorts of odd stories which could be told, but one odd minor point is the use of the term "forepart" by the House of Purdey, instead of "fore-end".

To illustrate the traditional Purdey sidelock I have chosen a pair of guns made in 1887. They are unusual since they have three pairs of barrels, but apart from this they illustrate to perfection the Purdey tradition as they lie there in the solid oak case, the barrels protected by velvet bags and with instruction for care and use inside the case lid.

RIGBY

A very fine photograph of a Rigby underlever hammer gun taken by Mr. R. Chesmore of Harrogate has been lying in my "In" tray for some time looking at me with what can only be described as a measure of reproach. The photograph is, I think you will agree, exceptionally good, since not only does it show the Rigby gun to advantage but, because of the angle from which it was taken, the photograph is lent a certain impact. Also seen in the original is the style of lettering used by Rigby, which became almost a trade mark with the firm. Talking of trade marks Rigby was one of the few firms with one – addorsed Rs or, put more plainly, Rs back-to-back!

If we turn for a moment from the gun to the firm whose name it bears, the first thing which strikes us is the date of foundation, 1735, long before percussion, let alone breechloading, guns were thought of. Surprisingly, the firm flourished in Dublin until it was sold in 1892 to the firm of Truelock and Harris. As an aside, I have often thought what a truly splendid name for a gunmaker "Truelock" is. One just couldn't go wrong with a name like that!

As one might expect, the Dublin end of the firm was renowned for the excellence of its duelling pistols and some of the finest examples of this type of weapon bear the name of Rigby. Equally distinctive were the Damascus barrels used by the firm on pistols, guns and rifles. These were more deeply etched so that the harder metal was brought into relief and to the knowledgeable such barrels needed no name on the top rib – they were Rigby barrels.

There was another distinctive feature of the percussion Rigbys: the additional notch or third bent to let the cock be raised slightly above the percussion cap to allow the weapon to be safely carried and yet ensure that the cap could not be dislodged from the nipple.

The firm of Rigby set up in London, and in 1860 John Rigby devised a method of forming cartridge cases from coiled sheet brass. Rigby Match Rifles were used with great effect in the great rifle competitions in the second half of the nineteenth century, not only by the "gentry" but also by members of the firm!

The London end of the business had, from 1866, a most prestigious address at St. James's Street W1, where they remained until 1955. In the early years at the London

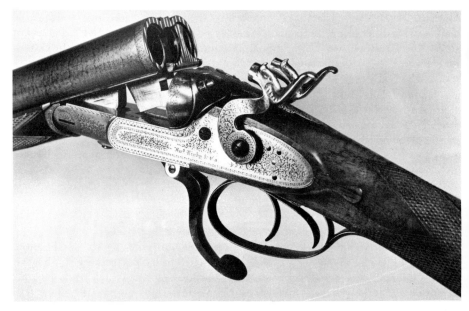

A very fine, restored Rigby hammer gun still in active use.

address John Rigby senior spent most of his time as Superintendent of the Royal Small Arms Factory at Enfield, Middlesex. During this period the London business was managed by his son Ernest John Rigby, who had gained valuable experience in the Birmingham Small Arms factory and, in addition, had followed in his father's footsteps by winning a number of prizes at competitive rifle shooting at the Bisley Meeting.

The Rigbys were well known to a small select group as builders of extremely fine target rifles and also for the manufacture of high-quality sporting shotguns. It is for their work in connection with the manufacture of sporting rifles, both double and magazine, that the firm is perhaps best known. For example, they introduced the first .450 calibre cordite rifle and this was followed by the Rigby .470 and the famous Rigby .416 for the big game magazine rifles.

Rigby made rifles of .577 calibre firing 100 grains of cordite behind a 750-grain bullet. Even with a rifle weighing 14 lb. this is quite a combination for anyone to handle, and in the 1930s Rigby offered their .470 in a best-quality double sidelock for £147. Let me make it quite clear that the price was £147 even in 1930!

The Rigby shotgun illustrated is earlier than 1930 and probably dates from before 1900. The barrels are fine Damascus, but they do not display the Rigby "finish" mentioned earlier. Bolting is by an underlever which is pushed down and forwards, while there is a small "pedal" on the right which clears the guard and assists in opening. This gun is an example of a "vintage" weapon saved from the scrapheap by careful restoration and, although I haven't seen the gun itself, the photograph shows that care and thought have been given to the problem of restoration. Mr. D. A. Mills of

Harrogate did the work and I hope that the present owner Mr. T. Hare appreciates that not only does he have a gun with an historic name but one which he can be proud to own. Increasingly, careful restoration is saving guns from destruction (for in years gone by they would have been placed on the anvil in the workshop and clouted with a hammer) and allowing those with a discriminating taste to own a gun of quality.

CHARLES ROSSON

I have received a number of queries on the subject of Charles Rosson. Since the information on my files was quite meagre I asked for help from readers, and, as usual, this was forthcoming, for which my thanks. If we summarise the data contained in the literature we first of all look for facts about the firm in *English Gunmakers* by Bailey and Nie. Checking first of all in the Birmingham section we find a number of gunmakers by this name. The earliest listed is Thomas Rosson, 1838, 22 Lancaster Street. Charles Rosson is listed from 1840 to 1872 at 56 Hatchett Street and also for part of this time at 19 Livery Street. Charles Jnr is shown as being at 20 St. Mary's Row from 1873 to 1882, and there is a G. Rosson at 1 Whittal Street from 1857 to 1861. During this period no firm by the name of Rosson is listed in the London directory so none of the firms listed above appears to have been sufficiently large to merit London agents or addresses.

In my own Birmingham gunmakers listings I have no mention of the Birmingham Rosson makers or any indication of the extent of their activities. No mention of any relationship between the various firms can be traced. In the provincial gunmakers list compiled by Bailey and Nie we find Charles Rosson in business in Warwick at 46 Market Place from 1859 to 1870. We ask whether *this* Rosson is any relation to the Birmingham Rossons – and, once again, we don't know.

If we then move into the twentieth century, but only just, we find that Charles Rosson is listed at 4 Market Head, Derby and at 13 Rampant Horse Street, Norwich. A further check is always advisable on the inventiveness of our quarry. In this case we come up with an answer, and another mystery. Charles Rosson of Market Head, Derby, Gun Manufacturer, obtained patent protection for a cartridge-case ejector in 1889. This ejector could be applied to both hammer-guns and hammerless guns.

Then we can have a look at the members of the Gunmakers Association, where we find a Mr. C. S. Rosson. The note I have against this name is, Gunmakers, Norwich, sold out to Charles Hellis & Sons Ltd. But I have no date for this. This, then, is about the sum total of information available from the literature. However, Mr. Wilson drew my attention to the fact that in the book *Experts on Guns and Shooting*, Teasdale-Buckell mentions that Charles Rosson of Derby was apprenticed to John Frasier and also worked for Hollis & Sheath in Birmingham. He is credited with the invention of a "try-gun" and a cartridge-loading machine capable of filling 2,000 cartridges an hour.

Mr. Hodgkinson of Derby told me that the original style of the firm was Dobson & Rosson. To prove the point I then received a photograph of the trade label which tells us that Dobson & Rosson were to be found at 4 Market Head, Derby and that the firm was "from Edinburgh". A quick look at Bailey and Nie to see if they have listed

Dobson & Rosson shows they make no mention. Mr. Pember mentioned his Dobson & Rosson hammer-gun marked 4 Market Head, Derby and bearing W. Anson's patent No. 9454.

Trade label with an intriguing reference of "from Edinburgh".

Mr. Hodgkinson went on to tell me that he could just remember meeting Charles Rosson and that the style of the firm changed to Charles Rosson & Son at the turn of the century. "Young Rosson", as the son was known, continued the business until about 1950 when the stock was sold off and the firm ceased to trade. Then from Mr. Stoodley (who very kindly sent me a copy of the Charles Rosson patent) came details of his Rosson gun No. 8097. Then we move to Stockholm where another Charles Rosson gun exists. This is No. 33074 and the owner, Mr. Ehrencrona, sent me details, from which I learned the gun was a side-by-side double finished in what we might call "London-style" stocked to the fences, and all-in-all a desirable gun. It is much later than Mr. Stoodley's gun, which is not stocked to the fences and has the earlier pattern of back-action lock with a bar-lockplate. The other Rosson, C. S. Rosson of Norwich, is also of interest since they sold a gun with a most unusual slide opening – but that is another story!

C. S. Rosson advertisement, c.1930.

JOHN A. SCOTCHER OF BURY ST. EDMUNDS

The gunmakers of the second half of the nineteenth century can be placed in several categories. First, there were the "great" makers of the capital, the capital not only of a country, but of a rich and powerful empire. Then came the important makers of the great centres of population, many of whom enjoyed, and had earned, a reputation as great as the fashionable makers of London's West End. Then came the makers to the trade, the Birmingham gunmakers who made guns to order and put someone else's name on rib and lockplate. Last, but by no means least, were what I call the country gunmakers. Many of these made guns in their entirety, others did most of the work, but bought in locks and furniture from the suppliers in Birmingham and Wolverhampton.

As the years went by, fewer country makers actually made guns. More and more parts were made elsewhere, until at last the gun was made to their specification and bore their name, but all the work was done in Birmingham. The history of many of these small country gunmakers is unknown. In their day they were an important part of the sporting scene and the owner or proprietor an important and respected figure in the community. However, with the passing of the years, information and records of the history of such men become increasingly hard to come by. Old records have been lost and names and events forgotten.

It is therefore with some considerable satisfaction that I received a letter from Gareth Jenkins of the Moyses Hall Museum, Bury St. Edmunds, giving me details of Suffolk gunmakers. A very complete list of the gun trade in Bury St. Edmunds was provided, dating from 1782 to the present day. Details of the three present firms in the gun trade were also included, Horrocks, Clayton and Anglia Arms. The recording of firms at present or recently in business is important, since it is only by such records that the historian of tomorrow will have access to information we so sadly lack today.

One of the most important of the Bury St. Edmunds gunmakers was John Adams Scotcher. From Mr. Jenkins' researches it appears that Scotcher began business in 1864 at 17 Market Hill. In 1868 the name was changed to 17 Meat Market and then the address was again changed to 4 The Traverse, from about 1900. Without local knowledge, one might think that Scotcher had moved twice. This does not appear to be the case; he stayed where he was, but, as so often happened, the street name or number was altered. Again, as so often happened, Scotcher took over premises which were previously occupied – in this case by William Young, who had been in business as a gunmaker from 1823 to 1858. What happened in the intervening years from 1858 to 1864 is not known. Scotcher's business may have been established at an earlier date but not recorded. In 1896 the style of the firm changed to J. A. Scotcher & Son, the son being John Gepp Scotcher. J. G. Scotcher apparently lived on the premises in 1912 and his father at 30 St. Andrew's Street South, where the chimney-pots bear the initials J.A.S.

Some nine Scotcher guns are known; all are breechloading, and those for which I have details are of good quality with a number of pleasant detailed touches to the finish which raise them from the ordinary to guns of quality.

Through the courtesy of Gareth Jenkins, I am able to reproduce a photograph of the

Scotcher trade label.

trade label of J.A. Scotcher and also a photograph of the premises. A careful examination of the original prints shows that the firm were selling Allcocks fishing tackle and Curtis & Harvey's "Smokeless Diamond, Amberite and Ruby" cartridges. Whether the two figures in the doorway are the Scotchers, father and son, is at present unknown, but it is possible.

One of the Scotcher guns in the museum collection is No. 2375 and has a conventional rotary underbolt, whereas the other back-action hammer-gun is a top-lever with J. Thomas's patent Vertical Grip of 1870.

Scotcher seems to have gone out of business in 1912, and in 1916 the premises were taken over by Henry Hodgson, who remained in business until 1952 at No. 4 The Traverse. After a lapse of six years, we find Robert Horrocks and Violet Clayton at No. 4A The Traverse and at the same address the style changes in 1971 to Robert M. & D. Clayton where, according to Mr. Jenkins, they are still in business. So, from the available records, this part of Bury St. Edmunds, in spite of several changes in name, remains firmly wedded to the gun trade as it has been since the first quarter of the nineteenth century.

For those with special interests in the gunmakers of Bury St. Edmunds, I strongly recommend a visit to the Moyses Hall Museum, Cornhill, and if you have any guns by Suffolk gunmakers, then Gareth Jenkins would be pleased to have details of them for a forthcoming book, *The Gun Trade of Suffolk*.

The Scotcher shop front in the late nineteenth century.

W. & C. SCOTT & SONS

These past few months have, for me, been a period of almost total unrest owing to the need to change houses. The problems of finding a house with sufficient accommodation for my records and several hundred books, not to mention a wife and children, are considerable, and our first effort was not a resounding success. So much so that throughout the stay in the house one had the feeling that one was only a guest and that tomorrow the bags would be packed and the family would be on the move again.

One thing that these changes have caused is a thorough clean-out of old rubbish and this has even included a careful examination of old negatives to see if the collection could be pruned and the useless discarded. Amongst the old 35 mm negatives I came across the illustration shown here. This gun is part of my past and although I have never owned it I have used it on one or two occasions and feel a very strong affection towards it. "It" is a W. & C. Scott double 12-bore sidelock ejector made before the First World War and once the proud possession of my good friend W. A. C. Paton.

The firm of Scott occupies an important position in the history of British gunmaking and survives (1971) as the Scott of Webley & Scott. The business of W. & C. Scott was founded in 1834 by William Middleditch Scott at 79 Weaman Street, Birmingham, and carried on by his sons W. M. Scott and J. C. Scott. The firm transferred its premises to Bath Street and then to Lancaster Street, where the Premier Gun Works was established.

The firm was responsible for many inventions in connection with sporting shotguns, the earliest being the top-lever spindle patented by W. M. Scott in 1865. Further improvements were made in top-lever work, bolting, fore-end attachment, elimination of wear on the joint pin, and in 1875 the feature which can be seen on the gun illustrated appeared – windows!

Originally the windows provided in the sideplate were quite large, but with the passing of the years they were made smaller and smaller until the window become a "peephole" rather than a window. The reason for the window was "to ascertain the position of the discharging mechanism in hammerless breechloading shotguns". The patent had provision for a hinged or sliding door if the glazed window appeared inappropriate. The Scott gun was well made, delightfully engraved and, of greater importance, Allan Paton could shoot with it. That is until I found out that it was not proved for smokeless powder. Off it went to be proved "for nitro" and back it came – rejected. My feelings can be imagined. It was at my suggestion that the gun was sent for proof and my only consolation, slight though it is, is that my suggestion may have prevented an accident. The Scott was rebarrelled and, since it had already been restocked following an earlier accident on the marshes, all that was left was the action and the fore-end. The opportunity was taken to alter the chambering and boring. The weight of the barrels was then different, the balance changed and somehow the old Scott never seemed the same after its "major operation".

Anyway, the gun was sold and that was that. Some years later I was in Italy and had made a special journey to see an Italian "country" gun shop. The shop chosen was at Castelnuovo above Carrara where the marble comes from. Here, in what we would

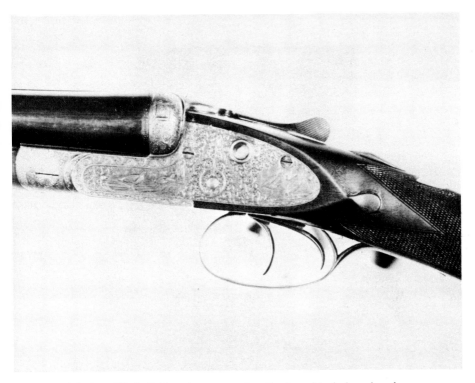

The later W. & C. Scott has conventionally shaped lockplates but the
"little window" can be seen and through it the fact that the left-hand
lock is cocked.

call a market town, was the shop of Piero Gualtierotti, a noted clay bird shot and a
connoisseur of fine shotguns. I asked what sort of gun he used and was told that he
used an "English gun", a gun of which he was very proud, because he left the shop in
our care and went home to bring his gun to show me.

When I was handed his best-quality Scott I recognised my old friend, the Scott which
had belonged to my friend Allan Paton. There was disbelief on the face of Piero; he was
too polite to mention it outright but this was taking gun expertise too far. That is until
I mentioned certain little minor scratches and marks under the fore-end, the marking
on the flats and the slight loss of plating from a corner of the escutcheon. These clues
re-established my veracity, and fate and the fortunes of a W. & C. Scott shotgun were
discussed and described to all the customers who came into the shop for the rest of that
day.

W. & C. SCOTT: GUNMAKING RESILIENCE

Not so long ago the future of Webley & Scott Ltd appeared uncertain. Now it seems

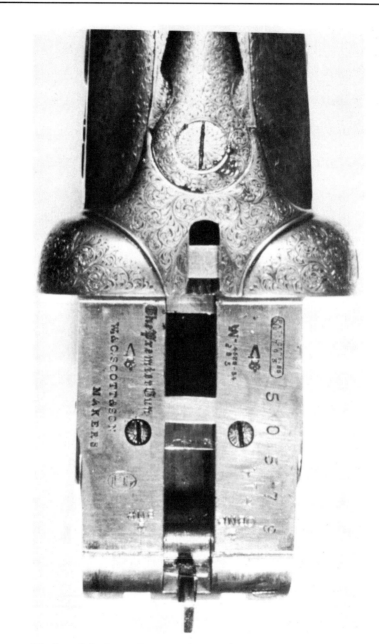

The bar of the Scott "Premier" shotgun showing serial number, patent numbers, trade mark, address and grade of gun.

that a way has been found to keep this firm alive and so preserve some of the traditions of the past. Most people know that Webley & Scott was formed in 1897 by the amalgamation of W. C. Scott & Son and P. Webley & Son.

What is perhaps less well-known is the extremely important part that W. & C. Scott played in the export field towards the end of the nineteenth century, and, to repeat what I have written in the past, it is no exaggeration that Scott could lay claim to being the best-known British shotgun manufacturer, particularly in the North American market and what we now refer to as "our former colonies". This was not based on volume of output but on the practical contribution to gunmaking and the high standard of the guns made for these markets.

By the turn of the century two guns were being offered, the "Premier" and the "Imperial Premier" at £82 and £112 respectively. Both were fitted with the Scott rectangular cross-bolt and block safety bar-locks, while the quality of workmanship and materials was of the highest.

For some time now I have been receiving catalogues and material from Dr. John A. Crawford of Oregon, and recently he sent me a facsimile Scott catalogue of 1922. This was extremely interesting because I was able to compare what was on offer with the range described in an earlier catalogue of 1910. This catalogue was used to illustrate an article on Scott which appeared in *The Shooting Times* of 10–16 May in 1979. There I mentioned that the two firms had amalgamated and that Scott guns could still be had bearing the Scott name, although made by the new firm of Webley & Scott. I have been able to find an illustration of the Scott gun once owned by Allan Paton, and you can see that the flats of the action bear patent numbers, "W. & C. Scott & Sons, Makers", and, in Gothic script, the description "The Premier Gun". Also on the flats is the trade mark used by Scott, a castle with a flag flying within an oval. Someone with a "Premier Imperial" should also have much the same markings although that gun will bear the name "Premier Imperial".

Now we come to the interesting part. John Crawford sent me a splendid photograph of one of the Scott guns in his collection. This Scott gun, No. 40534, was shipped round the "Horn" during the 1880s to Portland, Oregon where it belonged to Henry Winslow Corbett, a US Senator and one of the founders of Portland. The gun has the name W. & C. Scott & Son, the London address, 10 Great Castle St., Regent Circus, London and the name "Excellentia Triplex". This is a name new to me; it does not appear in the literature or in the catalogues I have. John Crawford kindly sent me a photocopy of the E. C. Meacham Arms Co. of St. Louis, Missouri, issued 1884, which shows a gun similar to the Scott No. 40534, but the catalogue refers to the gun as the "Premier". So, we are left with the mystery of the "Excellentia Triplex" and the question that naturally arises is whether this term was used for export guns only and not on the home market; and, even if this is the correct solution why the 1884 catalogue does not mention this term, it certainly was a very splendid one, even in an age when all gunmakers appeared to have had a classical education and guns bear names like "Facile Princeps" and "Desideratum".

If you do have a Scott double sidelock please take a close look at the name on the barrels and also any names on the action flats. I would be very interested to find out if Scott guns bore any other names such as "Unique", "Reliance" and "Victoria".

Coming right up to date, guns by W. & C. Scott now bear the names "Bowood" and "Chatsworth". As mentioned above, the uncertainty concerning the future of this firm now appears to have been resolved. The name W. & C. Scott has been retained, following a decision by Webley & Scott to cease manufacture of double shotguns. The people who would have been made redundant determined to remain in the shotgun business, and, financed by the Harris & Sheldon Group, a new company was formed under the name of W. & C. Scott, with a factory bearing the appropriate name Premier Works. The factory is located at Tame Road, Witton, Birmingham and not far from the Eley ammunition works. (W. & C. Scott is now – in 1985 – owned by Holland & Holland Ltd.)

The Birmingham gunmaker has over the years shown a remarkable resilience in the face of economic adversity, government indifference and the destruction of the foundations of the industry. The fact that Scott is a name still to be found on British-made shotguns is testimony to this rugged resilience and I wish them well in the years to come. Certainly, if past tradition is any guide, the future of W. & C. Scott is assured.

W. & C. SCOTT'S PREMIER HAMMERLESS GUN

Guns which bear the name of Scott have always aroused my interest. The reason is rather unusual, for guns by Scott seem to have a story attached. They aren't guns which are stored, or just used – things seem to happen to them and their owners. You will have read of Allan Paton's Scott which I found in Italy in Piero Gualtierotti's gunshop in Castelnuovo. More recently (*The Shooting Times*, 20 May 1972) there was a Scott sold by Henry Monk of Chester. Both of these guns have the Scott "windows" or, more correctly, "The Patent Crystal Indicator".

I know that the earliest Scott gun with the Crystal Indicator in the lockplate had lever cocking actions. With the introduction of automatic barrel cocking, the shape of the action body and lockplate altered and the earliest Scotts of this type have a safety bolt on the left-hand lockplate. Then comes the Scott illustrated in the 20 May 1972 article. Now we have the Scott No. 34034 illustrated here. I had a problem with this. Russ Kranich, who brought this gun to my attention and who provided splendid photographs, gave me two prints. It was a difficult choice to decide which to use, but this one, I think, shows the excellent engraving to advantage.

It's worth having a look at this engraving. The scroll work is typical fine English but the birds are particularly good. They remind me of one of the finest Birmingham characters I have ever met, Mr. Harry Morris, gun engraver. Mr. Morris is, alas, no longer with us, but in my younger days I used to spend my evenings in his workshop in St. Mary's Row where he did his best to make me aware of the skills and techniques of the gun engraving craft. He mentioned many times the man who taught him, and let me see rubbings of his work. I'm reminded very much of this by the style of engraving on the Scott gun.

Unfortunately the records of Scott have been lost, so, unless we can find other Scott guns of known provenance, we must guess at the date of this example. Such evidence as we have – the address, 10 Great Castle St., Regent Circus, London, and the fact that

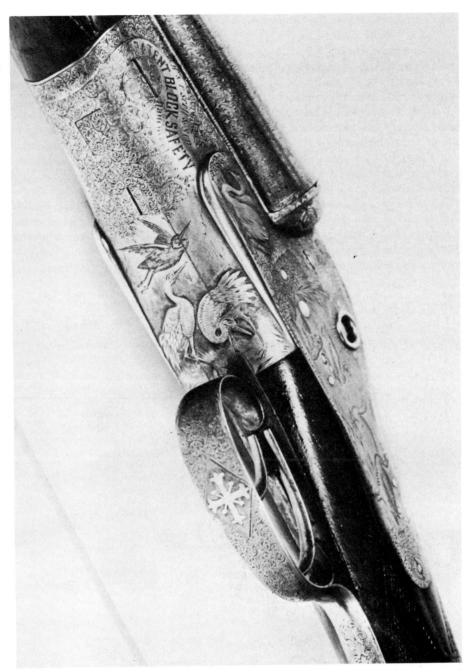

The engraving of this W. & C. Scott hammerless gun is particularly fine;
note the early style of "crystal indicator".

it has vents in the face of the "break-off" – would put the date of manufacture in the late 1880s. Not much to go on but we do know a little more about its later life.

The earliest owner was an ex-Prussian officer who settled in the Perkiomen Valley of Pennsylvania. Here, in the 1920s, he established a dry goods store and became quite successful. He was less successful in his passion for the ponies, and his habit of betting large sums on horses which finished last cost him his prized possession, his W. & C. Scott. The new owner used the gun regularly and left the gun to his son, who had a termagant of a wife who made his life so unbearable that the Scott was used to try to put an end to his torment. His wife, hearing the shot, summoned the doctor, who found that the owner was very much alive. In answer to the doctor's question he meekly replied, "Well, it was dark and ... I missed." The Scott, no longer holding pleasant memories, was given to the doctor in payment for his futile visit.

Fortunately the gun was rescued from sterile storage by Russ Kranich, a local rough shooter and springer spaniel field trialler who used it to good effect. The boring of the Damascus barrels was rather tight, the close patterns providing a good excuse for the missed pheasants. Recently the Scott has changed hands once again and it has now found an honourable resting place in the private collection of Martin H. Ritter.

SILVER & CO. OF CORNHILL

The fame of many gunmakers, both London and provincial, spread far and wide; some

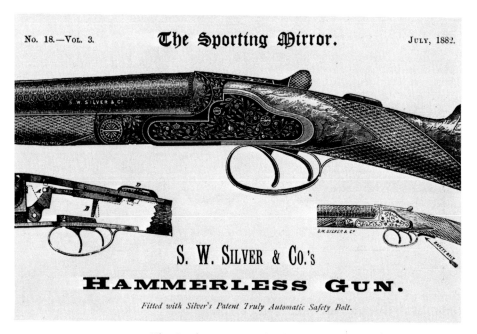

Silver's advertisement of July 1882.

were renowned for their shotguns, others for rifles. Some specialised in target rifles, some in big-game rifles, while others made wildfowling guns and punt guns. Then there were those firms whose fame rested upon one invention. With the passing of time it was forgotten that they were ever gunmakers; their name being solely associated with the special "patent" item.

If we have a look at A. G. Parker & Co.'s catalogue (this firm became Parker-Hale Ltd. in 1936) we will find an illustration of an anti-recoil pad, Silver's Pattern. For many years when you talked about a recoil pad for either a high-velocity rifle or a heavy shotgun the term was practically synonymous with the name "Silver". Even today the current Parker-Hale catalogue refers to the Silver recoil-pad and it is interesting to realise that the original patent for this recoil pad, which has been so widely copied, is dated 1874. The original design was rather complicated and it wasn't until 1886 that the simplified version made from rubber-faced vulcanite was introduced.

S. W. Silver & Co.'s premises were at 67 Cornhill, London but little is known of the founder of the firm or of its subsequent history. An early advertisement advises that an illustrated catalogue is available of every article of equipment for "Sportsmen, Colonists, Settlers, Explorers and Travellers, on application to ..."

This conjures up a splendid vision of a never-ending stream of intrepid Empire-Builders wending their way to Silver of Cornhill. What must have been the thoughts of the shop assistants as these bronzed heroes of the great outdoors came to have Silver's recoil pads fitted or to buy a patent "Transvaal Rifle & Gun"? I don't know what the shop was like, for Cornhill was not the "fashionable" gun centre – this was much further west – but Cornhill did have at least one other gunmaker in 1855, namely Edward Bond, and near at hand was the Minories, the historic centre of London gunmaking.

Most of Silver's gun patents were devoted to safety devices of one form or another. There were safeties in the tang of the trigger guard; another plan had the safety lever in the top strap where it would be depressed by the ball of the thumb when the gun was fired, and yet another automatic safety was incorporated in the butt plate so that the gun was "safe" until placed against the shoulder ready to fire. Few of these devices appear to have withstood the test of time. Several that I have seen in recent years have been rendered inoperative by taping them with adhesive tape or copper wire.

Rarely encountered in this country today is Silver's "Transvaal Rifle and Gun". This was a Martini-action to which could be fitted interchangeable barrels, either smooth-bored or rifled and, in addition, each barrel was supplied with the necessary bullet moulds and equipment for reloading.

It is very possible that some of the Silver & Co. shotguns survive and perhaps remain in useful service, but whether any with safety devices of Silver's design are still used is less likely.

Although the name Silver may be forgotten to all but a few with surviving guns by this maker (it is too much to hope that the "Illustrated Catalogue" might have survived) the name of Silver will be remembered for some years to come because of the invention of the recoil pad. Today rather splendid pads can be purchased with "white line spacers" and other eye-catching additions, but Silver was first!

J. & W. TOLLEY, BIRMINGHAM

A question often put to me in letters from readers is: "I have a gun by Messrs. 'X'; was he a good maker?" How does one categorise gunmakers? What makes a "good" maker? I suppose "a 'good' gun" is the correct answer. The *great* gunmakers were something different. They did not just make good or even great guns; they altered the course of events by invention, innovation or style. As to the question, "Did the man who made *my* gun make good guns?", the answer lies with the present owner. You have a gun bearing his name: what is *your* verdict?

Not long ago I received a letter from a reader telling me that he had a number of gun catalogues from the 1930s period and asking whether I would like to see them. A "Yes, please" letter went off by return, and in due course a parcel of catalogues arrived and it is from the Tolley catalogue of 1934 that the illustrations here are taken.

I do not have a Tolley catalogue myself, although I have an early Tolley self-cocking gun, and in *The Shooting Times* for 10 April 1971 I wrote about a Tolley double 8-bore rifle which a long-time friend had been kind enough to let me photograph. The rifle was fitted with hammer back-action locks and was stocked with a pistol hand and a cross-bolt to the fore-end. Locking was secure with a rotary underbolt and I regret that I was not able to fire what must be quite a remarkable rifle. On the top rib is the address St. Mary's Square, Birmingham. The earliest address I have for the firm is 22 St. Mary's Row and J. & W. Tolley appear to have started business there in 1859, moving to Loveday Street in 1878.

An advertisement of 1862 tells us that the firm were "Gun, Rifle and Pistol Makers, Contractors for Military Arms, Breech Loading Guns etc., also all guns suitable for the African Markets". In the ten years after 1862, production from the Birmingham trade was the highest ever achieved. Much was military: the American Civil War followed by wars in Europe did much to stimulate demand. In the end, however, many of these arms came back onto the market and, added to this, the development of mass production techniques in America meant that this country, for the first time, was capable of supplying much of its own requirements except for double shotguns which Birmingham and then Belgium continued to furnish for many years.

By the 1880s Tolley had moved again and acquired a retail outlet in London at 1 Conduit St., in the West End. In addition to their new "Perfection" hammerless gun Tolley also were able to supply wildfowl guns in all bores up to and including 4-bore and Express and Big-Game rifles up to and including double 4-bore.

Tolley were keen to advise their customers that they were "Makers by Special Appointment to the Persian Royal Family". The firm was also well known for its punt guns specialising in Snider actions and a formidable weapon with a "screw-breech". Some of these guns must have survived since it would have required major demolition to destroy them!

It is when we ask ourselves what is the exact category we would place the firm in that we come up against a problem. However, one patent appears against the names of J. & W. Tolley – that for a breechloading action which in 1879 was given only provisional protection. One of the mysteries is the relationship between J. & W. Tolley and Henry Tolley, also of Birmingham, who was by far the more prolific

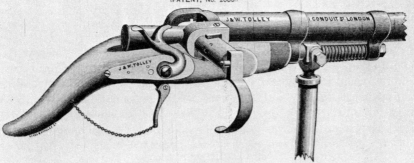

J. & W. TOLLEY'S
"HANDY" PUNT GUN
WITH PATENT BREECH ACTION.
(PATENT, No. 2083.)

The above Sketch shows our latest contribution to Wildfowl Shooting in the "Handy" Punt Gun, for which the following advantages are claimed :—

HANDINESS.—The weight is about 35 lbs., as against 80 to 100 in the ordinary Punt Guns: a boy can carry it on his shoulder for miles, in removing it from one shooting to another.

STRENGTH.—The absence of a hinge or falling-stock gives it great stability, while the form and arrangement of the Breech Action are massive—very noticeable in so light a Gun. The amount of friction in this Action is reduced to a minimum.

SIMPLICITY.—No Gun could have fewer parts in its Action; there is simply one stout cross-bar, which contains the striker: this is the whole of the Breech Action. To load : pull out the breech cross-bar by the handle on the side—when the cartridge chamber is exposed ready to receive the cartridge—push the cross-bar back into its place, and the Gun is ready for firing. The empty cartridge cases are extracted quite clear of the Gun. In this action there are no delicate bars and rods to get disarranged.

SHOOTING.—This Gun is the first Punt Gun that has received in its boring the same delicate treatment as a Shoulder Gun. Hitherto Punt Guns have been very roughly turned out as respects the bore of the barrel, consequently the performance was poor compared with the Shoulder Guns, taking into consideration the resources in the Gun, its weight, bore, length and charge. We have now remedied this by giving to our barrel the same boring as in our long-range Shoulder Guns (see special sheet). The result is that, with this Gun, we get *vastly* improved shooting, and a much smaller, handier, and less expensive Gun will do the work for which punters have been in the habit of using the usual large and heavy Guns.

SPECIFICATION.—*Weight,* 35 lbs.   *Bore,* $1\frac{3}{4}$ in.   *Charge: powder,* 20 to 25 drachms.   *Shot,* 7 to 9 ozs.
          Length of barrel, 5 *feet.*   *Price,* **£35.**   *Recoil Apparatus,* **£4.**

LARGE-BORE PUNT GUNS are made with the above Action at the following Prices:—
$1\frac{1}{4}$ in. bore, **£42.** $1\frac{1}{2}$ in. bore, **£48.** $1\frac{3}{4}$ in. bore, **£56.**   2 in. bore, **£66.**
Recoil Frames, **£5** extra.   Barrels over 7 ft. are charged £3 per foot extra.

J. & W. TOLLEY,
Pioneer Works, BIRMINGHAM, & 1, Conduit St., Regent St., LONDON.

Tolley advertisement of 1884.

inventor. Henry Tolley was perhaps best known for his patent top extension. He worked in Weaman St. and appears to have ceased trading in 1892.

J. & W. Tolley continued in business with premises at 10 Vessey St., and their catalogue shows that they were "late of 59 New Bond St." My records indicate that the firm was taken over by Holloway & Naughton, but when this was is at present unknown to me.

Tolley made some very interesting and unusual guns in their time. They also exported guns all over the world, and, although I don't think that they could be classed as "great" gunmakers, they certainly deserve to have something placed on the historical record for posterity.

VICKERS LTD.

My first contact with the firm of Vickers came through the purchase of a .22 rimfire target rifle which was used for indoor small-bore rifle shooting. It was bought second-hand in Steelhouse Lane, Birmingham and served me well during my membership of several rifle clubs. I restocked it and still have it. Vickers made two target rifles, the Grade 1 and the Grade 2 which, in 1929 cost £7 10s. and £6 15s. with a Vickers rearsight and a Parker-Hale foresight respectively. The action was a modified Martini and, although never as popular as the BSA range, it was accurate and well made. When production ceased I cannot say, but at some time the name was changed and one of the rifles was known as the Vickers "Empire".

As well as the .22 rifles (which, as an advert in the 28 May issue of *The Shooting Times* for 1927 assures the reader, could be had for target and sporting shooting) a range of central-fire rifles and shotguns was also offered. I have not encountered the .22 sporting rifle but the "Express Rifles" were based on Mauser '98 actions and offered in two calibres, the .242 Magnum Express and the .318 Magnum Express. The .242 was developed by Vickers and, according to their literature, had a muzzle velocity of 3,000 ft/sec. It can best be compared with the .243 Winchester and the .244 Remington, and it has long been obsolete.

The .318 was a successful cartridge developed by Westley Richards about 1910 for their bolt-action rifles and became a popular cartridge for non-dangerous African game. About the same time BSA introduced their range of bolt-action sporting rifles based, not on the Mauser '98 but on the Enfield P14 action. They, too, had a special cartridge of quite advanced design, the .26 rimless Nitro-Express which, although listed as a "rimless" cartridge, was actually a belted rimless case similar to the H. & H. designs. Neither the BSA nor the Vickers Express rifles enjoyed commercial success. Production must have been relatively small (today production figures are unobtainable).

Vickers Ltd., later to be Vickers Armstrong Ltd., were armament manufacturers and their venture into sporting firearms was unusual. BSA, on the other hand, had been formed by a consortium of Birmingham gunmakers in an attempt to ward off the threat posed by the establishment of the Royal Small Arms Factory at Enfield. Vickers did have an interest which BSA did not enjoy – the automatic pistol. As Vickers Sons & Maxim Ltd., they were U.K. agents for Deutsche Waffen-und Munitions-fabriken of Berlin and instrumental in arranging trials for what we know today as the Luger pistol. These trials took place before the British Small Arms Committee in 1900 and it is a quirk of fate that the basic action of the Borchardt-Luger owed much to the earlier toggle-link mechanism of the Maxim machine gun, made by Vickers.

Further efforts were made by Vickets on behalf of DWM, without success and then the outbreak of the First World War put an effective stop to negotiations. The story did not finish, however, since one of the notable "mysteries" is the story of the "Vickers Luger" purchased by the Netherlands Indies Army shortly after the end of the First World War. Even today it is not known if Vickers merely acted for DWM in the transaction, assembled DWM Luger components in the U.K., or actually manufactured Luger pistols on machinery supplied by DWM.

One of the most interesting aspects of this story concerns the Mauser '98 actions used for Vickers Express rifles. Were these also from DWM? The bitterness and resentment which followed the First World War would ensure that any relationship between Vickers and DWM would be shrouded in secrecy. The effectiveness of this secrecy, coupled with the passing of the years makes it now impossible to discover the true story.

International conspiracy, however, cannot be the cause of the mystery which still surrounds Vicker's manufacture of shotguns. The best known was the single-barrel, semi-hammerless ejector gun sold under the name "Vanguard". We are told that the Vanguard is made from British materials, by British workmanship throughout and that the barrel is forged from Vickers steel. The Vanguard guns bore London proof marks, which was understandable, if they had been made at the Crayford Works; but Vickers also offered the rather rare Vickers "Imperial" double sidelock. This employed a back-action coil-spring sidelock similar to that patented by Baker, but what is of greater interest is their "best" sidelock. This appears, from the illustrations, to have been a "best" London gun with Chilton locks, and, although the barrels are made from Vickers nickel steel, this is possibly the sole contribution by Vickers to the actual manufacture of this gun.

I have never seen either the "Imperial" or the "Best Quality" Vickers side-by-side double guns although one has just "surfaced" in Australia! We go back again to the years just after the First World War. In March 1919 the Australian Government offered a prize of £10,000 for the first flight made by Australians from Britain to Australia in a British aircraft. Vickers Ltd. had just the aircraft, the Vimy. Too late to make an impact on the war, the Vimy became immortal as the first aircraft to make a direct Atlantic crossing. This was in June 1919, so it is not surprising that Vickers entered the Vimy for the Australian flight. Flown by Captain Ross Smith of the Australian Flying Corps and navigated by his brother Lt. Keith Smith with Sgts. Bennett and Shiers as mechanics, the Vimy left Hounslow at 8 a.m. on 12 November 1919, reaching Darwin at 4.10 p.m. on 10 December, after flying 11,130 miles. The Vimy, G-EAOU, was presented to the Australian Government by Vickers and survives to this day, along with the Vimy of Alcock and Brown which is preserved in London.

So far we are going on fact; now we move to heresay. The story goes that Captain Ross Smith was presented with a shotgun by Vickers Ltd. after his successful flight. What better shotgun than a Crayford-built Vickers "Best" sidelock? The Vimy was built at Crayford Works but G-EAOU had been built by Vickers at Weybridge. Did Vickers build the "Best" shotguns at Crayford or have them made for them elsewhere; if so, where?

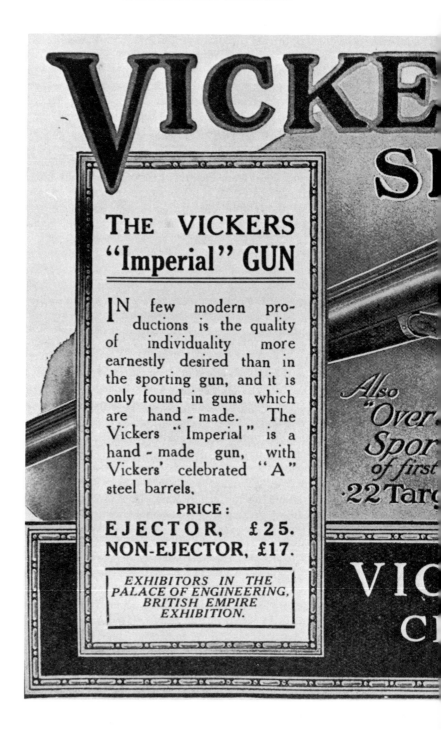

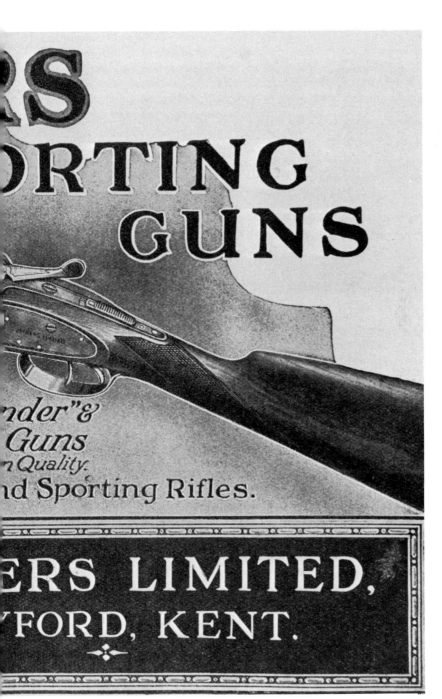

The Vickers advertisement in the April 19th issue of *The Shooting Times* for 1924.

The Aviation Dept. of Vickers went on to even greater things – the Spitfire and the Viscount – but what happened to the sporting gun department, if indeed there ever was one? Vickers today do not have the answers but there may be someone who does remember or who has the relevant literature. If so, I would be most interested to learn more about the guns and rifles made by Vickers or sold by them, and any facts about the presentation shotgun now in Australia would delight the owner and satisfy my curiosity.

WALLACE & AGNEW, EDINBURGH

One of the most fascinating aspects of my interest in firearms is the inescapable fact that there is always something new to learn. In September 1975 I wrote an article on MacLaughlan, gunmaker of Edinburgh, and used as an illustration his trade label,

John Dickson's trade label from the 60 Princes Street address.

which could be dated to between 1808 and 1817. The card label was 3½ in. by 2¾ in., with the dominant figure 8 right in the middle. It took me a while to realize that this was the street number of MacLaughlan's premises in Lothian Street, Edinburgh but it was not until I saw the label illustrated here that I appreciated that this was the usual style for labels of the period.

The John Dickson label is plainer than the MacLaughlan but readers may remember a very much later Dickson label which splendidly illustrated the whole panorama of Princes Street. In telling us that John Dickson & Son were gunmakers at 60 Princes St., Edinburgh the label gives two clues which help in dating it and, therefore, the case to which it was attached and the contents. But first let us look at the contents of the case which, after all, are our chief concern.

The case contains a pair of percussion, single-shot pistols, full stocked to the muzzle, with octagonal twist barrels and a captive swivel ramrod. Silver sideplates protect the wood of the stock where the flat bolt that secures the barrel passes through the wood and, although damaged by having the hammer spur probably deliberately removed (since it is missing on both pistols) and showing evidence of past corrosion, the pistols are of good quality and desirable from the collector's point of view.

One of a pair of pistols by Wallace & Agnew of Edinburgh.

Looking more closely at the pistols we find that the name on them is not the same as that on the trade label, although the pistols are fitted to the case which bears the label. The name on the barrels is "Wallace & Agnew, Edinburgh", and the makers' name, but not the locus, is repeated on the lockplate. Wallace was a famous Edinburgh gunmaker who was first listed in 1776. James Wallace was the son of Thomas Wallace, a smith in Carron, and, instead of following his father's trade, he was apprenticed to Francis Innes of Edinburgh, who was one of the first people to offer for sale the new

Forsyth guns on the detonating principle. In 1795, having completed his apprentice-ship, James Wallace set up in business with a member of the Innes family as the firm of Innes & Wallace at 25 North Bridge, Edinburgh.

In 1806 the firm took on as an apprentice John Dickson, when they were at 187 High St. Later the firm moved to 63 Princes Street, one of the most fashionable addresses in Scotland.

In 1841 the style of the firm changed from J. Wallace & Son to Wallace & Agnew but still at the Princes Street address. A year later the firm was described as Agnew & Co. John Dickson & Son were first listed a few doors away at 60 Princes Street in 1840–1 and by 1844 Agnew was no longer listed.

The last change important to our story took place in 1849–50 when John Dickson & Son changed their address from 60 to 63 Princes Street, the old address of Wallace. It would be reasonable to suppose that John Dickson bought the stock from Agnew when the firm went out of business and that the pistols were then cased and labelled by Dickson between 1844 and the change to the new address in 1849/50.

Of the three gunmakers in this story, Agnew is a bit of a mystery. I remember hearing references to "old Agnew" but whether or not a relative of the firm worked for Dickson in later years I cannot confirm. One can but speculate about the reasons which resulted in the various changes of address. That they were real cannot be denied but one cannot help wondering why Dickson moved from 60 to 63. I may be accused of creating a story where none exists, while the reason for the change was quite simple. Agnew went out of business and No. 63 was a bigger and much better shop. Often a change of address of but a few numbers in the same street was merely due to the post office renumbering the street, a not uncommon practice in those days. This did not happen here, of course, since both 60 and 63 were occupied simultaneously by gunmakers.

Often, in looking at old firearms, one speculates about the owners. In the case of these pistols I cannot help wondering about the makers and the story that lies hidden behind the various moves, the partnerships and the accidents of fate which allowed John Dickson to survive as a going concern to the present day.

The shop at 63 Princes Street was by no means pretentious but well known for the stuffed lion's head and other trophies in the window and this must have fired the imagination of many a small boy as he walked with his parents along the famous Edinburgh thoroughfare. Dicksons later moved to Frederick Street, not all that far away, and in true Edinburgh tradition, there on the other side of the street was the famous firm of Alex. Henry. Both must have watched each other carefully from 1938 when the Dickson move took place until Henry's (which had been bought out by Martin's of Glasgow) was finally taken over by the sole survivor, John Dickson & Son.

Other parts of the story remain to be filled in, possibly by the appearance of more trade labels from gun cases sold by Wallace and by Agnew. The story *is* incomplete so that I know there is the possibility of discovering more and that there is the slight, but totally rewarding, chance that *all* the story will be told. It has happened to me before, but only once!

WARRILOW OF CHIPPENHAM

Not long ago I was searching through the thousands of negatives that have accumulated over the years and I came across two photographs of a rather nice box-lock "made" by Warrilow. Prints were made but before they could be marked the pencil broke, and I made a mental note to place the numbers on the prints so that I could locate the negatives again and from the number perhaps locate some data on this gun. The prints turned out rather well but of course I forgot to put the identification numbers on the prints. Half a day has been spent searching for the negatives: they are not on the card index so this time the system has slipped up.

As one can see, this is no run-of-the-mill box-lock. We cannot, in all honesty, call the gun an Anson & Deeley since not all box-locks are based on the Anson & Deeley hammerless action.

It can be seen from the photograph that the gun has a Greener-type cross-bolt extension and, unusually for a box-lock, the bar has shoulders. The fences are well executed and the fine scroll engraving is nicely done. The stock has sunk panels and drop points and fancy chequering. If one then has a look at the top of the barrels, one can see how the fences were finished, the file-cut broad rib and the words "Full Choke" on the left barrel and "Cylinder" on the right one. The name of the "maker", James B. Warrilow, can just be seen in the panel on the rib and quite prominently the legend "Patent Clip Lump, May 31, 1884". The barrels are Damascus and nicely engraved at

Note the Damascus barrels on this modern "Rounded Action" sidelock.

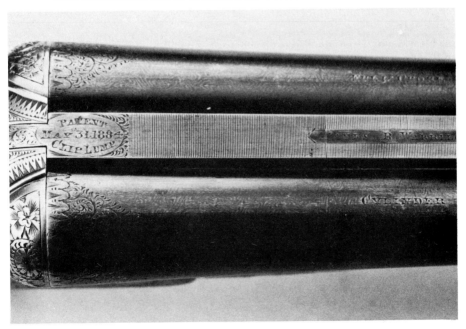

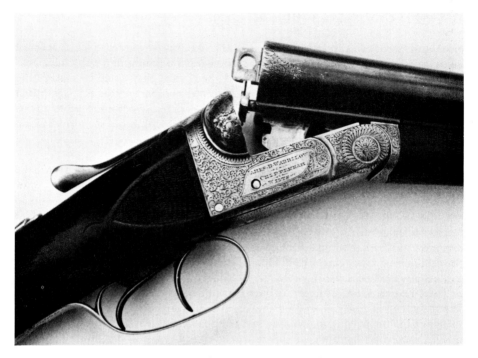

The Warrilow gun showing the sunk side panels and the Greener-type
cross-bolt.

the breech, and we have a well made and interesting box-lock which belies its name,
since it does not have the box-like look of many A & D-actioned guns, the shoulders
and rounded action appearing to reduce the length of the action bar.

One question always asked when one comes across a gun with a name that is not
well known is "Did they make the gun? If not, who did?" My feeling is that Warrilow
did not make this gun. I have little or no evidence, I don't even have my notes when the
photograph was taken, but the feeling is there. Perhaps it is because the name and
address on the bar of the action do not exactly fit in with the panel, the space being left
for this purpose. If one then asks, "Who did make it?" my answer would be C. G.
Bonehill, Belmont Firearms & Gun Barrel Works, Belmont Row, Birmingham.

To go back to the man whose name is on the barrel and action. I know that the firm
was in business in 1908 and that the full style was "James Blakewell Warrilow,
Railway Works, Chippenham, Wilts." Yes, the word "Works" does make me think a
little but if the name is anything to go by, Mr. Warrilow made railway engines not guns
so perhaps the works was alongside the railway.

Why Bonehill then? The reason is that the patent date given on the barrel is for a
box-lock action and a fore-end fastener. Another patent, taken out on the same day as
Bonehill, protects his idea for a prolonged rib and a special web which provides not
only the underlump but also the underflats. The breech end of the barrels is cut away to

accommodate the "all through" lump which is described on the gun as a "Clip Lump".

So what appears at first sight to be an ordinary box-lock is shown even by simple visual examination to be something more and, on further investigation, a number of interesting features appear. Anyone with any information on Mr. James B. Warrilow of Chippenham might perhaps drop me a line, and if there is any information on what went on in the "Railway Works" this would be most welcome.

WATSON BROS., PALL MALL

Perhaps my greatest interest in firearms lies in the unravelling of the many problems which confront the researcher into early breechloading hammerless guns – the guns of the closing decades of the nineteenth century. Many, because of a conventional external appearance, are overlooked until something goes wrong and a strange and interesting mechanism is exposed for examination. With guns other than those which appear to be sidelocks the difference in the mechanism from, for example, the standard Anson & Deeley, can quite often be guessed.

Such was the case when I was handed the 12-bore non-ejector by Watson Bros., 4 Pall Mall, London, not long ago. The date of the gun was not too difficult to discover: this style and address appear to have been used for quite a short period, from about 1885 to 1894, which would probably place manufacture between those two dates – near enough for all practical purposes.

I was fortunate to be able to examine this gun, since the external appearance was sufficiently different to make me curious about the type of cocking mechanism and lockwork employed. Apart from the name "Watson Bros." on each side of the action bar, and the full name and address on the top rib, the sole remaining clue was the words "Carlton Patent Hammerless" on the small "box" beneath the bar and in front of the trigger guard. Proof marks were those of 1875, which were themselves altered in 1887. Simple arithmetic then narrows down the date of manufacture to the years 1885, 1886 and 1887.

With the gun in front of me and the opportunity to take it apart and inspect the "works" instead of having to work from photographs as I often have to do, the next problem was to discover who was responsible for the design of the cocking mechanism and the lockwork. A search showed that this was none of the Watsons, but research elsewhere for quite a different purpose provided the linking clue. In my research on Watson I had discovered that the firm had been founded by Thomas William Watson and that after trading under this name for a period the firm had then been known as Watson Bros., reverting later to Thomas W. Watson. This information had been obtained as a result of very much earlier work on the firm of Atkin, Grant & Lang. Watson had been taken over by Grant & Lang in 1935, some three years before Charles Lancaster had been acquired and shortly after F. Beesley. So, Watson's were in very good company at 7 Bury Street, St. James's.

How exalted the company was I had yet to discover! I had thought that the important connections were in the closing years of the life of the firm, but this was not so. Further research revealed the fact that Watson was the son-in-law of a very famous

Birmingham gunmaker named William Tranter. To most people the name Tranter is linked with revolvers, and although Tranter had a marked influence on the development of the British revolver, this was by no means his only interest in what was to become, in his lifetime, the gun industry.

The name Tranter was to link all the loose bits of information together because I remembered having seen a drawing of a shotgun action patented by him which had a rather odd, old-fashioned box underneath the action bar. A search of the records showed this to be so; the action used by Watson was that patented by his father-in-law in 1882 and, with the aid of the patent and being able fully to dismantle the gun, I was able to discover details of the rather unusual type of action.

The Tranter action never became popular. It was complicated and slightly unwieldy and the external box did detract from the appearance. It offered no advantage over the earlier Anson & Deeley (patented in 1875) and few appear to have been made; fewer still have survived. Unfortunately, the barrels are no longer in proof and their condition is such that I would not like to risk using even black-powder cartridges; so how the gun would perform under field conditions remains a mystery.

WESTLEY RICHARDS

The firm of Westley Richards was established in 1812 and in June of that year the Americans declared war on Britain. Westley Richards supplied double-barrelled muzzle-loading pistols to cavalry officers who fought in the American War of 1812 and they also supplied weapons to Wellington's armies in the wars against Napoleon which ended in the Battle of Waterloo in 1815. William Westley Richards, the founder, was born in 1788 and he died in 1865. During his working life he was responsible for a number of inventions connected with the muzzle-loader; one was highly praised by no less an authority than Colonel Peter Hawker. Although founded in Birmingham, the firm was not typical of the Birmingham trade, and its premises were in the old High Street quite some way from the gun quarter. A London retail outlet was established in 1815 at 170 New Bond Street, under the management of William Bishop, who was known to generations of shooting men as "The Bishop of Bond Street". The London end of the business grew in fame and fortune.

In Birmingham, Westley Richards, the son of the founder, took over the business from his father in 1840 and a further series of important inventions did much to influence the development of guns, rifles and revolvers. It has been said that the firm enjoyed the highest reputation of any Birmingham gunmaker, and apart from the contribution made on the military side (the Westley Richards Monkey Tail carbine), sporting shotguns received attention: 1858, drop-down barrels; 1861, drop-down and slide-forward barrels; 1862, the famous top-lever and "doll's head" extension, and, in the same year, patent rifle-sights. In 1864 the top-lever design was modified to improve the operation, and in 1866 the Monkey Tail capping breechloader was further improved. The stream of inventions continued until Westley Richards retired in 1872 and that year saw bolt-action and sliding breech-block designs. In 1878 his last patent covered the locking system for the drop-down barrel gun.

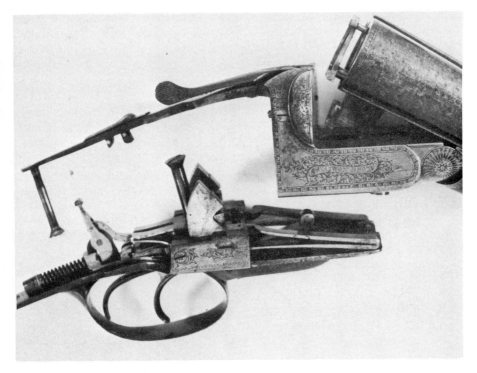

Tranter's patent action, sold by Watson Bros.

This remarkable man died in 1897, having lived through the most exciting period in the development of the British shotgun and, as we have seen, having made a notable contribution to that development himself.

With the retirement of Westley Richards, the firm was fortunate enough to find another outstanding man, John Deeley, to take charge. Deeley had joined the firm in 1860 and, between 1873 and 1907 he was partly or wholly responsible for some 17 patents. Of these, there is no doubt that British Patent No. 1756, taken out jointly with W. Anson in 1875 is not only the most important of the patents associated with the firm of Westley Richards, but it can be said with confidence that it is one of the most important of all the nineteenth-century patents, protecting as it did the world-famous box-lock Anson & Deeley action.

This was the first practical shotgun to be cocked by the fall of the barrels, and it was also the first practical re-design of the action of a double-barrelled shotgun and one which reduced the number of components considerably. It would be impossible to guess at the number of A & D and A & D-type shotguns which have been manufactured since 1875 and the fact that guns of this type, similar in concept and design to the original, are still being made is more than adequate testimony to the brilliance of these two men.

The A & D-action sporting shotgun quickly became very popular, and Westley

Richards licensed others to manufacture it. Numerous "improvements" also appeared. Of the improvements to the original, two ideas were of significance, both patented by John Deeley. The first was an intercepting safety and the second, hand-detachable locks.

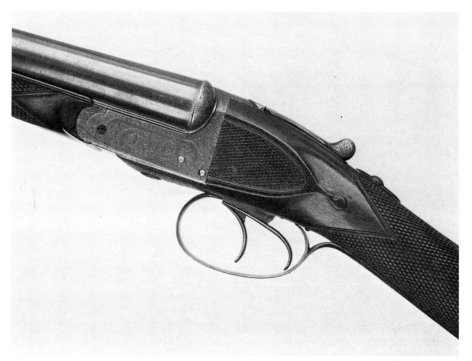

The Westley Richards Anson & Deeley No. 1. A truly historic gun.

It is fortunate that the firm has managed to retain in its possession the first Anson & Deeley gun made, and this is the gun which illustrates this article. As you can see, the gun bears the inscription "The First Anson & Deeley Hammerless Gun, Patented 11th May 1875". The remarkable thing about this gun is that it could be taken to any shoot today and used without comment well over a century after it was built. Unlike so many prototypes the Anson & Deeley looks "right" from the start. Possibly the only features which might betray its age are the shallow fences.

In 1896 the firm finally outgrew the premises in the High Street and moved not to the gun quarter but (again keeping to themselves) out to a factory in Bournebrook, on the south side of the city. This is where you will find them today. Things have changed but, once again, A & D guns and rifles are being built. Some seventy-five per cent of the capacity of the works is concerned with the manufacture of highly specialised tools and dies. Some of the "space age" machine tools which are used in this side of the

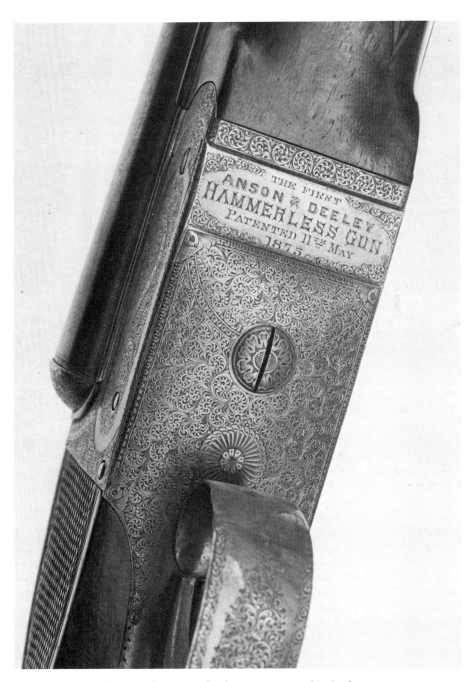

So that there can be no mistake the gun is engraved "The first Anson &
Deeley Hammerless Gun".

business are also used in the manufacture of the Westley Richards guns and rifles of today. There is a happy blend of the best of the old and new and the techniques employed for gunmaking are those best adapted to the kind of work involved.

It should be placed on record that a Westley Richards fixed-lock 12-bore has a delivery time of about year. Price is about £2,500. A similar gun, with the famous "hand-detachable" locks, has a delivery time of 18 months to two years and the price is (1983) in the order of £6,500. Prices vary, since each gun is made to the customer's exact requirements, and an interesting aspect of having your gun made by Westley Richards is that, when you place your order, you are given the serial number(s) of the gun or guns. You can then visit the factory at any time until your gun is completed to watch its progress and talk to the craftsmen involved.

Westley Richards is rightly proud of its long and distinguished history and it is very pleasant to record that the company is not resting on its laurels, considerable though these may be. The firm is fully engaged in building what will undoubtedly be the heirlooms of tomorrow.

GILES WHITTOME, GUNMAKER

The manner in which firearms are made varies enormously. On the one hand we have modern, mass-production methods where required skill is built into machinery while at the other extreme it is possible for one man alone to make an entirely satisfactory gun.

Today, in this country, use of specialised machine tools is restricted to manufacture of military weapons and, to a lesser extent, the manufacture of simple bolt-action sporting rifles. However, the needs of the high-quality sporting shotgun market cannot be met by these manufacturing techniques. It is not that modern technology could not produce weapons of this type, but, quite simply, that because of the low demand it would be far too expensive to employ the highly sophisticated techniques that are now available for such low-volume production. Nor, on the other hand, is it possible for one man to make all the parts of a sporting shotgun himself, as part of an economically viable enterprise. It can be done as a "one-off" exercise and it has been done in recent years, though largely to satisfy the individual's sense of personal achievement.

For a commercial enterprise something different is needed. One cannot get a number of people who can all, as individuals, make identical things. It is expression of the individual's sense and feeling for craftsmanship which make the objects of their attention desirable. The alternative is one which was adopted hundreds of years ago – specialisation. The advantages of specialisation from the production aspect can be readily seen in the manufacture of bows and arrows during the Middle Ages. Even today, many of the specialised skills developed are remembered in surnames such as Bowyer, Shafter, Fletcher.

In the manufacture of simple firearms the task was divided into the making of the locks, the barrels and the stock. In the North of Italy whole villages were "specialised" in this manner and the gun was subsequently assembled, tested and sold from a central point such as Gardone in the Val Trompia. In this country the gun trade developed along these lines in Birmingham, increasing specialisation arriving with the use of power for barrel making and for the forging of certain gun parts, which were then supplied to the trade.

By the mid-nineteenth century the trade had become so highly specialised that even a relatively simple weapon like a muzzle-loader could pass through 50 or 60 hands before completion. Obviously for the system to work well these skills had to be co-ordinated.

Two broad classes of supplier emerged. The first was a time-served gunsmith with a general knowledge of gunmaking who set up on his own. He might employ journeymen whose skills and craftsmanship were known to him and to whom certain tasks were given. As an alternative he could own premises and let out space, a bench, light and even tools, to craftsmen who would work for him but also be free to offer their skills to others in the trade. This provided a very desirable degree of flexibility to cope with fluctuations in trade and could often mean that skilled men could be kept employed when otherwise they would have to be paid off or be idle.

So far, we have two methods of manufacture which were well suited to the production of sporting shotguns: the first, where the entire operation was carried out under one roof by people employed by one man and the second, where the operation was carried out by self-employed craftsmen, sometimes under one roof but often dispersed over a specific area. Some of the skills needed were of such a specialised nature that few "gunmakers" could ever aspire to having these operations under their own roof. Tube making, lock making and engraving are good examples.

The second means of co-ordinating manufacture differed from the first in that the man responsible, and whose name and address quite often appeared on the gun, was not a gunmaker in that he had special trade or craft skills. He was what we would call today an entrepreneur, contractor or even businessman. His skills lay in the co-ordination and organisation of the various skills, and purchase of raw materials perhaps, and his was the decision on what was to be made, quality, quantity, markets and methods of sale. He also had responsibility for the final firearm. His was the responsibility for ensuring customer satisfaction.

Some of the most commonly asked questions are, "Who made my gun?"; "Did *they* actually make it"; and "Were they *gunmakers*?" As you can see from what has been a somewhat lengthy preamble, the answers are not easy to find. The name on the gun might be that of man long since dead, or a firm or, in rare cases, the gun might bear one name on the outside of the lockplate, another on the inside, the engraving might be signed by someone else and the barrels bear yet another name.

The name on the rib and the outside of the lockplate is the name of the man or firm responsible for the complete gun and, quite recently, I had the chance to meet someone whose name is on the ribs of some extremely fine-quality shotguns and rifles, Giles Whittome.

Giles explained from the very first that he is not a "gunmaker" himself: that is to say, his skills are not those of a barrel maker, lock maker or stock finisher. He is an accountant. This, when one looks at it, is probably the most appropriate skill needed for survival in this age of government intervention and trade manipulation by tax law. Giles solicits orders for the unusual, the unique, and the frankly mind-boggling in

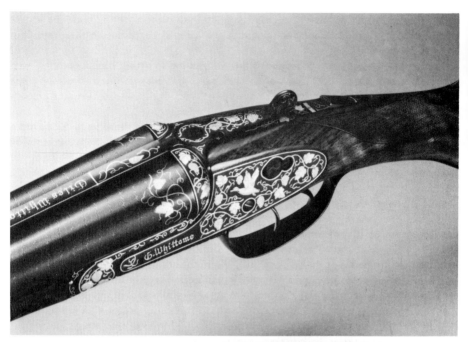

This gun bears the name of Giles
Whittome. The locks are "quick
detachable" and the ornate gold inlay
has been extended to the breech end
of the barrels.

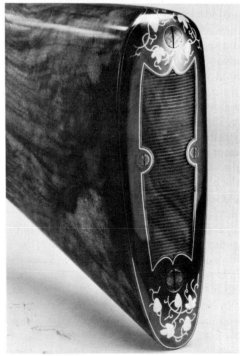

The finely figured stock is finished off
with a skeleton butt plate, also inlaid
with gold.

firearms and, provided that what the customer wants can be achieved by skilled craftsmen (within the constraints imposed by safety), Giles will endeavour to comply completely with wishes.

Fundamental changes in the way the gun trade organises itself mean that no longer is it necessary for the craftsman to work in the gun quarter, within walking distance of the gunmaker. Probably the first to break the traditional nineteenth-century mould was the engraver. Today, many engravers have reverted to what one might almost call a cottage industry. They live in pleasant rural surroundings and operate in a manner more in keeping with the eighteenth century than the twentieth. With what can only be called the virtual demise of manufacturing industry in many parts of the country who is to say that this will not be the way many things will be made by the end of the century?

Giles has a finger in many pies and the manufacture of *armes de luxe* is but one of them. He does not live in any of the "centres" of gunmaking but draws on the skills of many specialised craftsmen who do work for the London trade. Many of these people have also followed the lead of the engravers and no longer are cohabitants of a gunmakers' warren, and the younger craftsmen (and their wives) appear to find this way of working more congenial. A co-ordinator is, however, needed for much of the work and it is here that Giles comes into his own.

The gun illustrated is a good example of the work which is "assembled" by Giles Whittome and which bears his name. Made to the highest standards of quality, the style is impeccable. In some respects the gun is technically advanced but in others somewhat anachronistic. The embellishments, the gold inlay work, may not be to the taste of those raised on the more sober decoration of the traditional London trade but it must be remembered that for decades the London (and Birmingham) gun trade has made guns for people who live in other parts of the world and whose tastes in these matters differ from our own. The quality of the decoration is the highest, but it is when you look closely at what is a double side-by-side sidelock, that you realise that it is not just the decoration that seems a little strange. This gun has Damascus barrels!

The truly magnificent case which houses this gun has a space for snap caps. However, these snap caps are not the usual chrome-plated type, they too are made from Damascus steel! A technical feature of the gun is the trigger mechanism. Again this is not what it might seem. The front trigger can be used as a "single trigger" with the option of reverting to conventional use with the rear trigger. The stock is of the finest wood, beautifully finished; and a classic touch in keeping with the use of Damascus barrels is the decorated skeleton butt plate. The final touch is the fore-sight. The head of a dog, in gold, with ruby eyes!

Black and white photography cannot do full justice to the splendour of this gun and its case. This piece is a true gunmaker's *chef-d'oeuvre*. I am delighted that we still have craftsmen in the gun trade with the skills needed to produce what can only be described as a work of art and that we still have entrepreneurs of the stature of Giles Whittome who can "realise" *armes de luxe* to delight and astound present and future generations.

THOMAS WILD, GUNMAKERS, BIRMINGHAM

The definitive history of the Birmingham gun trade has yet to be written. Tantalising glimpses of the past are provided from time to time, but it is sad that as the years pass by more and more information is lost to us. The survival of data on gunmakers whose names ring down through the years is important to us, and some have a longer history than at first might be expected.

One of the reasons for the lack of early documentation is that gunmaking in Birmingham was free from corporate restriction, although we know that a payment was made to the Birmingham gunmakers in 1690 by the Treasury on the authorisation of the Office of Ordnance. The amount was considerable, £1,016 18s. 0d., and a further contract was obtained for the supply of muskets at the rate of 200 per month. The ability to carry out the work to the standards required and to manufacture in the quantities mentioned leads us to believe that the Birmingham gunmakers were already well established, and certainly as the eighteenth century opened some 400 Birmingham gunsmiths petitioned Parliament to stop the persecution of the London Guild.

The eighteenth century saw an increasing demand for arms due to the Jacobite Rebellion, and in 1723 we find recorded the name of Benjamin Watson; later the name of Watson appears again with that of Ryan in connection with the formation of a committee for the erection of a Proof House, the firm of Ryan & Watson being in business from 1777 to 1830. The style reverts to Benjamin Watson in 1830, and in 1857 the firm of Thomas Wild is first recorded, later to be bought out by a relative, Rowland

A & D gun by Wild from his last catalogue showing the "fancy back" to the action.

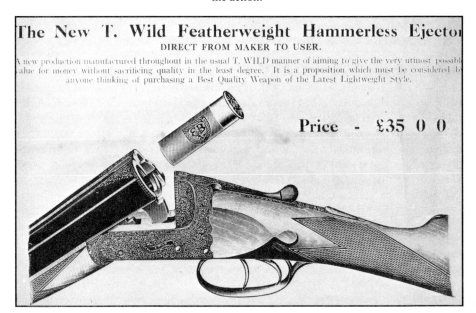

The New T. Wild Featherweight Hammerless Ejector
DIRECT FROM MAKER TO USER.

A new production manufactured throughout in the usual T. WILD manner of aiming to give the very utmost possible value for money without sacrificing quality in the least degree. It is a proposition which must be considered by anyone thinking of purchasing a Best Quality Weapon of the Latest Lightweight Style.

Price - £35 0 0

Watson. Although today the firm of Thomas Wild is still in business, it is directed by yet another Watson, Mr. R. H. G. Watson.

The firm of Thomas Wild is important because it is one of the few Birmingham firms known to the public, since most firms produced mainly for the trade. The manufacture of sporting weapons increased and the "birding trade" (as it was known) became more important as the Birmingham makers contributed not only to the numbers but also to the technical excellence of the sporting gun.

Exactly what the individual contribution of the firm of Thomas Wild was during the second half of the nineteenth century is unknown to us, but from their last catalogue issued in 1937 we can see the extent of their business. As well as the "Special" grade sidelock illustrated, with Anson fore-end, Southgate ejectors and Scott spindle, available in 12-, 16- and 20-bore, Wild produced six grades of A & D ejector guns, some with ball fences, others with what the trade called Webley fences. The best grades had scroll back-ends to the action body and could also be had with "sunk" side panels. The prices varied from £60 for the sidelock down to just under £9 for a plainly finished A & D non-ejector. Top-lever hammer-guns were also offered, with both bar- and back-action locks, the cheapest of which was £7 (the comparable Belgian gun being offered at just under £4).

Guns by Thomas Wild will be found to bear the name "T. Wild" on the action and "T. Wild, Birmingham" on the top rib. Today Wild do not issue a catalogue but "make to order"; but it would be of interest to discover how many Thomas Wild guns are still in use for, as we have seen, the firm can be traced back to the earliest years of the gun trade in Birmingham.

JOHN WILKES OF BEAK STREET

As you turn off to the right from the splendour of Regent Street down Beak Street into Soho you move into a different world, almost a different time, for the area bounded by the four circuses, Oxford, Piccadilly, Cambridge and the less well-known St. Giles, is full of interest, full of history. As you move deeper into Soho you can sample gastronomic delights, the best fish and chips in London in Old Compton Street, glad rags in Carnaby Street, the pub in Poland Street where this poor scrivener used to meet Tim Sedgwick, one-time editor of *The Shooting Times*, and then move on to the "delights" of the modern "pornographic palaces" of today.

Every nationality has been represented here in Soho at one time or another; Greek Street reminds us of the Greeks who fled to this country; the French Huguenots brought with them their skills; and Soho has always been an area replete with skills from tailoring to gunmaking.

A Venetian artist who called himself Canaletto moved into 41 Beak Street and stayed for four years; Karl Marx lived in Soho at 26 Dean Street; and, along with all the other trades that were to be found in the streets, lanes, squares, yards and mews of Soho, were the practitioners of the gun trade. Thomas Perkes was to be found in Duck Lane, a patentee of shotgun actions. Over a century ago, Thomas Parkin made gun barrels in Soho, James James made gun cases and William Norcott sold gunmakers' tools. Charles Fisher, John Hoskins, and S. & C. Smith were all gunmakers in Soho, whilst just beyond the boundaries in Regent Street, Oxford Street and St. James's were to be found the "gunmakers of quality".

Alas, many of the gunmakers of quality are no longer to be found in their prestigious premises, but in Beak St., Soho, a gunmaker is still to be found – John Wilkes at No. 79. It would be nice to be able to say that the firm had been in Soho since 1830. This we cannot do, for at the beginning of the nineteenth century the Wilkeses were in Birmingham – where, exactly, we don't know. We do know that in the 1860s the business was prospering, largely on account of the Civil War in America.

With the surrender of the last Confederate Army at Shreveport, New Orleans on 26 May 1865, the war ended. A year later a family upheaval nearly wrecked the Wilkes gun business. The John Wilkes of the period did not arrive for work and an investigation brought to light the fact that John had taken all the money from the bank, mortgaged the business to the hilt and absconded to America. The younger Wilkes brother, Tom, went to America to search for John and for a time worked at the Colt Armoury and with Singer's to gather enough capital to search for John and to replenish the family coffers. It is part of the family history that Tom did in fact locate a John Wilkes, Gunmaker, in a small town near St. Louis; but by the time he arrived the bird had flown and Tom returned to England. A business was established in Soho at 1 Lower James Street, Wilkes & Harris, and the year was 1894. Mr. Harris was not a gunmaker; he looked after the books and when the Wilkeses decided that they could do this just as well themselves, the firm became John Wilkes in 1895. This is the name it has borne ever since. In St. James's was the famous firm of James D. Dougall, formerly of Glasgow, with whom the Wilkes had both family and business relationships. The John Wilkes who died in 1968 aged 84 remembered sleeping on a pile of heather in Dougall's shop at the time of Queen Victoria's Diamond Jubilee. Whether this is authentic or not depends very much on where the date was correct, for the Jubilee was in 1897 and Dougall had died on the train of a heart attack in January 1896! Wilkes could not take over the Dougall business and the firm remained in Lower James Street. It is important at this stage to realise that James Street is in Soho, Golden Square, to be exact, and must not be confused with St. James's. Golden Square has another claim to fame for here it was in 1849 that John Snow, the first specialist anaesthetist in the world and one of the earliest epidemiologists, investigated a severe outbreak of cholera. The houses in Golden Square were not supplied with water from pipes but drew the water from surface wells. One former resident of Golden Square was the widow of William Eley, who had left the square to live elsewhere. She died of cholera, although living outside the area – it was later proved that she had been in the practice of sending a servant to draw water from "the sweet well" she had been used to; this caused her death. The John Wilkes of today told me the location of the well, which is now suitably marked, and I understand that this is a place of pilgrimage for students from all over the world.

John Wilkes, Gunmaker, London.

The pump for the well was in Broad Street, Golden Square and the Wilkeses moved here in 1925 after a brief sojourn in Gerrard Street. The outbreak of cholera had been stopped, incidentally, when John Snow on being asked by the Guardians of the Parish, "What should we do?" had replied, "Take the handle off the Broad Street pump!" In 1950 the Wilkeses moved from Broad Street to their present address in Beak Street, where in spite of ever-rising costs they remain to this day.

The Birmingham end of the business closed in 1933 and all the gun work is now done on the Beak Street premises. The years between the wars saw quite an output of guns from Beak Street: sidelocks, box-locks, rifles – both doubles and a bolt action of a particularly pleasing design. Shotgun cartridges were also sold under their own brand name, "Doughty", and a pun on the name of the younger brother in the family, "Tom-Tom". After the Second World War, during which all sorts of highly specialised firearms had been produced, guns and rifles were still being made not only on special order and for the "shop" but also for some of the "bigger" names who no longer had the facilities they formerly enjoyed.

Today John and Tom Wilkes still work away at the bench, taking time off now and again to discuss some problem with a customer, who can be a French aristocrat, a rich American, or the local plumber who brought his gun in to have a new top-lever screw made – which was made by John as he talked to me about the past and the present.

What the future holds is difficult to say. People no longer "live over the shop" and travelling costs and "time" have increased, as has the cost of living in what one might call "the eighteenth-century London". Trying to carry on a business, with the overheads and restrictions imposed by a twentieth-century bureaucracy is increasingly difficult. John and Tom Wilkes still manage to produce a London-style "best" sidelock shotgun to order, a quality gun with a long tradition to back it. Wilkes is unique in London and, as a family business with five generations behind it, not a little unusual in Britain as a whole – long may it continue to do business.

Index

Figures in italics refer to illustrations and captions